GIACOMO MEYERBEER
A Life in Letters

HEINZ AND GUDRUN BECKER

GIACOMO MEYERBEER
A Life in Letters

Translated by
Mark Violette

Reinhard G. Pauly,
General Editor

AMADEUS PRESS
Portland, Oregon

For Mareike

Translation © 1989 by Amadeus Press (an imprint of Timber Press, Inc.)

ISBN 0-931340-19-5
Printed in Hong Kong

Amadeus Press
9999 S.W. Wilshire
Portland, Oregon 97225

Library of Congress Cataloging-in-Publication Data

Meyerbeer, Giacomo. 1791-1864.
    [Correspondence. English. Selections]
    Giacomo Meyerbeer, a life in letters / [edited by] Heinz and
Gudrun Becker ; translated by Mark Violette.
        p.   cm.
    Translation of: Giacomo Meyerbeer, ein Leben in Briefen.
    Bibliography: p.
    Includes index.
    ISBN 0-931340-19-5
    1. Meyerbeer, Giacomo, 1791-1864. 2. Composers--Correspondence.
I. Becker, Heinz, 1922 June 26- II. Becker, Gudrun. III. Title.
ML410.M61A4   1989
782.1'092'4--dc19
    [B]   89-45
                                                        CIP
                                                        MN

Contents

List of Illustrations

Illus. 16: Caricature of the 1850 premier of *Le Prophète* in Berlin, by Wilhelm Scholz. The head of the donkey is a likeness of the manager Karl Theodor von Küstner (*Fliegende Blätter*, 1850).

Illus. 17: Eugène Scribe. Photo by Nadar, ca. 1850.

Illus. 18: Meyerbeer approx. 1854. From a lost oil painting by Jäger.

Illus. 19: *L'étoile du Nord*, Stuttgart, 1854. Anonymous woodcut in the *Illustrierte Zeitung*, vol. 23, Leipzig, 1854.

Illus. 20: Portrait of Homage, ca. 1855.

Illus. 21: Caricature by Wilhelm Busch for *Dinorah*, Act II: The shadow dance (*Fliegende Blätter* 1860).

Illus. 22: Minna Meyerbeer, née Mosson. Oil painting by Meyerbeer's son-in-law, Gustav Richter, ca. 1860 (original lost).

Illus. 23: Giacomo Meyerbeer. Photograph by Numa Blanc, Paris, 1861.

Illus. 24: *L'Africaine*, premier April 28, 1865: Act III, Scene 6. Drawing by Auguste Anastasi (*L'Illustration*, Paris, May 6, 1865).

Illus. 25: Meyerbeer on his death bed, Paris, May 2, 1864. Illustration by E. Rousseau (Meyerbeer Archives, Berlin).

Illus. 26: Arietta "Soave istante" for the tenor Giovanni Battista Rubini (unpublished, private collection).

Illus. 27: Meyerbeer's burial at the Jewish cemetery in Berlin, Schönhauser-Allee, on May 9, 1864. Drawing by M. L. Loeffler (*L'Illustration*, Paris, May 28, 1864).

Introduction

When Wolfgang Amadeus Mozart died on December 5, 1791, Giacomo Meyerbeer was three months old to the day; Richard Strauss was born barely a month after Meyerbeer passed away on May second, 1864 in Paris during rehearsals for *L'Africaine* [The African Woman]. Meyerbeer's life spanned the height of Viennese classicism, the Romantic period and the onset of modern music drama. This was also the age of Jewish emancipation, which extended beyond Prussia and was filled with hopes and disappointments.

Jacob Liebmann Meyer Beer did not contract his last two names to Meyerbeer until 1810. He was born into an environment characterized by affluence and wealth. His father, Juda Herz Beer (1769–1825) had been living in Berlin since approximately 1785 and married Amalia (formerly Malka) Liebmann Meyer Wulff (1767–1854) in 1788. She was the eldest daughter of the so-called "Croesus of Berlin," Liebmann Meyer Wulff, who had made his fortune delivering supplies to the Prussian troops and as the director of the Prussian lottery. Juda—later called Jakob—Herz Beer knew how to increase his wealth; he ran a sugar refinery in his house at 72 Spandauer Strasse, maintaining branches in Hamburg and Gorizia, Italy. In 1815, Beer was considered the richest individual in the city of Berlin. He was interested in culture and in improving the social standing of his fellow Jews, taking on important activities in the council of elders of the Jewish community in Berlin and being very active in the movement to emancipate the Jews. As a youth, Meyerbeer had already been confronted with problems stemming from his Jewish heritage. Unlike the Mendelssohn family, the Beers did not convert from Judaism and in 1812, Meyerbeer made a formal vow to his mother promising that he would always remain true to his father's religion.

In 1816, Friedrich Wilhelm III awarded the *Luisen Orden* (medal of honor) to Meyerbeer's mother in recognition of her charitable activities during the Wars of Independence. She furnished the family home according to the customs of high society of the day and was able to bring the cream of society, members of the court, artists, and intellectuals into her home which, complete with its own concert hall, provided an attractive atmosphere for musical performances. This was how Meyerbeer came in contact with the great artists of his time at a very early age. In keeping with aristrocratic tradition, he was educated by private tutors; it was evident that the goal of emancipation and freedom could be reached only with the assistance of a comprehensive education. In 1807, Meyerbeer was placed under the tutelage of the Jewish scholar Aron Wolfssohn (born ca. 1754) who performed the role of major domo, aiding Meyerbeer in taking his first steps into the outside world. His music teachers included Franz Lauska (1764–1825), the court piano teacher who taught him starting in 1798, as well as Clementi (1752–1832) and Abbé Vogler

Illus. 1: Meyerbeer at the age of eleven: Oil painting by Friedrich
Georg Weitsch (owned by the family).

(1749–1814) when they stayed at the "Beer" house. Thus, Meyerbeer
enjoyed a princely and unusually comprehensive education which
assisted him in his later artistic development. A sense of diplomacy, for
which he later was famous, was thereby instilled in him at an early age. As
a boy, his maturity was noted by the critics on the occasion of his first
public performance (1801) as a piano playing Wunderkind. The fact that
he was Jewish was especially noted because at the time Jews did not even
enjoy Prussian citizenship and had not been very active in the world of
music. It became Meyerbeer's historic taste to pave the way for Jewish
participation in European musical life. This journey was not easy and
even in 1821, when recommending the young Mendelssohn to Goethe,
Carl Friedrich Zelter jokingly remarked: "it would really be a miracle if
the Jewish boy ever became an artist."

In 1807, the two year period of sporadic composition studies with
Carl Friedrich Zelter came to an end. Because Meyerbeer had been drawn
to dramatic composition from the very beginning, he became a student of
Bernhard Anselm Weber (1766–1821), conductor of the royal opera, but

Illus. 2: Carl Friedrich Zelter; Lithograph by Heine based on a
painting by Begas, Deutsche Staatsbibliothek, Berlin.

soon outgrew him artistically. As a result, Weber recommended his
talented pupil to Germany's foremost music theorist, Abbé Joseph Georg
Vogler in Darmstadt. It was here, together with Carl Maria von Weber and
Johann Gänsbacher, that Meyerbeer experienced his artistic apprentice-
ship and acquired extensive knowledge of counterpoint and dramatic
composition. At the same time, he devoted himself energetically to
improving his abilities as a pianist, bringing them to such heights that in
1816 Carl Maria von Weber referred to him as "most likely Europe's best
pianist." In 1812, Meyerbeer ended his studies with Vogler and, after brief
sojourns in Munich, Vienna, Paris, and London, set out for Italy in 1816.
For eight years he traveled throughout that "land of the sun" and
presented six operas written in Rossini's Italian style, each one more
successful than the one preceding. The crowning point of his success was
the performance of *Il Crociato in Egitto* (1824) which, as Heinrich Heine
later exclaimed with astonishment, caused a public "frenzy."

The name Meyerbeer became famous throughout Europe. When, in
1824, he was invited to begin rehearsals of "Crociato" in Paris, Meyerbeer

11

had achieved the goal of his young life: Paris.

His father's death on October 27, 1825 gave Meyerbeer occasion, as the oldest male in the family, to establish his own household. On May 25, 1826 he married his cousin, Minna Mosson (1804–1886), in Berlin. She was the daughter of one of his mother's younger sisters. Their firstborn children, Alfred and Eugenie, died while still in infancy. Their three surviving children, Blanka (1830–1896, the future Baroness von Korff), Cäcilie (1837–1931, the future Baroness Andrian Werburg) and Cornelie (1842–1922, married to the Emperor's court painter Gustav Richter) outlived the parents.

Although Meyerbeer never gave up his permanent residence in Berlin, he was more at home in Paris than in his native city. The premiers of all his later operas, with the exception of *Das Feldlager in Schlesien* (The Encampment in Silesia), took place in Paris. It was there, in 1831, that the premier of his *Robert le Diable* (Robert the Devil) caused an unprecedented stir in the opera world. The success of this opera quickly spread the world over, making Meyerbeer the most famous operatic composer of his time. François Le Sueur, Berlioz' teacher, stated succinctly that the age of pleasurable music had given way to the age of music with character. Rossini, whose *Guillaume Tell* was the most extensive and carefully written opera of his career, had closed the doors on operatic composition; Meyerbeer now had no real rivals or serious competition until the appearance of Richard Wagner and Giuseppe Verdi.

Les Huguenots (1836) surpassed even the spectacular success of "Robert", and by 1900 it had been performed 1000 times in Paris. Although Meyerbeer was Berlin's first and only native composer to gain world renown, the Berlin theaters closed their doors to *Les Huguenots;* the Office of Censorship would not allow the performance of the opera for religious reasons. In Munich and other cities located in Catholic states the work, which told the story of the gruesome events of the Saint Bartholomew's Night Massacre, was only allowed to be performed with a modified plot and a different title. Not until Friedrich Wilhelm IV came to power (1842) did censorship in Prussia relax somewhat, thereby allowing the Berliners to become familiar with this famous opera of their native son. In the same year, the new King summoned Meyerbeer to return to Berlin to take over Spontini's position as Music Director General. This was an unprecedented event: Meyerbeer's appointment in 1842 signaled the first time that a Non-Christian had held a public office in Prussia. Meyerbeer was not only the director of the court opera but also director of the King's private court music. Along with this appointment, Meyerbeer was awarded the order Pour le Mérite in the "peace category." The King offered Felix Mendelssohn Bartholdy the position of director of church music, but he did not accept and worked in Berlin only sporadically. In 1846, Meyerbeer, too, left his official functions de facto and was granted a leave of absence for an indefinite period of time. He continued to hold the position of director of church music, but it was only a figurehead appointment. The royal family, above all the future Empress, Princess Augusta, gave Meyerbeer nothing but support and recognition while the Berlin public and, to a large extent, the music world in Germany, was rather reserved and even hostile in its criticism of his music. In a time of growing nationalism and in the aftermath of Napoleonic rule, people in his homeland were unable to respond objectively to the principal representative of French grand opera.

Schumann's negative review of *Les Huguenots* lacks insight and Rellstab's foolish comments regarding Meyerbeer's work border on the insulting. Wagner's later attacks are summed up in his essay "Das Judentum in der Musik" (Jews in the Music World), which brings the dangerous prospect of anti-Semitism into play. In France, however, Meyerbeer was appointed Commander of the Legion of Honor after the premier of *Le Prophète* in 1849 and was considered a national composer of sorts, even though he was referred to as the leader of the "German school." The intertwining of different national styles in Meyerbeer's operas, hailed as universalism in Mozart's music, was celebrated in France as unfettered internationalism. In Germany, however, his critics dismissed him as a mere eclectic. That Meyerbeer gave 19th-century opera its decisive thrust, that his operas, when measured against later musical extravagances, still retained relatively modest dimensions, was hardly recognized in Germany. Only today is the experimental side of his work gradually coming to light. Meyerbeer's use of the newest instruments of the day— bass clarinet, bass tuba, sathorns—created remarkable, exquisite sound combinations and paved the way for the development of modern concepts of tone color. Wagner's musical drama and esthetic concepts would not have been imaginable without Meyerbeer's forays into program music, but all of this has been knowingly and willfully supressed.

Meyerbeer created scenes (recognition and exorcism scenes in *Le Prophète*) and roles (Marcel in *Les Huguenots,* Fides in *Le Prophète,* Selica and Nelusko in *L'Africaine*) which were without precedent and could not be duplicated without creating an obvious imitation. Meyerbeer also had a very distinctive style. That he was unsuccessful in consistently maintaining this style in his large operas could be interpreted as a fault, but that was not the general consensus at the time. Sprinkling his stage works with conventional numbers—arias, duets, choruses, ballet interludes— provided more than just a glittering showcase for singers and dancers. There were also commercial considerations such as publishers and opera directors who had to be pleased. In order to exist, the Paris Opéra depended on the general public with its Grisettes and Lorettes and their beaus. The sale of vocal scores, the many arrangements of popular excerpts for piano, two instruments or even solo flute, financed the costly printing of the full scores and also served as advertisements for the operas.

Rossini's esthetic credo, which he still espoused in 1868 shortly before his death, was summed up in the word "Diletto" (delight): the true goal of all music should be to delight. Meyerbeer did not subscribe to this artistic philosophy. He paid a great deal of attention to the nature and demands of his librettos, always being involved in their writing. One need only compare a comic opera such as *Dinorah* to *Le Prophète* to recognize the wide spectrum of artistic expression at his command. This was also true of his many *romances* and *mélodies,* songs in the Italian, German or French styles. Wagner remarked, in praise of Schumann's music, that it contained nothing "Meyerbeerish," saying that Meyerbeer had no personal style, nothing distinctively his own. Still, Wagner expressed a different position in his essay on Meyerbeer's musical esthetics. When it came to the art of joining contrasting musical forms, great variety in musical transitions, the expansion of harmonic processes, and the experimental development of modern orchestral color, Meyerbeer laid a firm foundation for later operatic composers. Meyerbeer's influence can still be heard in Verdi's work, up to and including *Don Carlos* and *Otello.*

Because of the virulence with which Meyerbeer's work and person were attacked in Germany, his historic contribution has, as yet, hardly been established impartially. Misunderstood nationalism and anti-Semitic thought clouded judgment. Schumann's *"Huguenot* Review" and Wagner's writings and comments regarding Meyerbeer have had a lasting and unfortunate influence on Meyerbeer's image. Still, only what is significant and successful provokes resistance—that which is inconsequential disappears by itself.

Meyerbeer's life ended on May second, 1864, in the midst of preparations for the premier of *L'Africaine.* He was not to attend the first performance of his last opera. Scribe, the librettist, had died in 1861. When, on April 28, 1865, the curtain went up in the Paris Opéra on the posthumous premier of *L'Africaine,* not only the French Imperial couple but Europe's political and cultural elite honored Meyerbeer by their presence. The opera was greeted with stormy ovations; the applause spread beyond Paris, creating yet another world success for Meyerbeer.

Meyerbeer's death was considered the end of an era. The obituaries in the German newspapers were as contradictory as always when evaluating Meyerbeer's work. In Paris, however, his loss was deeply felt. "The music world has lost its master" wrote the opera director, Nestor Roqueplan, in his commemorative article. Meyerbeer's role as a unifier of people and the importance of his cosmopolitan view of music, which at that time had heavy polical overtones, were recognized more than ever before. During the memorial service at the Gare du Nord, which was attended by great numbers of people, Emile Ollivier, representative and future cabinet leader, emphasized these qualities of Meyerbeer's work in his eulogy:

> He created a harmonious bond between the two nations. May the name Meyerbeer, and the memory of our mourning the man who came to us from across the Rhine, cement this precious bond between two sister nations who should never again be separated. May this bond grow ever stronger between the fatherland of Beethoven, Mozart and Meyerbeer and that of Hérold, Halévy and Auber.

In 1863, Meyerbeer stipulated that in the event of his death his estate should be closed for reasons of confidentiality. He wanted to avoid the publishing of letters that might compromise his colleagues who were still living. According to his will, the music manuscripts, diaries, and sizable library were deposited in the Prussian State Library in 1916, but the documents and letters remained in the possession of the family until 1952. At that time Hans Richter, the last grandchild (died 1955), turned this material over to the Staatliches Institut für Musik-forschung, Stiftung Preussischer Kulturbesitz. These "Meyerbeer archives" contain a large portion of his correspondence, including hundreds of letters which were either turned over to the family after his death or bought back by the family at auctions. Included also were the appointment books which Meyerbeer carefully kept, several "brouillons," i.e., rough drafts of letters, and a copy of the diaries which Wilhelm Altmann, then director of the music department of the Berlin State Library, had made in 1916. Altmann's planned publication of the diaries never took place due to objections from Meyerbeer's heirs.

During the chaotic war years, the archives survived in private hands in Berlin and little was lost in the postwar period. Still, even in Meyerbeer's lifetime important pieces of correspondence and valuable music manuscripts fell into unknown hands.

Richard Wagner's letters were and still are, for the most part, lost although Georg Kinsky published a large number of them in 1934 in the *Schweizerische Musikzeitung* without revealing the owner's name. As early as 1886, Wagner's letter from Koenigberg (February 4, 1837) had been printed in the journal *Der Zeitgeist* [the Spirit of the Times]. Though there are a large number of letters by Carl Maria von Weber in the archives it is evident today, based on the notes in Meyerbeer's diary, that many of these have also been lost. Weber's letters to Meyerbeer's parents and brothers are missing altogether. It is also remarkable that not one single letter from Meyerbeer to Weber has come to light. There are also large gaps in the family correspondence: Meyerbeer's letters to his brother Wilhelm, who attended to Meyerbeer's artistic interests in Berlin while Meyerbeer was living in Paris, might answer some very important questions. The surviving correspondence between Meyerbeer and his wife is far from complete due to their constant traveling. While Meyerbeer's official letters survive in the Prussian State Archives, some of the personal material was found in the "broullions." Comparisons with the fair copies and diary entries show the accuracy of the drafts which have been proven to be reliable sources. With the help of these rough drafts and diary entries, the letters included in the 1869 biography of Meyerbeer by Jean F. Schucht, which departed greatly in style and content from Meyerbeer's other letters, were exposed as obvious forgeries. Schucht, who wanted to use the first publication of these "never before published" letters as advertisement for his book, had only corresponded with Meyerbeer regarding a loan and employment. His attempted deception is an indication of the intense interest in Meyerbeer's letters after the composer's death.

Large portions of the once extensive correspondence have either been given to or purchased by the Bibliothèque Nationale and the Bibliothèque de l'Opéra de Paris, the Prussian—now German—National Library in Berlin (GDR), the Vienna Public Library, the National Library in Vienna, and the Washington Library in the USA as well as many other libraries. Private collections can be found today throughout the world and from time to time are put on the manuscript market once again.

To support the scholarly edition of Meyerbeer's letters and diaries published by Walter de Gruyter in Berlin, Alfred Berner and Hans-Peter Reinecke, the directors of the State Institute for Music Research in Berlin, as well as Rudolf Elvers, director of the music department in the National Library, Prussian Cultural Foundation, have acquired many of Meyerbeer's writings.

*   *   *

By respecting Meyerbeer's wishes that his estate remain closed, his heirs accepted the fact that much in Meyerbeer's life would remain hidden, that mere guesses and fabrications would falsify the composer's image, that publicists and scholars, in an effort to advocate their own particular protagonists, would decry Meyerbeer's personality. It was not until his document estate was opened in 1952 that a reliable representation of his life was possible, opening the doors to an important chapter in the history of European music, one in which Meyerbeer played an important role.

*   *   *

Letters are conversations with distant partners in which an immediate, spontaneous reaction, an intellectual and spiritual attitude toward the recipient, is communicated. They are a medium in which the writer reflects on his relationship to the person he is addressing, taking the recipient's likely reaction into account, soliciting, admonishing, pressuring, teaching, and requesting. Tone and word choice are not only a reflection on the addressee, they also reveal the climate of the relationship, indicating security, demands, devotion and affection. Much more than merely informative, letters are slices of life. Often a line jotted down hastily can provide greater insight than a beautifully written, carefully formulated and wordy epistle. As a mirror of life, letters are more than an autobiography, which is often clouded by hazy recall. Letters carry the aura of the time in which they were written and therefore of something genuine.

Since the multi-volume scholarly edition of Meyerbeer's correspondence, published by these editors, is usually only available in larger libraries, the idea of presenting Meyerbeer's life in letters in a more

16

restricted framework arose from the desire to familiarize a larger group of people with his personality and his place in history. Furthermore, the larger edition is not yet complete due to lengthy preliminary work. The text of the larger edition is also multi-lingual with large sections in French which often precludes its use by some students and scholars. Therefore, this selected edition provides a welcome opportunity to publish these letters in translation. We have made every effort to be as true to the original text as possible. Another advantage is that there are letters included in this volume which will not appear in the multi-volume edition for some years to come. They lend special significance to this collection because they are being published for the first time. Letters are also included which were found after the publication of Meyerbeer's correspondence had begun, such as his letters to Pezzi. These, too, are being published for the first time. By carefully choosing from the hundreds of Meyerbeer letters, the authors have attempted to provide a well-balanced picture of all periods of his life and to promote greater understanding of the composer's work. This includes Meyerbeer's position in his family, his relationship to his parents, in particular to his mother, the "Nonne," (the Italian term for Grandmother, given her by the family) to his wife Minna, to his daughters, friends, colleagues, opera directors, to the aristocracy including the Prussian royal court. Letters to Heinrich Heine demonstrate Meyerbeer's intervention on behalf of the poet, others indicate his support for Richard Wagner. Concerns with Jewish questions which played such an important role in Meyerbeer's life have not been excluded. The social convictions of the millionaire Meyerbeer had to be addressed as well. Another very important subject is that of Meyerbeer's musical-dramatic concepts and his role in the preparation of the librettos. Here, the letters to his librettists Scribe and Dumas offer valuable insights.

Every selection process sacrifices completeness. There are gaps which one would like to see closed. On the other hand, concentration on the essential does provide one advantage: it stresses what is essential. In the multi-volume edition, where attention is paid to many details, including the replies to letters, essential elements are apt to be hidden or lost altogether. In the present edition, these essentials, such as Meyerbeer's personality, are given greater emphasis. The decades of Meyerbeer's life are condensed, outlining more clearly the contours of his life's journey. We become aware of the foresight, assurance, and determination of a man who, gaining moral strength from the religion to which he was deeply devoted, pursued his life from the very beginning with conviction. This self-assurance can also be seen in his manner of expression, in the often careful, diplomatic language which sometimes even attained literary heights.

In order to understand the letters and their background, explanatory comments are inserted to provide the necessary information. Only rarely have the letters been shortened to exclude the most ephemeral information. There are also drafts of letters from the very detailed notebooks, the "brouillons." A comparison with existing original letters has often confirmed the reliability of these draft books while diaries and appointment books verify the content and the fact that the letters were mailed. These "brouillons" contain the "carbon copies" of Meyerbeer's letters. It is understandable that they lack the usual salutations.

The editors decided in favor of modern spelling in order to facilitate reading. The multi-volume edition of the letters with original spelling is available for scholarly use. For the same reason, there are no footnotes in this edition. Italics are used to indicate material underlined in the original.

Bochum/Grindelwald, Chalet Guarda val 1982

Editor's postscript, 1989:
Since 1952, the Meyerbeer Archives had been in the Staatliches Institut für Musikforschung in West Berlin. In October 1984, the collection was returned to Meyerbeer's heirs; in the spring of 1987 it was auctioned off by Sotheby's of London. Today it is located in the Music Division of the *Staatsbibliothek Stiftung Preussischer Kulturbesitz* in West Berlin.

GIACOMO MEYERBEER
A Life in Letters

*On April 15, 1810, Meyerbeer arrived in Darmstadt with his brother
Heinrich, his tutor Aron Wolfssohn and a servant. He had come to take a
master class in composition with Abbé Vogler, the most renowned music
theorist and organ virtuoso of his time. This master class in composition was
to signal the completion of Meyerbeer's studies. Since Meyerbeer was
already an excellent pianist, Vogler also encouraged his organ playing and
had even hoped that Meyerbeer would choose a career as an organ virtuoso.
Vogler's pedagogical far-sightedness is exemplified by the fact that he also
familiarized his students with necessary business practices by showing
them the correspondence he conducted with his publisher. He also demonstrated his trust in Weber and Meyerbeer by revealing his income to them.*

*The following is the earliest complete letter known to have been written
by Meyerbeer. It is the only letter from the year 1810.*

1. To A. Kühnel

Hessen-Darmstadt, August 9,
1810

Esteemed Sir,

Due to the absence of Baron Carl Maria v. Weber, Privy Counsellor
Vogler has asked me to answer your esteemed letter of August third.
Accordingly, I have the honor of informing you that the Privy Counsellor
has agreed to sell you the 12 chorales in question for a price of 8
Friedrichsd'or. This will exclude six copies which will be for his own use
and to be given to friends as gifts. I am convinced that you, as I, will find
this fee to be most reasonable.

I agree with you completely when you state that these chorales are
not suitable for everyone. However, I believe that they are timeless
because, even though changing fashions and tastes may destroy present
musical forms, the laws of harmony cannot be shaken. They are rock
solid, and excellence achieved in this area will last, as is most certainly the
case with these chorales.

Of the four-part a capella hymns you wish to engrave, the Privy
Counsellor would like to give you 12 pieces, at the same price of 8
Friedrichsd'or. You will also receive an esthetic and critical analysis of the
same. These hymns include four antiphons, Salve and Ave Regina: regina
coeli and alma redemptoris. In addition, o salutaris hostia, o sacrum con-
vivium, etc. I believe that you will use these pieces frequently and in a

wide variety of ways because their lovely, flowing vocal lines and ease of execution make them just as suitable for use in musical societies as their majestic style and artistic counterpoint do for performance in church. This is especially true of churches whose means do not permit the use of an orchestra.

The analyses provide an additional advantage, causing these pieces to be extremely useful and effective study material for young composers (and indeed for many older composers as well).

With regard to the eight-part hymns, the Privy counsellor is asking one Friedrichsd'or for each. For now, he does not have any organ concertos or theoretical works. The success of these negotiations will be very decisive for future business dealings.

Finally, I am very pleased to take this opportunity to thank you once again for the many favors you so kindly extended to me when I was in Leipzig 18 months ago with Kapellmeister Weber [Bernhard Anselm Weber] from Berlin. Rest assured that I have no greater wish than to be of similar service to you in the near future.

Incidentally, I now have the good fortune to study under Privy Counsellor Vogler and to belong to the small group of his students with whom he, at his advanced age, once again reviews the entire spectrum of his musical observations and experience. This has also provided me with the pleasure of sending you this written testimony of my respect and the opportunity to express once again my best regards to you.

Yours truly,
Meyer Beer

Please give my best regards to Mr. Riem
P.P. The Privy Counsellor expects payment for his manuscripts to be made in gold and via mail coach.

*   *   *

In May of 1811, Meyerbeer was in the care of his teacher Abbé Vogler in Darmstadt. On May eighth of that same year Meyerbeer's lyrical rhapsody Gott und die Natur *[God and Nature], set to text by Dr. Aloys Schreiber, a professor in Heidelberg, had been performed in Berlin at the Royal National Theater under the direction of Bernhard Anselm Weber. The success of this performance encouraged the young composer to plan more concerts in his native city. These would include works by his friends in the "Harmonic Society" who published their reviews under previously agreed upon pseudonyms. One member of this group was Gottfried Weber (1779–1839), jurist and State Attorney at the ducal court in Mannheim, who later made a name for himself as a respected music theorist. The double concerto by "the great man," i.e., by Meyerbeer, is mentioned in the following letter. It was also reviewed in the Allgemeine Musikalische Zeitung in 1813; the composition "by Meyerbeer, the genius" impressed the listeners as being "too dark and thus did not enjoy general applause." Due to the Beer family's prominent position in Berlin, Meyerbeer was able to procure the services of first-rate virtuosos and singers for his planned concert. Gottfried Weber, probably the most ambitious* member of the *"Harmonic Society,"* even managed to publish an article on Meyerbeer's oratorio in the widely read *"Zeitung für die elegante Welt" [Journal for the Elegant World]*. In this article, he refers to Meyerbeer as a *"superb pianist"* and *"well-known composer"* who had achieved *"great fame"* with his latest work.

2. To Gottfried Weber in Mannheim

Hessen-Darmstadt, May 22, 1811

Dear Brother,

Who is Mr. Henning, you ask? A very competent composer and violinist who even had the good fortune to compose, with the great man, a double concerto for violin and piano. Next fall I want to arrange a concert for the boy, one that will make all of Berlin sit up and take notice. And you, old boy, will consider it a great honor to have your works performed at this concert. For this purpose I am sending him: 1) my new Symphony in E-flat Major, 2) Vogler's *Trichordium* (that has not yet been heard in Berlin), 3) the Turkish Overture from little Weber's [Carl Maria von Weber] *Abu Hassan,* 4) the double concerto I just mentioned to you by Henning and myself which he will perform with one of my pupils, and finally, 5) your *Deucalion,* which is why I will send an express letter to Iffland so that he can take over the declamation. The work will be performed by an orchestra and chorus of 60 people under Weber's excellent direction. In addition, there will be several concertos and arias performed by the foremost virtuosos and singers. I give you my word: as soon as the ticket office opens, it will be stampeded. I will arrange for the trumpet fanfare after the concert.

I would like you to consider not performing the music in Mannheim before this concert. I would like to hear from you within the next two weeks as to whether you can have your piece finished by fall. If not, it would be to your great disadvantage for I most likely will not be in Germany over the next two years and will therefore not be able to work as actively in your behalf.

I have received two letters from little Weber along with three copies of his *"Momento Capricioso."* Two of those are probably for you. I will send them along to you with tomorrow's mail together with his letters to me. In addition, I will enclose a small 'Cantata' I composed last week for my father's birthday (Nota bene: in three and a half days). I can never take pleasure in the work I've done until it meets with your approval, you scoundrel.

What was the response to my Oratorio you ask? Its success exceeded my wildest expectations. Even during rehearsals, the music caused such a stir that music enthusiasts came pouring in by the hundreds. The performance enjoyed the success that composers had already predicted during the rehearsals. Friends and enemies, strangers and acquaintances alike were all seized by the same enthusiasm. The morning after the performance, several famous composers and poets (including my outspoken opponents) sent the most flattering notes and letters to me; countless poems were dedicated to me and even to Schreiber. I have enclosed a few of these silly little things as well as a newspaper which includes a few more, also the reviews from both Berlin newspapers which you will, no doubt, find flattering enough. The reviews are all the more surprising because they were written by enemies. One of them (the one I have underlined) is by my notorious opponent Rellstab who wrote about me so viciously a few months ago. What humiliation it must have been for this miserable fellow to be forced to praise me in spite of himself!

The choir and orchestra both performed splendidly. Schmalz, Gern and Eunike sang magnificently, especially Eunike. When, during the rehearsal, someone shouted to him that he sung like an angel, his reply was: "the music indeed comes from heaven." (Now, don't make such a face as you read this, you old goat).

Since then, I have been offered seven subjects for future operas. To sum things up, the public is wonderful and quite taken by this music.

I am quite sure that you do not believe that I am going into such detail merely to indulge my vanity; after all, who knows better than we how much the success or failure of a work is a matter of chance and what erroneous and slanted perceptions usually influence public tastes. We really cannot take very much credit if a work succeeds. Given the sort of relationship we have, I would even go so far as to say it is my duty to inform you of all the details, just as I did when my *Psalm* was poorly received. But enough of this for now. As things stand at present, you can confidently slip 8 to 10 pompous lines about this work into the "Badische Magazin" to whet the Mannheimers' appetites.

Now that the music will certainly be engraved, it is one of my greatest wishes to hear it again in order to reassure myself about countless things of which I am still not certain. In case you try to accomplish this but have difficulty writing out the full score, I could manage that here because I have an excellent copyist. However, it would have to be done immediately, in four weeks at the latest, because I will be leaving soon and my publisher cannot wait much longer.

I have very openly expressed my greatest wish to you. Now you must be equally frank in telling me whether there are any circumstances or obstacles that would prevent you from fulfilling it. In the event that you are able to overcome the difficulties and perform the work, please do not fear that I will then continually bother you with my music. On the contrary; for your reassurance, I would like to give you my written word never again to set foot in Mannheim.

Recently, I saw a new newspaper: "Süddeutsche Miszellen Für Leben, Litteratur und Kunst" (South German Articles on Life, Literature and Art). It is published in Karlsruhe and a certain Mr. Rehfuss is said to be the editor. Why isn't this our publication? Karlsruhe is located in your state; write to them or have "Mr. Unknown" [A.v. Dusch], our beloved creature, write; this fellow does nothing for our society.

Write and review ad vocem. When you read the Berlin newspapers you will see that those people do not even know how to praise someone effectively. They didn't even mention the "Chor der Elemente" [Chorus of the Elements from the oratorio *Gott und die Natur*], and I am willing to bet that they cannot even figure out its meaning. It was the same with Chorale No. 10 ["Er war, er ist und er wird seyn Kraft," (He was, he is and will be the power)]. How would it be if you selected a couple of excerpts from that marvelous letter you sent to me on this subject, a short one and a longer one. You could send the first one to the *Morgenblatt* and the second one to little Weber (since you are on bad terms with the "Musikalische Zeitung"), who could then send it to Härtel under his own name. (This is why I am returning the letter you sent me.) I would ask you, however, to prepare the excerpt at once so as to preempt the Berlin reviews. As for reviewing the rest of the concert, you can stick entirely to the Berlin newspapers which, by the way, I expect returned tomorrow because I have urgent need of them. Are you listening? You can have them copied at my expense because we need them for our records. I hope that your journalistic efforts will not be deterred by the fact that you, in Mannheim, are reviewing a work performed in Berlin. After all, you could have correspondents there, or have been there on a short visit yourself.

What is our brother Rock doing? Why isn't he active? Have him write to Castelli in Vienna (as a traveler), send a list of employees at the Mannheim theater (which should impress him), complain about the decline of sacred music and, in doing so, highly recommend your Masses. He can also mention something about Berlin: he can heap praise upon *La vestale* by Spontini and *Deodata* by Maestro Weber, because they are very popular with the Berlin public. The first one is popular because of the ingenious mixture of the Italian and French genres, combining heavenly singing with proper declamation and imaginative orchestration (albeit sometimes a bit too active); the second one owes its popularity to its energy and powerful declamation as well as to its dramatic spirit which can be heard in all the choruses. Reichardt's "Taucher" [Diver] was not well received. He should sound disappointed about that, because Reichardt does very commendable work. He might also make some comments about B. A. Weber's Concert spirituel and include mention of my Oratorio, for which you can give him some directions.

Giving a concert in Darmstadt would be all but impossible now, although I would like to meet Mr. Tollmann; please give him my best regards.

Samori won't be performed for another three to four weeks.

I have not yet received the "Hymnen".

I am greatly indebted to Dusch for his poem. I will go into more detail about that in my next letter, because I have to close for now.

Your true brother Philodikaios

I desperately need my hat. For God's sake, please see to it that I get it.

*   *   *

Carl Maria v. Weber, who had formerly studied under Vogler with Meyerbeer and who was also a member of the "Harmonic Society," went on a concert tour to Berlin in mid-February, together with Heinrich Joseph Baermann, the famous clarinetist from Munich. He arrived on February 20 and stayed at the home of Meyerbeer's parents at 72 Spandauerstrasse. However, Meyerbeer's trip with Vogler was delayed until the beginning of March. In Würzburg, the first stop on their journey, he completed his opera Jephtas Gelübde *[Jephta's Vow] on April 6. It was performed on December 23, 1812, at the Munich Court Opera. Any contribution by Meyerbeer to the* Allgemeine musikalische Zeitung *has not been proven. The review of compositions by Gottfried Weber (July 29, 1812) was attributed by G. Kaiser to Carl Maria v. Weber.*

3. To Carl Maria von Weber in Leipzig

Hessen Darmstadt, January 8, 1812

Dear Brother,

Thank you for the New Year's greetings, and I wish you all the blessings and luck that one soul can stand.... In your letter, you presented me with the pointed and philosophical question as to whether it is you or I who is an ass. After having searched from Aristotle to Schelling, I finally think I have the fundamental answer; neither of us. All joking aside, if one of us was guilty of not writing, it certainly was not I. Several months ago, I wrote a letter to Gottfried Weber that dealt entirely with *your* affairs. I asked him to send it along to you which, as he wrote to me, he has done. So it is you who owes me a letter. This would not have prevented me from writing to you, if it were not for another important cause: my *laziness*. Luckily, you were lazy too, so enough said.

Since I received your letter just yesterday, yet want very much for you to receive my response while you are still in Leipzig, I am writing you on a day filled with things for me to do. As a result, my news to you will be brief and to the point.

I will begin your letters for Berlin [recommendations] in a few days; I will send them to one of the four locations you gave me. I do not yet know which one, so please inquire at each post office.

I take it for granted that you will be staying at my parents' house. They are already looking forward to your visit and have asked in several letters when you would be arriving.

Samori [opera by Abbé Vogler], which was supposed to be presented in October, will be performed on Sunday the 12th for sure. Eight days later is the first performance of *Hermann von Unna* [opera by Abbé Vogler], and four days later we travel to Munich.

My opera will be finished in two weeks. It would have been finished a month ago if I had not rewritten part of the plot. This resulted in my having to make many musical revisions.

K. Wagner's opera [*Nitetis*] was performed on 26 December, and neither the text nor the music went over well at all. (Incidentally, please keep these comments very much to yourself).

Wohlbrück was called to Munich and will be the director of the *Vorstadttheater* (suburban theater). He has committed himself to both of us.

The publicity campaign in the Berlin papers should begin in eight to twelve days.

The old lady, Papa's [Vogler's] sister, died two weeks ago.

(Most important): Speak of me to Härtel as someone whose essays would be very desirable. I say this because I want to send him reviews of Giusto's [Gottfried Weber] vocal quartets and French singing method. If you would like to write something about the quartets in the *Musikalische Zeitung,* it would be better to do so in another paper because I can then write a very detailed review and thereby impress the editorial staff of the Musikalische Zeitung, so that they will want to remain in contact with me.

*　*　*

On April 22, 1812, Meyerbeer noted the following in his diary: "at noon I ate at the guests' table [table d'hôte]. The "young lovelies" hurt me to the innermost region of my soul and ruined my entire day. When will I finally learn to resign myself calmly to the unavoidable?" All his life, Meyerbeer had suffered from displays of anti-Semitism. Nevertheless, he remained true to the family faith as he had promised at the deathbed of his grandfather, Liebmann Meyer Wulff.

4. To Amalia Beer in Berlin

Munich, August 30, 1812

Dear Mother,

Upon my return two days ago, I found the sad letters and was then certain that the hopes I had carried with me were but dreams. I cannot and will not try to provide comfort, for I myself am too devastated and know how little comfort cold words of sympathy provide in the face of intense outbreaks of sadness and grief. Please remember, dear mother, that our pain would drive us to the brink of insanity if your health were to suffer as a result of this terrible loss. Try to avoid the vivid memories and take whatever medicine you can to dull the piercing pain; I ask this of you with tears in my eyes.

Wolff's letter went right to my heart. Yes, if Grandfather had even a glimmer of consciousness on his deathbed, it must have been a comfort to him to know that his children will never leave the faith he so warmly embraced. Therefore, please accept a promise from me in his name that I

Illus. 3: The mother: Amalia Beer, née Liebmann Meyer Wulff. Oil painting by Carl Kretschmar (State Institute for Musicology, Berlin).

will *always* live in the religion in which he died. I do not believe that there is any better way to honor his memory.

Please forgive me, but I am unable to write more today.

Farewell
Meyer B

*   *   *

At this point in his life, Meyerbeer was still considering a career as a virtuoso pianist. When he was only 14 years old, his performance of a Mozart piano concerto was greeted with wild enthusiasm in Berlin. Vogler wanted to make him Europe's premier organ virtuoso and in 1808 Carl Maria von Weber, in the dedication of his Momento Cappriccioso, *referred to Meyerbeer as "Compositore e Professore di Cembalo" (composer and professor of piano). In 1815, Weber hailed Meyerbeer as "one of the greatest, if not the greatest pianist of our day." However, the trip with Johann Baptist Gänsbacher (1788–1844) did not take place. The Wars of Independence (1813–14) eliminated all travel plans. Meyerbeer headed for Vienna to wait out the war and to continue studying.*

5. To Johann Baptist Gänsbacher in Prague

Mannheim, January 16, 1813

Dear Brother,

Words cannot describe what a great pleasure it was for me to find your wonderful letter upon my return here. Your affection for me, dearest of friends, is no grater than the sincere love I shall always feel for you. The professor also sends his greetings and was delighted to receive news of you. I see from your letter that you know of my "Jephta's" success, but you don't know how much blood and sweat I put into it before it was performed. Thank heavens it is over at last. Before my departure I played again in an orchestra concert, and I am said to have earned more applause than any other pianist in the history of Munich. The audience went beyond applauding to shouting in a frenzy. I must admit this marvelous reception was more than even I expected. After the second performance of my opera, the Queen sent me the first flattering compliments via her lady-in-waiting (Countess Taxis) and gave me a strikingly beautiful diamond ring.

I would be very grateful if you would put this in a newspaper in Prague or Austria. Of course I realize that a political newspaper does not publish music reviews, but it need be only two lines (perhaps it could come at the end of a political article from Bavaria), it could read something like this: "On December 23, 1812, *Jephta's Gelübde,* a grand opera by the composer J. Meyerbeer, was premiered to an enthusiastic audience. Her Majesty the Queen gave the composer a beautiful ring after the second performance."

This would more than suffice, dear brother, because experience has shown me that two *lines* in a *political* journal have more effect than two *pages* in a literary journal.

And now to our trip to Italy: this was actually the reason why I waited so long to answer your letter. I really wanted to say something conclusive about the trip, but was unable to do so because I was still rehearsing my opera. However, now I can say something specific because tomorrow I am going directly to Paris and will stay there from six weeks to two months at the longest. I will arrive in Italy at the beginning of April as long as the political climate does not prevent the journey. Therefore, I will write you about this again when I am in Paris. But why the devil do you write that you cannot make the journey this year, you rascal? Because you did not receive the support you expected from Bozen? You should allow a dear friend, a brother, to offer you what you do not hesitate to accept from strangers. In the event that your oversensitive pride (which, unfortunately, you demonstrated in Munich) were to prevent this, then you should at least allow me to be your banker and advance to you the money for this year (since, as you wrote, you probably will not receive anything from Bozen until the end of next year). You can repay me next year. I will even accept interest, if you so desire, even exorbitant interest: for every hundred Gilders, one new Canzonette.

All joking aside, dear brother, do not let your oversensitive pride prevent you from enjoying and profiting greatly from this once-in-a-lifetime opportunity of traveling together through Italy. Just think how we could stimulate each other to work, how much more each of us would benefit from exchanging our impressions. Do you attach no value to the spiritual boost of traveling through that paradise in the company of a friend? I impatiently await your reply, which you will please be so good as to send to Paris, in care of Mr. Worms de Romilly. As I did in Munich, I would ask you to keep our plans as quiet as possible (not even our brothers are to know).

You will receive my oratorio *Gott und die Natur* [God and Nature] and the Canzonettes with the next mail.

I spent some pleasant days with Gottfried Weber and Dusch, and they send their greetings.

Your,
Meyerbeer

*   *   *

In 1804, Aron Wolfssohn, a scholar from Breslau, published an essay ". . . An impartial discussion of the accusations recently directed at the Jewish community" and spoke out in favor of a new direction for Jewish life. In 1807, he was hired by the Beer family as a tutor for Meyerbeer and his brother Heinrich; it was he who accompanied the two brothers to Vogler in Darmstadt. He also had the composer's absolute trust, as can be seen in several letters and drafts of letters. The letter to his mother refers to the beginning of the Jewish New Year, the first of Tishri, September 22, 1814.

6. To Professor Aron Wolfssohn in Berlin

[Vienna, September, 1814]

[. . . .] This silence is the reason why I have not yet mailed the long and important letter I wrote to mother at the New Year. I would like to wait until she finally ends her silence. The letter was a collective response to several frustrating inquiries. I have put off answering time and again because, as you know, one always postpones unpleasant matters. Of main concern is the question which, as it was put to me by Mother, most certainly was communicated to you earlier. This is why my response to her (as contained in this letter) would perhaps be of some interest to you. It is the request to come to Berlin in order to perform the opera *Jephta*. Last year, when the Prussian government encouraged the youth of the land to volunteer for military service I felt that, based on my view of the situation and, to a certain extent, on my own personality, it would be in my interest to avoid heeding this call. My views have remained the same, but I have come to the conclusion (unfortunately, too late) that at such moments one simply cannot have convictions. In times of crisis, the moment itself decides and evaluating in relation to the present and past becomes pointless. Following this line of reasoning, I cannot hide the fact that I have been disloyal to the state and I fear that this decision will carry the scorpion's sting that will poison my honor for the rest of my life. To make things even worse, my brother Wolff and others who have been to Berlin have told me what outrage and bitterness the Berliners reserve for countrymen who did not heed the call to arms. As a result, I could be subjected to all kinds of unpleasant repercussions. However, even if an exception were made and I were to be spared, it would pain my conscience. I would feel the silent hills mocking me and the whispering of the trees would be contemptuous laughter to my ears. I would see accusations coming from even the most unlikely sources and every joke would throw me into a rage. This is the reason why I cannot come to Berlin now; not until there is peace and the citizens put down their weapons once and for all and have forgotten all swaggering heroics. A return under the current conditions would be so horrible that, even if the government called upon us expatriates to return home or my parents threatened to use force to bring me back, I would have to put a bullet through my skull were I unable to find any way around that command.

*   *   *

In 1813, Duke Ferdinand Palffy von Erdöd took over as sole director of the Theater an der Wien and of the Kärntnerthor Theater where, on October 20, 1814, Meyerbeer's opera Wirt und Gast *[The Host and the Guest] was premiered under the title* Die Beiden Kalifen *[The Two Caliphs]. It was also performed later in Dresden under the title* Alimelek. *The work was not a success— predictably so, because of the poor preparation about which Meyerbeer complains. The noticeably confident sounding letter written by the 23-year-old shows signs of the future rehearsal fanatic who spared nothing when it came to rehearsing his own works or those of others.*

7. To Count Ferdinand Palffy von Erdöd in Vienna

[Vienna, ca. October 15, 1814]

Three days ago, in response to my urgent statement that my current situation makes it impossible for me to wait out more delays in the production of my opera, Your Excellency assured me that the performance would take place on Friday. Now you have just informed me that it will not be performed until Tuesday. As if that were not enough to demonstrate to me how hollow these assurances have been, the scene painters informed me that they would not be ready until Tuesday because they had other work to do. The rehearsal then ended before one single note was performed because half of the cast never even put in an appearance. Under such circumstances, I have to wonder if these delays are not at least partially deliberate. As accomodating as I have been to Your Excellency regarding the legitimate delays, continually postponing my journey so as not to hamper the performance of the opera, I must now state that given this unfortunate experience, I will not hesitate to use the right accorded to me in writing and cancel the production of this opera if it is not performed by this coming Wednesday at the very latest. This performance will only be possible if the rehearsals are divided up as follows: since Mr. Stegmaier will rehearse *Moses* daily with the chorus, there must be two morning rehearsals on Thursday and Friday. From 9 to 10 o'clock, the chorus will rehearse *Moses* followed by my opera. This will not be too taxing if we rehearse only Act one on Thursday and only Act two on Friday so that the chorus only rehearses one hour on each day. Both acts will be rehearsed on Monday and Tuesday and the opera, after sufficient rehearsal, would be ready for performance on Wednesday. If Your Excellency and the stage directors of the opera are satisfied with this rehearsal schedule, I would be happy to postpone my trip once again as a renewed demonstration of my devotion. If, however, this arrangement does not seem adequate, then I do not believe that the opera can be performed on Wednesday and I will be forced, given my current situation, to retract the opera from the stage. Whatever Your Excellency's decision may be in this matter, it is most urgent that I receive a response *in writing* before today is over so that, in the event that the rehearsals and hence the opera do not take place. I do not needlessly postpone my trip, especially since before my departure I owe myself and my friends among the general public an explanation as to why I have taken these steps. Otherwise those who do not know that this opera should have been in performance since August 20 might be alienated.

*   *   *

During his 18-month stay in Vienna, Meyerbeer devoted himself to his studies and performed from time to time in private salons. It was during this time that he met Beethoven. Tomaschek provided Beethoven's often-quoted exclamation after the first performance of the "Battle" Symphony: "this young man was assigned to play the large drum. Ha! Ha! Ha!—I wasn't at all happy with him. He did not strike it properly and was always too late. Therefore, I really had to give him a dressing down. Ha! Ha! Ha! This may have upset him. Nothing will come of him. He does not have the courage to strike at the right moment." Meyerbeer's encounters with Louis Spohr were more positive. Spohr was in Vienna at the time working on his Faust and he often asked Meyerbeer to play sections of his work on the piano "at which he excelled."

At this point, Meyerbeer was anxious to realize his plans to continue his studies in France. He left Vienna in mid-November and traveled to Paris via Munich.

8. To Jacob Herz Beer in Berlin

[Vienna, November, 1814]

Twenty-four hours after I wrote the above, I received two letters from you dated October 11 and 15. Please explain to me, dearest Father, why you have suggested that I cut short my trip to return to Berlin to hear an opera of mine that I have had more than enough of here? Why do you want me to see a doctor in Berlin when there are dozens (both famous and obscure ones) here? For years you have known that I consider Paris to be the ideal arena for my education in musical drama and that I have a great passion for French opera. You also know how much I have longed for this. Is it my fault that for a year now the war has prevented me from making the journey? Did you not write to me in Mannheim yourself, urging me to return to Vienna and wait out the war, and did you not give me every assurance that nothing should stand in the way of my journey? (I still have that letter.) You might reproach me for not starting on my journey as soon as peace was declared. Indeed, this was my intention. However, if you only knew how bad things were for me in the spring, you would most certainly forgive me. Later there was the production of my opera which, as you know, was subjected to countless delays. I am well aware that a delay of 18 months is very expensive for you. However, am I to blame, or is it the times in which we live? Many times I have asked you to be frank with me in this regard and not to say anything to anyone but me if you felt that I spent too much money. One word, and I will limit my expenses to a level you find acceptable. I do not place a high premium on caring for my person, and making this a lower priority would be very easy for me.

Incidentally, I am aware of the reason why you suddenly want me to return. From Professor Wolfssohn's last letter I have ascertained that the Berlin Theater is looking for a second director and that [B.A.] W[eber] is not adverse to suggesting me for the position. His fear of hiring a *great* talent with a will of his own is probably as great as his hope that I will be a *small* talent and will adhere to *his* will. He is wrong about me on both counts. However, this is not my concern (the error would be his loss). I would consider this a very acceptable and honorable position if I had

Illus. 4: The father: Jakob Herz Beer. Oil painting by unknown painter (owned by the family).

already completed my musical studies. But you know that I have always considered familiarity with the French and Italian theater to be indispensable. This is why I cannot, under any circumstances, return to Berlin until I have made both of these journeys. I believe this to be of the utmost importance to my musical training and would not let anything in this world prevent me from going, even if I had to set out on foot and wage battle against the raging elements.

It grieves me to realize how incapable I have been recently of pleasing you, even though my actions correspond to your previous wishes. Earlier, you complained that I had not staged anything here and now that I am doing so, you write that you do not understand that I am presenting an opera that did not go into rehearsal until August. There was a time when you were in complete agreement with me regarding my travel plans; now, when I am finally about to have this opera performed (the political situation has no influence on this), you want me to return. I implore you to allow me to complete this final stage of my artistic education in peace. Please do not ruin the one focus of my life, the unhindered study and practice of my art, by constantly expressing your dissatisfaction (which causes me great pain). If you take this away from me, you will have robbed me of the one single pure source of inspiration in my life. I must close for today. It is too late to reread what I have written here, but my pounding pulse tells me that I may have involuntarily put myself into a mood in which I may have said too much too strongly and with too much bitterness. If this is the case, please do not take everything I've written literally. I ask you, Father, to be patient with me until such time that circumstances around me change and return to me the composure that the last six weeks of misfortune have taken from me. It was not the opera's lack of success which upset me: as a young composer, a young composer of operas, I would be unabashedly over-confident if I never considered the possibility that a new opera of mine might not be a success. It was the battle against the unending deceit, teasing, and cabals, from the first day of rehearsals to the performance, which have exacted their toll from me and exhausted me.

Your Devoted M.

*　*　*

At the end of December, 1814, Meyerbeer arrived in Paris. Paris, the center of Europe, the cosmopolitan city, stimulated and intoxicated the young composer. He wrote to Gottfried Weber: "the wondrous works of art and nature, and especially the theaters have such an overwhelming grip on my entire life and have instilled in me such a spiritual addiction to pleasure that I go from museum to museum, library to library, theater to theater with the restlessness of the wandering Jew." He spent half of every day in the library studying scores and music theory. On November 30, 1815, he journeyed to London with his brother Wilhelm. Here, too, he spent evening after evening at the theater, studied singers and orchestras, visited museums and, most importantly, sought out the famous pianists of the day: Ries, Klengel, Cramer, Kalkbrenner. He did this so as to establish his own position in the phalanx of piano virtuosos. In December of 1815, the two brothers once again set foot on French soil. A bit later, at the beginning of 1816, Meyerbeer traveled to Italy; it was there that he planned to complete his education. Rossini's star was beginning to rise at this time while mediocrity spread around him. Meyerbeer traveled the length and breadth of Italy, all the way down to Sicily where he compiled folk songs. He became acquainted with Gaëtano Rossi, the librettist, with Pietro Lichtenthal, a correspondent for the Allgemeine Musikalische Zeitung, and with Franz Sales Kandler, the writer and journalist. In 1817, Meyerbeer staged Romilda e Costanza, *his first Italian Opera. This was followed in 1819 by* Semiramide *in Turin and* Emma di Resburgo *in Venice on June 26. "Emma" was performed 74 times and established Meyerbeer's reputation in Italy. Kandler reported in the Austrian Allgemeine Musikalische Zeitung that Meyerbeer's opera had scored a complete victory over its heralded predecessor, Rossini's* Edoardo. *Experts saw him as the man capable of doing great things to reform Italian opera.*

9. To Franz Sales Kandler in Venice

[Venice, June 27, 1819]

Dearest Friend,

The friendly and spirited letter I received from you yesterday has acted as a *liquore annodino* [pain-killer] and once again rejuvenated me in the final stages of a drawn-out work which had almost exhausted me. I now have recovered the courage I had almost lost. The gracious letter I received from you today fills me with joy and gratitude. It would be superfluous to tell you that your approval is more flattering to me than that of a foolish, unknowledgeable audience. You know yourself and you know me. However, what I would really like to thank you for is the care you took in overlooking what I *had* to do for the sake of the public, as well as the true friendship you demonstrated in seeking out what I had attempted to do for the sake of art in this opera. I say this because I am more than convinced that you were well aware of what could have been done differently. I will consider "Emma" my most fortunate production if it contributed to creating an artistic and amicable bond between us. I have so much respect for you that I also fear you somewhat, my dear friend. Last night, at each of the opera's weaker moments, there were butterflies in my stomach when I thought of my friend, Kandler. I will be at your residence at precisely six o'clock tonight, so that we can begin our lengthy discussion on art. I will also provide you with all the musical information that you require with respect to "Emma." You can have the score if you so desire (from which, as you mentioned, you could draw examples to support your views), or any complete section, in the event that you would like to send it along to the Wiener Musikalische Zeitung as a musical supplement. In short, you can have anything that I could offer you. The only thing I cannot give to you is my heart, for you have already stolen it from me.

I send you my greetings and embrace you in spirit until I can do so in person this evening.

P.S. Do not scold your messenger for taking so long to return. I was looking among my papers to see if I might find one of my little riddle-canons so as to write it down on your note. This is what has taken so much time. However, I found nothing and must ask you to be patient for another 24 hours. Adieu once again.

Your friend in body and soul,
Meyerbeer

In bed at 11 o'clock!

*   *   *

The engagement of Nicolas Prosper Levasseur (1791–1871), the most prominent French bass who, in 1820, created the role of Carlo Belmonte in Meyerbeer's opera Margherita d'Anjou *in Milan, did not take place. However, it probably was*

Levasseur who provided Meyerbeer with his link to the Paris opera. A few years later, in 1831, Meyerbeer wrote specifically for him the role of Bertram in his opera Robert le Diable. *This was the beginning of Meyerbeer's rise to world fame.*

10. To Nicolas Prosper Levasseur in Paris

Venice, May 21, 1823

Dear Sir,

With the greatest of pleasure I recall your wonderful interpretation of your role in my *Margherita d'Anjou;* since your performance I have often hoped to benefit once again from your great talent. I may have such an opportunity now. The management of the large Teatro La Fenice in Venice has invited me to compose a new opera seria for the next carnival. I happen to know that they have not yet engaged a bass and that they are a bit unsure as to whom they should choose because they want to have a singer of the highest possible caliber. I would very much like to suggest you, but before I do this I would have to know if your commitments in Paris would permit you to come to Italy during the carnival season. I would also need to know what your fee would be. The season begins on December 26 and runs through March 20, however, the singers must be in Venice at the beginning of December for rehearsals. I remember hearing you say, dear friend, that only an engagement of six months or a year would bring you back to Italy. I must tell you that the Teatro la Fenice can make you no such offer because this theater is only open during the carnival season. Could you please give me your response as soon as possible so I can inform the management. Whatever the outcome may be, let me say how great a privilege it would be for me to see you again and to write a role for you in my opera.

Please send your response to Jacques Meyerbeer c/o Mr. Samuel Guerber & Company in Florence. In the meantime, it is with the greatest admiration that I remain your devoted servant and friend.

Jacques Meyerbeer

11. To Nicolas Prosper Levasseur in Paris

Milan, July 5, 1823

Dear Sir,

Your silence has been torture for us. It cannot take more than 20 days at most to receive a response from Paris to a letter sent from Venice. It has been 36 days and we still have heard nothing from you. I did everything in my power to postpone the engagement of another bass and I must say that Mr. Crivelli demonstrated tremendous good will in this matter because he would have very much liked to have hired you. However, he could not wait any longer because he was obliged to provide the management with a complete list of the ensemble by the end of June. As a result, he hired a certain Mr. Zuccoli on the 25th in your stead—your letter arrived on the 28th. I forwarded it to Mr. Crivelli immediately and he, as I, is deeply disappointed that we have lost you for this year due to your late response. However, he requested that I inform you that he has leased the large theater of Venice for five years and would like to engage you for the following season. He also said that he would write to you directly about this. This is all well and good for him and for you, but *I* have been robbed of the pleasure of composing for you in this carnival season. I have also informed His Excellency, the Governor of Milan (who is currently supervising the Teatro alla Scala) of your good intention to return to Italy. He admires you greatly and would be delighted to engage you for next Spring in the event that Mr. Remorini, with whom we have been negotiating for quite some time, does not come for that season. This could very likely be the case. The situation will be clarified very soon and I will have the honor of communicating it to you.

I was very flattered by the passage in your letter referring to the supportive comments made by the director of the French Opéra regarding my modest talent. Would I be interested in composing for the French stage, you ask? I assure you that it would be a much greater honor for me to write for the French opera than for all the Italian theaters put together (incidentally, I have already performed my works in the most important of these theaters). Where else but in Paris can one find the immense resources that French opera offers to the composer who longs to write truly dramatic music? Here we are suffering from a shortage of good opera librettos, and the public enjoys only one musical genre. In Paris there are wonderful librettists and your audiences show an interest in all types of music, as long as the music is imaginative. Paris, therefore, offers the composer a much greater opportunity than can be found in Italy. You might wonder why, given my feelings, I have not yet attempted to write for Paris. Well, here we are told that French opera is fraught with difficulties and that a composer must usually wait years before coming out with an opera. This tends to intimidate us. I would also have to admit that, in this regard, I have been spoiled in Italy where people have shown keen interest in me. However, I realize that this is due more to my public's exceptional indulgence than to my own small merits.

Please be assured of my greatest respect with which I have the honor to be

Your most devoted servant,
Jacques Meyerbeer

* * *

The first performance of the opera Il Crociato in Egitto, *the Florentine production of which Meyerbeer reported to the critic and editor of the Gazetta di Milano,* took place on March seventh at the Teatro La Fenice in Venice. Meyerbeer was *wildly celebrated and for the first time attracted international attention. Several years later, when writing of his impressions while in Italy, Heinrich Heine wrote "Never before have I seen such frenzy as during a performance of* Il Crociato in Egitto, *when the music's sometimes soft and melancholy tones suddenly changed to passionate agony. This frenzy is called* furore *in Italian."*

With "Crociato" a long era in the history of Italian opera came to an end: the era of the castratos. Out of great admiration for his incomparable vocal and interpretive abilities, Meyerbeer wrote the title role of his work for Giovanni Battista Velluti (1780–1861), the last famous castrato, whom Meyerbeer continued to admire for years thereafter.

12. To Francesco Pezzi in Milan

Florence, June 3, 1824

My dear friend,

Have you completely forgotten me? Ages ago, I completed the two pieces of your beautiful cantata, but the remaining pieces have not yet arrived although you wanted to send them to me (with a new text for the *Lamento*) eight days after I left for Florence. Am I not correct to fear (as I said when we spoke of this) that you have not yet made your full peace with me and do not yet trust me? If you have completed the remainder of the cantata, please send it to me in Florence where mail will still reach me. If you would rather hold on to it, I can pick it up myself when I pass through Milan in 12 days on my way to Berlin.

You have allowed me to provide you with news of my opera in Florence and I am delighted to do this because it was one of the most brilliant successes I have had to date. The opera was very enthusiastically received. At each of the first three performances, the audience called me up on stage four times. The singers received the same enthusiastic response after each of their principal numbers. Velluti had not enjoyed success in *Ginevra* [by Simon Mayr] because he was ill the entire time, however, my opera once again provided him with the opportunity to demonstrate the charm of his great and versatile talent. Time and again both his gentleness and energy unleashed storms of applause, even from his outspoken enemies. Our Tosi was indisposed during the first performance and could not perform in the manner the audience had justifiably come to expect. (Just between us, there was also a bit of ill will between her and Velluti on account of the roles.) In the second performance, she was in better voice and sang magnificently and the audience applauded her endlessly. The greatest tribute went to Reina, the tenor. He recreated the interpretation of Crivelli, for whom the role was written, perfectly and he, too, was enthusiastically applauded by the audience.

As I write this, there has still been no article about my opera in the

Florence newspapers. I will not send this letter until something appears in the papers and I can enclose it with the letter. Articles here tend to be poorly written, so it is my hope that you will keep the most essential points and change the rest by committing words to paper with the magical colors you employ in response to all subjects.

I dare hope that it is still your desire to do me the service you spontaneously promised me upon my departure from Milan. I would like to make an additional request: please publish your article as soon as possible, so that it appears in your newspaper before my arrival in Milan. I realize, my dear friend, that it is forward of me to request so much of you but your friendship and kindness have given me the courage to express to you all of my wishes which are contingent upon your goodwill and friendship.

Adieu; please accept my gratitude in advance. I remain your lifelong devoted friend.

Jacques Meyerbeer

*   *   *

On July 30, 1824, Rossini took over the direction of the Italian opera in Paris. Encouraged by the tremendous success of Crociato in Italy, *the General Manager, Sosthéne de la Rochefoucauld immediately invited Meyerbeer to come to Paris to stage his opera. Meyerbeer had achieved his goal; on February 23, 1825, he arrived in Paris to prepare for the first Paris performance. In May he returned briefly to Italy for rehearsals of his* Crociato in Padua. *However, he did not make the trip to London because the quality of the production of* Crociato in the King's Theater *was guaranteed by the presence of Barbaja's troupe and by Velluti. The London success was so great that the English music journal* The Harmonicon *published an unusually extensive article including almost 60 pages of excerpts.*

13. To Francesco Pezzi in Milan

Paris, July 10, 1825

My dearest friend,

I surely would not have hesitated to comply with your kind request that I write you immediately upon my arrival in Paris, had I not wanted to give you news concerning the fate of my *Crociato* in London. It was presented there on June 29. Our long relationship has shown me the interest that you, out of friendship for me, have taken in the success of my modest works. Therefore, I hope it will make you happy to know that the London production of *Crociato* was a total, brilliant success. Velluti made his English debut. During the first evening's performance he had to struggle against strong opposition. This opposition was not directed at his talent, but rather at his person because a portion of the audience considered it improper and immoral to allow a castrato to appear on the stage. Velluti remained calm and did not let himself be shaken by the murmurs and whistles.

He gloriously won over all of his critics and created a sensation. The English newspapers, articles from which I have enclosed in translation, reported that the second and third performances of this great artist were very well received. I do not think it is proper for me to tell you about the success of the music, but I can at least write about one fact which demonstrates how quickly its popularity has grown: eight days after the opening of *Crociato*, the English opera *Broken Promises* was performed, in which the trio and the romance ("Giovinetto Cavalier") from *Crociato* had been used with English text; my work was adapted on the spot.

I have the honor of enclosing in this letter some excerpts from English articles which were published in the Drapeau Blanc and in the Corsaire. I have selected these because they go into more detail than those published in the Journal des Débats, the Courier Français or other publications. You know what great respect I have for your journal. I would be very happy if, when translating one of these articles for your journal, you could inform the Italian public of *Crociato's* success in London. Your journal has helped so often to increase my small measure of fame that I dare hope you would once again demonstrate your goodwill on this occasion.

My brother is here as I write this, my dear friend, and sends you his greetings. I remain your

devoted servant and friend,
Meyerbeer

*   *   *

The Paris opening of Crociato, *took place on September 25, 1825 and was quite spectacular. The unquestionable success of the work impressed Frederick William III of Prussia who arrived the day after the opening and attended the second performance. As early as October ninth, he issued a Cabinet decree in which he invited Meyerbeer to compose a German opera. On October 17, Count Brühl asked Meyerbeer to produce* Crociato *in Berlin. Meyerbeer knew that he could get the recognition he so desired in his native city only if the success were nothing short of overwhelming. However, now that his greatest wish had been realized, i.e., to write a French opera for the Paris Opéra, the commission for an opera in Berlin was not all that attractive. The opera* Ines de Castro, *also mentioned in this letter and intended for the Teatro San Carlo in Naples, was never written either.*

14. To Count Karl von Brühl in Berlin

[Berlin, December 11, 1825]

In response to your inquiry as to whether there is already a German translation of the opera *Il Crociato in Egitto:* to my knowledge none exists.

39

Illus. 5: Meyerbeer ca. 1825. Lithograph by Constans based on a painting by Vigneron.

Many writers have asked me for the score, but I have always refused because I am convinced that *a German translation of Crociato performed on a German stage* could only have *very limited* appeal. I feel this way because of the text which, despite endless twists in the plot, remains monotonous and tiring and is so unmotivated and fragmentary that it would be anything but successful. There would be a particular problem with the role of Felicia which was inserted into the plot. This would not go over well with the drama-oriented audiences in Berlin. However, from a musical point of view (especially because of the ensemble pieces) this role has become so important that, despite its dramatic emptiness, it not only cannot be left out, but (because of the trio) its character cannot be changed. In the music itself, several aspects of vocal style (the result of the individuality of the Italian singers and the tastes of the Italian audiences) would not go over with a German audience, especially since it was written by a German composer. Yet these vocal structures, as arbitrary and unessential as they may sound, are so completely woven into the fabric of the work that even the tiniest alteration could destroy the work's overall effect....

As strong as my feelings are about not producing a German version of *Crociato* in Berlin, I have an equally strong desire to compose a work for the royal stage in my native city. It would take into account the fine singers in Berlin as well as the German audiences' tastes. Therefore, the invitation issued by His Royal Majesty fills me not only with a deep sense of gratitude for the trust my gracious King has placed in me: it also coincides with my own desire. Thus I am all the more grateful for this opportunity. This opera will be my first project as soon as I have completed two earlier works for which I am contractually bound. These are an Italian opera for the Royal Teatro San Carlo in Naples and a French opera for the Académie Royale de Musique in Paris. The latter must be ready for performance by the end of the coming year so that, from 1827 on, I shall be able to devote my full attention and concentration to the task of composing a work for Berlin.

*   *   *

Jakob Herz Beer died on October 27, 1825 in Berlin while Meyerbeer was still in Paris. A short time thereafter, on November 28, 1825, Meyerbeer became engaged to his cousin Minna Mosson. According to Jewish tradition he, as the eldest male member of the family, had to establish his own household as soon as possible after his father's death. Existing letters and documents shed no light on the young lovers' relationship. The wedding took place on May 25, 1826 in Berlin.

The opera Ines di Castro, *which had been planned for Naples and was based on a libretto by Gaetano Rossi, never got beyond stretches. Meyerbeer's growing reputation in Paris resulted in his settling all of his obligations in Italy: This was a remarkable confirmation of the fact that an opera's success in Paris, the secret capital of Europe, was more significant than a success, no matter how spectacular, in Italy.*

The first performance of Crociato *in Italian had already taken place in Munich in July, 1825. Meyerbeer here recommends the expanded French version, conceived for Paris, as the basis for the German translation.*

15. To Heinrich Joseph Baermann in Munich

Augsburg, March 9, 1826

My dearest friend and brother,

I was very pleased to hear news of you via Mr. Santini. I am very sorry that you would believe that my love for my old friends had weakened because I did not stop in Munich on my way to Milan. It would be unjust and even ungrateful on my part if I did not feel genuine attachment and gratitude to Munich (to say nothing of my personal love for my old friends there), because my musical productions were done there with so much care and goodwill. But, my dear friend, I am recently married and a very devoted husband. This is why I postponed my trip to Italy to the last minute and subsequently had to rush there to release myself from my obligations to the theaters there. I was actually able to get a few months' postponement from Barbaja regarding the new opera I am supposed to write in Naples. I have completely cancelled the one I was to do for the Scala in Milan. Instead, I was given the privilege of staging my *Il Crociato in Egitto*. It opened on Thursday, March second and was more enthusiastically received than anything performed at the Teatro alla Scala in years. On each of the three evenings I conducted, I was called up on stage four times. I have enclosed the Milan newspaper containing an article on this production because I have learned through Mr. Faubel and Mr. Santini that you are still very interested in my musical success. I also hope that you might be able to get an excerpt of it into one of the Munich papers given the fact that, as you mentioned in your letter, *Crociato* will soon be given in Munich in German, and that public interest is aroused if there is talk of a previous success of the same work (especially at so prestigious a theater as the Scala). If, my dear brother, you make use of the Milan newspaper for the above-mentioned purpose, I would request that you send the paper back to me in Berlin. I would like to bring it to my dear mother whose only comfort in life now is to hear or read praise of her son. Perhaps you are wondering why I did not pass through Munich on my return trip. Should I have come to Munich, after a twelve-year absence, only to stay for three or four hours? Would that have provided me or my friends with any measure of joy? I would not have been able to stay any longer because my bride knows my departure date and counts the hours until my return. She will probably even meet me in Leipzig. I, too, anxiously await the moment when my destiny will be joined with that of the woman with whom I hope to spend a lifetime of happiness.

Send my warm and heartfelt greetings to all my Munich friends who still remember me, above all to my beloved friend Poissl. Tell him that I heard about the love, friendship and care he put into the Munich production of *Crociato* and that I am deeply grateful to him for this. If he wants me to deepen my debt of gratitude, then he should wait a few months before performing the German version of *Crociato* so that I can send him a copy of the score as soon as I arrive in Berlin. It contains changes, cuts, improvements and *new pieces* that I have added since last year and from which the opera has greatly benefited. Please write to me in Berlin about his reaction so that, in the event that he agrees, I can have a score copied at once. According to what I have heard from Munich, Madame Vespermann seems much more suited to the role of Armando than Miss Schechner. Therefore, I hope Poissl gives the role to the former.

If you, as I hope, can provide me with information on all of these matters when I am in Berlin, please do not forget, as you did in your last letter, to give me news of your present life, work, and future artistic plans, for I am just as interested as always. I count on your continued friendship and love, and please believe, dear brother, that I will forever remain your true friend and brother,

J. Meyerbeer

* * *

In Meyerbeer's personal calendar, Robert le Diable *(Robert the Devil) was first mentioned on February 18, 1827. The opera was first intended for the Opéra Comique.*

Meyerbeer was well aware that plans for a German opera for Berlin would fail for lack of a good librettist. Who was capable of writing the libretto? There were no prominent librettists in Germany—even the opponents of Italian operas complained that German opera librettos were boring. The incentive he found in France was missing in Germany: it was not until 1844 that the payment of royalties, based on the French model, was introduced in Austria and Germany for librettists and composers. One-third of the royalties went to the librettist and two-thirds to the composer. They would now not only profit from the performance of their works, but also from the sale of the score, vocal scores, and arrangements. In this context, it is clear why Scribe did not want to give up his author's rights. As long as the score had not appeared in print, the authors held all rights, and performance of a work was contingent upon their permission. If permission was granted, the hand-copied performance material was turned over to the theater. In this way, the new work enjoyed a certain measure of protection so that rank amateurs could not come in and ruin the success of a new opera.

16. To Frederick William III of Prussia, in Berlin

[Berlin, July 16, 1828]

Most serene almighty King and Lord!

Two years ago Your Royal Highness was gracious enough to grant me the honorable opportunity of composing an opera for the Royal Theater of my native city. At that time, my first and foremost goal was to find a good opera text, for it is my conviction that dramatic music can only be created if it is based on truly dramatic material. Naturally, it was of the utmost importance for me to produce the very best of which my modest talents are capable so as not to appear unworthy of the great honor Your Royal Highness has bestowed upon me.

At the time, I also received a request from the Théâtre Feydeau in Paris to compose an opera for which the management had engaged the services of the renowned Mr. Scribe to write the libretto. I therefore asked Mr. Scribe if he would consent to having the opera performed at the Royal Theater in Berlin before being performed in Paris. Unfortunately, Mr. Scribe fell victim to a prolonged illness, after which he became involved in other projects. As a result, it took him more than a year to finish the libretto and when he finally did send me the work a few months ago, he retracted his previous consent to produce it in Berlin first. The reason for this decision (according to him) was that he had learned in the meantime that, if the opera were first produced outside France, it would fall into the category of a foreign work and no droits d'auteurs (royalties) would be paid. In the event that the opera were to be a success in France, the lost royalties would be more than he could forfeit. It is my belief that this fabulous work by Mr. Scribe, on account of its highly romantic setting, would be very suitable for German audiences. Therefore, it is my greatest wish to make my debut at the Royal Theater of my native Berlin with a performance of this opera and, as Your Majesty's most humble servant, I request that this opera be accepted as the opera I was commissioned to write for the Berlin stage, despite the fact that it must first be performed in France. The first performance in Paris is sufficient to ensure Mr. Scribe's royalties. I can then send the libretto and score to Berlin immediately. Since no other theater can perform the opera before the score is printed, the Berlin performance would preempt that of other theaters. In the hope that my humble request has the good fortune to meet with Your Majesty's approval, I remain Your Royal Majesty's most loyal servant and subject.

J. Meyerbeer

* * *

Meyerbeer's first two children, Eugenie and Alfred, died when they were each but a few months old. Blanca Meyerbeer was born on July 15, 1830 in Baden-Baden where Minna Meyerbeer often spent the summer months. This letter to Marie Patzig, a servant in the Meyerbeer household, demonstrates the respectful and friendly relationship Meyerbeer maintained with his household staff.

17. To Marie Patzig in Baden-Baden

[Paris, July 20, 1830]

My dear Miss Patzig,

I have just received your two letters dated July 16 and 17. Please accept my heartfelt thanks for your kind reports, and please be so kind as to send me a *daily* bulletin on the health of mother and child over the next two weeks. I wish I could see Minna every hour of the day in these first few weeks during which every passing day brings changes in the condition of mother and infant. Therefore, your daily letters would be more than a mere godsend; they would help quell the fears and anxiety to which the human heart is subjected when an individual is separated from his loved ones and hears no news of their well-being. Therefore, I rest assured that your kind heart will inspire you to fulfill my request punctually. Please accept in advance this expression of my utmost gratitude to you.

With the greatest of admiration,

Yours Respectfully,
Giacomo Meyerbeer

*   *   *

If one is to trust Heine's account in the "Letters Concerning the French Stage," he met Meyerbeer for the first time in Berlin in 1829. In 1828, Heine had published a favorable review of Struensee *by Meyerbeer's youngest brother, Michael, and this may have endeared him to the Beer household. Heine and Meyerbeer met again in 1831 in Paris, where the writer had decided to take up permanent residence and where he surrounded himself with many German journalists in exile. There, he followed with great interest the growing fame of this composer and fellow-German and wrote of Meyerbeer's success in the Augsburg "Allgemeine Zeitung." Fearing Heine's biting wit and flare for irony, as well as out of concern for the ailing writer, Meyerbeer was prepared on numerous occasions to pay Heine large sums of money. Misunderstandings and Meyerbeer's procrastination, which resulted in several of Heine's folk song texts never being set to music, finally led to a break between the two. Meyerbeer set only three of Heine's poems to music, probably because he preferred the dramatic French Chanson to the German Lied.*

 Later on, Heine drastically revised those feuilletons dealing with Meyerbeer that had appeared in the Letters Regarding the French Stage *and included them in a book. The revisions account to a reversal of his earlier opinions.*

18. To Heinrich Heine in Paris

[Paris, June 25, 1831]

Esteemed sir and friend,

 I have heard that you have written many new poems about spring which still remain in your desk, hidden from the public. Madame Valentin told me that you have given some of them to Mr. Hiller but that others have not yet been wed to music. Might I, in my modest way, be permitted to court this delightful maiden? You can send your response to Madame Valentin.

Yours with admiration,
Meyerbeer

*   *   *

"The score of Robert le Diable *is not only Meyerbeer's masterpiece, it is also a milestone in the history of music . . . it places Meyerbeer at the forefront of the German school. He is now their leader." Thus was François Joseph Fétis quoted after the glorious first performance of the opera on November 21, 1831. Meyerbeer was also enthusiastically praised as a German composer in reviews written in other French newspapers. As a result of the sensational success of this opera, Meyerbeer became a composer of world renown.*

Illus. 6: Caricature of the famous Gnadenarie ("mercy" aria)
(Cavatina) in the finale of Act IV of *Robert le Diable.*

19. To Heinrich Heine in Paris

[Paris, December, 1831]

Dearest sir and friend,

That you, the great poet, desired to hear my opera a second time was too flattering a wish to let go unfulfilled. Therefore, I have obtained tickets for a good box, the one belonging to my Cerberus-like director. I shall have the honor of sending them to you at two o'clock as I am unable to get

Illus. 7: *Robert le Diable*: stage design by Pierre Luc-Cherles Cicéri, lithograph by Benoist and Bayot.

them any earlier. A thousand thanks for the heavenly Lieder: what are we poor note-scribblers to do when the verses already contain so much music? Nonetheless, I shall make an attempt.

Yours sincerely and with
admiration,
Meyerbeer

*　　*　　*

Meyerbeer knew that, by Parisian standards, Berlin could hardly offer the same quality resources for the production of Robert le Diable. *Only Paris boasted a reputable "Conservatoire," a music academy as we know it today. It supplied the Paris Opéra with top singers and instrumentalists. Nevertheless, Meyerbeer had no reason to doubt the good will of Count Friedrich Wilhelm von Redern (1802– 1883), the general director. Marie Taglioni (1804–1884) danced the role of the sinful abbess Hélène in the famous ballet of nuns from the opera. It was this sequence that Edgar Degas later immortalized in two masterful paintings dating from 1871. This was the first time that a ballet sequence amounted to more than an ornamental insert or entertaining divertissement. Here it is an integral, characteristic part of the opera's dramatic concept. This heralded the beginning of a new opera genre which came to be known as "grand opera." It was not Rellstab who did the translation for the Berlin production, but Karl Winkler (also known as Theodor Hell), who was Meyerbeer's friend and stage writer.*

20. To Count Friedrich Wilhelm von Redern in Berlin

[Paris, February 4, 1832]

[. . . .] Baron von Humbolt . . . shared my opinion that Miss Taglioni's performance would not only be of great interest to the Royal Theater in Berlin, but would also be a great contribution to the success of *Robert le Diable* in Berlin. This will only be possible if arrangements can be made to delay rehearsals of this opera until Mr. Taglioni and his daughter are present. Furthermore, Mr. Taglioni has not only choreographed the ballet for this opera, but has also directed the very difficult staging and is familiar with all details regarding the sets, machines and the magic moonlight, all of which are difficult to manage but add great effect to the opera. Moreover, the role of the abbess Hélène in this opera was created by Mr. Scribe specifically for Miss Taglioni. She danced with the utmost perfection in the first four performances, after which a foot ailment forced her to take a six-week leave from the stage.

My second question concerns two of the sets: that of the abbey cemetery with the graves in the third act and that of the church in Act Five. Both of them are the products of a system which is so new (especially the manner of lighting) and create such a diorama-like effect that many other theaters already had small models made of the sets. I would like to know if the Royal Theater in Berlin would be willing to incur the expense for such small models of the sets by Mr. Ciceri. Should this be the case, Mr. Taglioni could then bring them along to Berlin.

I would also like to ask Your Excellency to engage Mr. Rellstab for the translation. This has always been my desire and I already mentioned it to Mr. Rellstab on the occasion of my departure from Berlin two years ago. If my request poses no problems for the theater, I would ask you, esteemed Count, to accommodate my wishes.

The score is still not completely finished. Copying began six weeks ago, but Mr. Scribe made many changes during the rehearsals which necessarily had to be entered into the score. As a result, it was impossible to use my earlier copy for I wanted to send to Berlin the same version which had been performed in Paris. However, the publisher had so many different arrangements made for all kinds of instruments that for three weeks I was unable to procure the score for my copyist. As a result, he was able to work on it only in spurts and starts. The day after tomorrow I shall receive the last numbers from Act Five, so I am sure that I can send everything off this week.

It is with the deepest and utmost trust in your lofty and liberal artistic perspective and in the support you have so kindly given me, that I place the fate of my "Robert" in your hands, your Excellency. I consider myself doubly fortunate in that this work, perhaps less imperfect than my others, is also the first to be performed in my native city under your guidance and protection . . .

48

In 1829, Alexandre Dumas (senior) (1802–1870) celebrated his first stage success with his Henri III et sa Cour [Henry III and His Court]. Meyerbeer had a keen sense of the young writer's dramatic talents and sought to work with him. Perhaps Meyerbeer's interest was also aroused by Spontini's remark that he would bring one of Dumas' opera sketches to Berlin. Meyerbeer wrote about this in his diary. However, the two men never did collaborate; Dumas complained later that Louis Véron, as director of the "Revue de Paris" did not give him any assignments and, as the opera director, insisted that Scribe write the libretto for Meyerbeer. As a result, all plans to work with Dumas failed.

The opera entitled Les Brigands (The Bandits) was to be a collaborative effort between Dumas and Meyerbeer whose musical sketches for this planned opera still exist. The remarks, quoted below, regarding the rhythms conform to an old operatic practice to which Meyerbeer remained loyal for some years to come: Meyerbeer occasionally composed arias or other vocal works without a text, only using so-called "monstres," i.e., rhythmical models. The only specifications were the general mood or type of the aria or the personality of the character singing it. The relationship between text and music remained of secondary importance.

21. To Alexandre Dumas in Paris

[Paris, Spring, 1832]

My dear colleague,

I have enclosed several examples of good musical rhythms which are suitable for the various genres and I have marked them—.

I would like you to use one particular rhythm frequently because it can be used on all occasions. The rhythm is as follows:

O Seigneur / ta clémence	[Oh lord / your mercy
a calmé / ma souffrance	has stilled / my suffering
ta grandeur / ta puissance	your grandeur / your power
egalent ta bonté	equal your kindness]

I am still counting on your permitting me to visit you between the hours of four and five P.M. Wednesday

Your humble servant,
Meyerbeer

* * *

In 1831, Thomas Monck Mason assumed the direction of the King's Theatre, the Italian opera house in London, and immediately secured the performance rights for Robert le Diable. However, by the time the work was premiered on June 11, 1832, it had been known in London for some time. In a veritable race against time, no fewer than three theaters had produced the opera, albeit illegally and inadequately. On January 23, 1832, the Adelphi Theatre came out with a parody entitled The Devil's Son. This was followed by the Drury Lane Theatre production of The Daemon on February 20 and the Covent Garden production of The Fiend Father or Robert of Normandie on February 21. The director of the Drury Lane Theatre had immediately purchased those selections from the opera which had just been published with piano accompaniment and then had the orchestra conductor write out instrumental parts as he saw fit. The ensemble pieces, recitatives and orchestral sections were provided by English composers because the original performance material of the opera was not available! Even though the "Times" condemned this as a type of vandalism, Meyerbeer was unable to prevent this mutilation of his work.

Meyerbeer's mother was known as "Nonne" within the family circle, meaning grandmother, based on the Italian word "nonna."

22. To Minna Meyerbeer in Baden-Baden

London, May 4, 1832

My idol!

I have just received your dear letter from which I see that you received my two letters from Paris and Calais. By the time you read this one, you will probably have received several from London, thereby alleviating all your anxiety. I hope you are now convinced that I am not to blame for the delay of these letters. Rest assured, my dearest, that, as lazy as I am about writing letters, this does not extend to you. My happiest moments of the day are those spent talking with you, my dearest wife. This is the way I would begin every morning, if it were not something I saved to cheer me up at noon. Since the only reason for my separation from you is to assist in the production of my opera, all other distractions (daily invitations to dinners, soirées, balls etc.) cannot compensate for the fact that the reputation of "Robert" has been devastated by the performances at Covent Garden and Drury Lane. It has gotten to the point that even the Italian opera house no longer holds out hope and my artistic reputation as a whole has suffered from this. Furthermore, Mason's sloppy management tries my patience to its limits 20 times a day. He is responsible for the Italian and German operas, the ballet and now also "Robert." I have to spend half the day traipsing around the theater in order to speak with him, then he promises me everything because he is the most good-hearted person in the world. However, 15 minutes later he has already forgotten everything he had promised. Imagine: the chorus rehearsals have not even started yet, and there has not even been any decision made as to whether the opera will be performed in French or in Italian. In addition to all of this, the French singers' vacation ends on June 15.

What pains me more than anything else is a letter Michael sent me from Berlin. The old mood of hostility there continues to work against me as it did before. Michael sent me an article from Berlin which appeared in the Leipziger Musikalische Zeitung in which I was bitterly accused of having dawdled so long with this opera that it was a demonstration of contempt for the King to send the score so late. There was also sharp criticism of the libretto, referring to it as being contemptuous of all decency and religion, and that no opinion of my music could be formed based exclusively on the individual excerpts performed in concerts, except to say that they have not been well received at all. It is just like those people, who have been kicking me for years, to attack me simply because I chose not to come crawling at the first invitation. Despite these bad omens, I would leave for Berlin on the 20th, on account of my opera (I have committed myself to work here with Mason until then), even if the opera here is not yet in performance. My only hope is that the opera in Berlin can be postponed until June 15, because my presence there will be of absolutely no use if I cannot have 18 to 20 days to rehearse. However, Michael writes that the opera must open at the beginning of June because Schaetzel is leaving. She may, however, stay longer on my account. These are unpleasant stories. I am willing to leave London as soon as my obligations here are finished (i.e., the 20th), even before the opera is performed here, if this means that I could be useful in Berlin. But if I stay on here and arrive in Berlin only a few days before the premier, thereby being of no use to the Berlin production, I would be losing one without being able to save the other. Please ask Nonne to write to him in this regard, and write him yourself and ask if he will do what he can (he does not seem to want to) to ensure that the opera does not open until the 25th. You and Nonne could also write him that you do not think it at all wise for me to leave the London production hanging if I cannot be of any assistance to the Berlin production. Michael's response can still arrive here before the 20th. I have already told Mason that I will direct the rehearsals until the 20th but will then consider my responsibilities fulfilled, feeling free to leave for Berlin. Nonne and you could make a commitment in my name that I will depart on the 20th, if I can be sure that I will be able to rehearse in Berlin until the 15th. Since the journey will take seven days, that would leave no more than 16 days for rehearsals—not a great deal of time for a work of this nature.

And now, my dearest, to the most important item in this letter, which I have left for last. Your health, my dearest, not only belongs to you, but also to me. I am very disturbed that your stay in Baden has not had a better effect on your health. . . . Farewell! A million kisses to our beloved angel Blanca. I have enclosed the review so you can see whether I am wrong to fear the worst from such enemies. N.B. I hear that the chorus rehearsals really started last night.

* * *

On May 31, 1832, Meyerbeer arrived in Berlin to begin rehearsals for the premier of Robert le Diable, which took place on June 20. At the beginning of July, he *traveled to Baden-Baden to be with his wife. On the 16th, he continued his journey to Bad Ems for a health cure. In August, he spent some time in Bad Schwalbach apparently having decided not to take a planned trip to Spa. Meyerbeer's comments regarding the planned opera* La branche d'if *(The Branch of the Yew) indicate that he was seriously considering composing a German opera for Berlin.*

23. To Alexandre Dumas in Paris

[London, May 23, 1832]

My dear colleague,

Why did your letter not arrive 15 days earlier? Everything could have been arranged as you had suggested. But now I am leaving London the day after tomorrow to travel to Berlin where I shall stay no more than 12 days before I am obliged to make another journey. Thus, we could not meet in Spa before the end of July, and this would be too late for our mutual interests. Incidentally, since we last corresponded I have received information about Betourné from Labarre. Betourné had written an opera libretto for Labarre, and Labarre told me that it would be very easy to make all the changes and cuts if they were given to him but as far as musical cuts were concerned, he did not have a great deal of expertise. You are knowledgeable enough in this area to be of assistance to him, and if we were working together we would not need anyone else. However, this is not what I would suggest. According to what you write, your collaboration with Scribe has been broken off and he is no longer associated with the work. Let us return to your original idea of bringing Nourrit in on the collaboration. He is very familiar with musical editing, very intelligent and of very noble and outstanding character. Since you have already ceded one fourth of your interest to Scribe, this collaboration should not subject you to new and difficult problems. This is what I envision, and if we were to sound out Nourrit indirectly, I am sure that he would accept the conditions (he admires your genius and he is fond of me, so he would greatly enjoy working with us). You would receive the remainder of the fee (three-fourths of the honorarium for the libretto) and your share from the sale of the score. He would then settle for half of your author's royalties (percentage of the opera's box office sales). However, since you have already ceded a fourth of these royalties to Scribe and since I do not want you to lose anything in this matter, I shall cede one-fourth of my royalties to Nourrit, as you would. If you agree to this, then the matter is settled. In any case, I shall write to Mr. Véron today and shall send him a signed contract. However, if I sign a contract stating that I shall deliver the score on a fixed date, then I must set the condition that you deliver a complete libretto to me in six weeks and that you deliver all changes that I request no later than one month after these requests have been made. I believe that Mr. Véron will sign the contract I plan to send to him because all I am asking of him is that he be able to assign roles according to my wishes, provide three months of rehearsal

Illus. 8: Alexandre Dumas, Sr. Photo by Nadar.

time exclusively for my work, and that he guarantee that the opera shall go into performance before the end of 1833. If Mr. Véron should, contrary to all expectations, refuse to sign this contract, then I would suggest to you that we do *La branche d'if* together. If I am in agreement with the plan after they have worked it out, I shall be prepared to pay a fee of 4000 francs if you permit me to perform the work in Germany before it is performed in Paris. As soon as you have sent the libretto, I shall present it there (in Berlin). If they like it, I shall return it to you with the first payment of 1000 francs. The remaining 3000 francs shall be paid to you on the day the complete libretto is delivered. Taking German tastes into account, there should be more action and more brilliant sets than was evident in your original idea. There must also be a happy ending. This would also be a good idea for the [Théâtre] Feydeau. If I am not in Paris we shall need the assistance of a man who is well versed in making musical cuts, and I believe that Nourrit is the man who could best serve our needs; all the more so if he could leave the fee to you and be satisfied with half of your royalties, laying no claim to your percentage of the sales of the score.

You can see, my dear friend, that we could begin working together at once if you so desire. As things stand now, I see no reason at all why Mr. Véron would refuse to sign the contract because I have made no unreasonable requests of him. Incidentally, you might present this request to him yourself (I am writing to him today). If you find that he is not prepared to work with us, you can begin work on *La branche d'if*. Adolphe Nourrit will stay in London for three more weeks. If you would like to take a trip, why not make London the goal of your excursion? Together, you and Nourrit could write half an opera in three weeks. In any event, my dear and loyal friend, let me know as soon as possible what your response is. Please address the letter to Mr. Meyerbeer in Berlin care of J. H. Beer.

Farewell and warmest greetings.

Your devoted,
J. Meyerbeer

*   *   *

When the curtain went down in London's "King's Theatre" after two o'clock in the morning on June twelfth, 1832, Robert le Diable *had been deemed a "colossal success." Nourrit and Levasseur, Mesdames Damoreau and Demerie, all of whom sang the leading roles in Paris, were given thunderous ovations. Even Monck Mason, the theater manager, having spared no expense for the stunning sets and elegant new costumes, was called up on the stage. But Meyerbeer's name was called out in vain—he had left for Berlin before the premier because he considered it his duty to his family, his native city and to the King to direct the final rehearsals of his opera himself. However, in puritanical Berlin where "foreign" opera was severely attacked, Meyerbeer lacked real friends and supporters—he could find these only among the very enlightened royal family. Rellstab dismissed Meyerbeer as a beginner, stating he knew "of not one single good—to say nothing of beautiful—piece of music" by Meyerbeer. There were reviews praising Meyerbeer's work, but after this performance he knew that his future home would not be Berlin, but Paris.*

24. To Minna Meyerbeer in Baden-Baden

[Berlin, June 24, 1832]

My dearest wife,

What must you think of me, seeing as I have not written you in so many days? But in my entire, long career I have never been confronted with a situation such as the one I am faced with now. When I arrived in

Berlin on May 31, I found everything to do with my opera in a state of absolute chaos. In order to prevent disaster, everything had to be started again from scratch. Not only the music, but all other aspects of the production as well; staging, costumes, sets, organ, etc. I had 18 days to accomplish this because I knew that Miss Taglioni had to leave on the 20th. Therefore, I had to do in 18 days what I had had four months to accomplish in Paris. As unbelievable as it may seem, I managed to complete this monumental task and was even able to compose a new dance piece for Taglioni. However, I literally spent every day from six o'clock in the morning to ten o'clock in the evening in the opera house, often having four to six rehearsals in one day. Only then, my dearest, did I go home and fall into bed until the rehearsals began again on the next day! Therefore, taking into account the enormous task I am confronted with here, I hope you will forgive me for something I have never before done, nor shall ever do again: to let 12 days pass without writing to you. Despite all of my Herculean efforts, this time would still have not been sufficient, had it not been for the goodwill, enthusiasm and hard work of the singers, chorus, orchestra and all of the theater personnel. They all demonstrated their commitment up to the very last moment; I cannot praise them enough. The King, Crown Prince and all of the Princes at court also behaved very kindly towards me and paid me the most flattering compliments in front of everyone, both during the rehearsals and the performance. The audience, however, treated me as despicably as it had before. Though I (upon Count Redern's request) conducted the performance myself, which is always considered a courtesy to the audience, and though the performance was, I assure you, exemplary from an orchestral and choral perspective, and though Schätzel was superb and Seidler and Blume were, contrary to all expectations, tolerable, the opera (the first performance of which was yesterday) was received so tepidly that there was no applause for an entire act or longer. The entire fifth act, which includes an organ piece and a trio, came and went without so much as a clap of the hand. I was called out on stage after the third act but only after Taglioni. In short, we could really call yesterday's performance a fiasco. There may have been factors in play which did not have anything to do with me personally. The entire parterre had been converted to stalls, and the heat was oppressive. Since the stage hands had not rehearsed the set changes, the opera lasted from 6 to 11 o'clock, an unheard-of hour for Berliners. I would like to think that, as my good friends have stated, this is the explanation for the opera's poor reception although I have my doubts. I shall know for sure after the second performance. Rellstab's review in the "Vossische Zeitung" was so scathing that I had to promise my brothers that I would not read it.

Yesterday I received the response from Ems. Joseph Mendelssohn arranged accomodations for us in the Four Towers from July 1 to August 15. It must be very beautiful because it costs 28 francs per day. God willing, the weather will be such that we can soon go there. I must relax here for two or three days before I leave because I am completely exhausted. Then I shall rush to be with you, my beloved Lily and, God willing, we shall spend quiet, happy days together with our child. Tomorrow, I have another meeting with Horn regarding you.

Do you still need the whey cure? Miss Milder has told me that she was cured of a stubborn hoarseness by taking a whey cure in Münstertal near Baden.

Farewell for now, my dearest wife. Give my love to Nonne, to your beloved mother, and to our angel.

Your,
Giacomo

*　*　*

On October 1, 1832, Meyerbeer wrote to his wife that he had to do a tremendous amount of musical and historical research in preparation for his new opera Les Huguenots. He plunged into the Psalms of Marot in order to assimilate the local color of the period, which was supposed to be the most important principle in Grand Opéra.

Contrary to Meyerbeer's expectations, Crociato was a tremendous success on its opening night, October 15, 1832, in the Königstädter Theater, the Italian opera house in Berlin.

25. To Minna Meyerbeer in Frankfurt/Main

[Paris, October 10, 1832]

My dear, adored wife!

I wanted to write to you yesterday, but the meeting with Scribe, Véron and Duponchel lasted longer than I had expected. When we were finished, the post office had already closed. Scribe has almost completed the first act [of Les Huguenots]. He is gracious and imaginative, but there is something he lacks which, in this instance, is very important. He does not have any feel for the local color of the chosen period. On the sixteenth, the first and perhaps even the second act shall be delivered to me. The contract has still not been signed. Both Véron and I dread the moment when two people who do not trust one another but need one another, as is the case with us, propose their contract conditions. We plan to do this the day after tomorrow.

I have not written to you about the opera's subject because it is difficult to describe. The story is almost completely fictitious but the period and the ending are historical; that being the St. Bartholomew's Day Massacre [massacre of the Protestants under Charles IX in 1572]. However, there are also some cheerful and lovely scenes in the first three acts. I ask you, my dearest Lily, not to tell anyone about this because this particular event has never before been presented on the stage.

The day before yesterday marked the 49th performance of "Robert." The box office took in 8600 francs and an additional 600 from subscriptions, making a total of 9200 francs. Several hundred people had to be turned away. Since the singers and the orchestra knew that I would be leaving soon, they performed with extraordinary enthusiasm. The performance was so good that there was even mention made of it in the newspapers. Boieldieu, who has not been in Paris for the last 15 months, saw "Robert" yesterday for the first time and sent me the enclosed note. I cannot deny the feeling of satisfaction I have derived from receiving positive comments from so excellent a musician as he so I enclosed it because I thought you would enjoy reading it as well. Please be so kind as to send it to Nonne in Berlin as soon as you have read it. Please do not forget to do this, dearest Lily, because I have already mentioned it to her and her joy is even greater than ours when someone writes favorably of us.

I received the letter from Wilhelm which you forwarded to me. In the letter, he mentioned that Cerf is doing *Crociato,* but not with Jaeger. Instead, he is using a certain Holzmiller who is a perfectly miserable tenor. He is also working with a score which has been horribly chopped up (from Graz, I believe). I mentioned this to the scoundrel in Berlin and I offered him my original score so that the missing sections could be added if he so desired, however, that pitiful rascal did not even bother to answer. This will once again give the Berlin reviewers the needed ammunition to produce scathing reviews.

Yesterday I read German and Italian newspapers and discovered that Miss Pasta had sung "Crociato" in Bergamo and that *Margherita d'Anjou* had been performed in Prague. Each met with only a lukewarm reception.

I am looking forward with great anticipation to your next letter which I hope will contain Stieglitz's response. A million kisses to you and our child and give my love to your dear mother and to Mokka from your

eternally in love,
Giacomo

* * *

Meyerbeer left Paris on October 31, 1832 and went first to Frankfurt where his wife was spending the winter. He also spent a short part of the winter in Karlsruhe and Baden-Baden; the family moved to Baden-Baden at the beginning of March. On March 22, 1833, Michael Beer, Meyerbeer's youngest brother, died in Munich. Upon his death, Meyerbeer traveled to Berlin to be with his mother. He had been staying in Bad Schwalbach since June second.

Princess Augusta of Sachsen-Weimar and Prince Wilhelm of Prussia were married in June of 1829. Meyerbeer had constant access to the court only after becoming Prussian General Music Director and director of court music under Friedrich Wilhelm IV.

26. To Minna Meyerbeer in Bad Ems

[Bad Schwalbach, July 22,
1833]

Sweet Lily, keeper of my soul!

I believe the reason I have not written to you in three days is because nothing worthy of mention has occurred in my isolated life here. I do not have anything to report to you today either except that I worship you and shall always do so. Surely you must know this! I am sorry to hear that the spring water goes to your head and causes the malaise you mentioned, but everyone with whom I have spoken claims that the Ems spring only has good after effects when it bubbles up during a cure. So let yourself be affected by it, dearest wife.

In your last two letters you made no mention of our child. Heaven forbid that there was a reason for this. I have had several frightening dreams about the child since I last visited. Please ask Miss Becker not to let our angel out of her sight for a second. Dreams can sometimes be premonitions or warnings.

I must recount to you an event of extreme embarrassment to me which occurred as a result of my near-sightedness. Yesterday noon as I was taking a walk after my bath, a woman came up to me and asked "Have you been here long?." At first, I did not recognize her at all, then I thought it was Marianne Saling. Given the fact that she and I have known each other for years, I took the liberty of replying with "So you are here, too!" However, the children and servants following this woman, and a closer look, convinced me that I had been mistaken. I had a strong feeling that it was Princess Wilhelm and I was correct. We had a long and friendly conversation and she asked with great interest about my new musical projects. She especially asked about dear Nonne of whom she spoke with great warmth. However, I have to admit that my embarrassment (as a result of having responded to her first question in so unbecoming a fashion) made the ensuing conversation difficult for me. The Prince was not there and I had never encountered him or her before; at least I had never noticed them. In order to make up for my inconsiderate behavior, I planned to formally greet everyone wearing a moustache because the Prince, as a general, probably wears one. Interestingly enough, the first person wearing a moustache whom I greeted was, in fact, the Prince. I had barely greeted him when he came over to me and we had a long and very friendly conversation. As he was leaving he asked to be remembered to my dear mother when I next wrote to her. He went on to say how fond they all were of that distinguished woman.

Is this not a touching story for a royalist such as yourself?

Farewell, dear Lily
Your eternally devoted Moor,
Giacomo

* * *

After the brilliant success of **Robert le Diable,** *Meyerbeer could afford to choose the time for the production of his new opera. When he was unable to come to any agreement with Véron, he paid the customary penalty of 30,000 francs and, with his wife, left for Italy with the score in his luggage. They arrived in Italy on October 30, 1833. Sections of* **Les Huguenots** *were reworked under the strong influence of Vincenzo Bellini's opera* **Norma.** *The role of Marcel, in particular, gained new, stronger contours.*

27. To Minna Meyerbeer in Baden-Baden

[Paris, September 5, 1833]

My dear, adored wife,

I cannot think of any better way to celebrate my birthday than to start it off by writing to you, my sweet Lily. I especially want to keep your lovely image in my head today in order to ward off melancholy; something which one should not feel on one's birthday. However, I cannot deny that I am not in the best of moods. Véron has again proven himself to be a brutal, worthless individual. I repeated to him what I had had Schlesinger tell him; that the condition of my wife's health had worsened and that, on doctor's orders, we had to spend the winter in Italy. Therefore, it would be impossible for me to come to Paris with my opera before the end of spring. I also told him that I knew very well that my contract required a penalty of 30,000 francs in such a case, which I was prepared to pay. I added that I hoped that his loyalty under these circumstances would be such that he would not demand this sum from me, especially since I allowed him to break his contract with me two years ago when we were working together on *Philtre* [an opera by Daniel François Auber] and I did not demand a 30,000 franc penalty. I stated that, if he insisted, I would pay it, but he would never receive my score. I cannot begin to tell you all the flattery and miserable, petty lies he used to get me to pay and still give him my score. We had two meetings (you can imagine how unpleasant they were) and we both stormed out of the last one. In order to give him time to think matters through and to assure that I did not become the loser I told him that I had to take a cure at the ocean resort in Dieppe and then would return via Paris. He could then give me his answer there once he had reconsidered the matter. Therefore, I am leaving tomorrow for 8 to 10 days. Meanwhile, Armand Bertin will try to reason with him. Incidentally, Bertin feels that the best course of action in dealing with Véron's sort would be to pay the 30,000 francs but to tell him that he can have my opera only on the day that he repays me the 30,000 francs. Bertin knows the opera business and feels that Véron will agree to this because he needs me too much. He hopes to earn 200,000 francs from my new opera.

"Robert" is more in vogue than ever; the 82nd performance (with Lafont) earned 7200 francs, not including the subscription receipts. The only thing that impresses Véron is success, so let us hope that Bertin is right. Incidentally, Bertin has paid me many compliments, saying that I am an exemplary husband to sacrifice so much money and fame from a new opera for the health of my wife. Nine times out of ten a reputation, for better or for worse, is achieved in just so false a manner as this. For the sake of your health, dearest wife, I hope that you have now finally overcome all of your doubts about this matter and are able to hold fast to the decision to make this trip to Italy. No matter how things will turn out here, I shall leave to join you at the end of the month. Farewell, keeper of my soul. May heaven bestow joy and blessings upon us by restoring good health to you and Nonne from whom I have still not received a word. My warmest greetings to your dear mother and our child.

Your ever devoted Moor,
Giacomo

*   *   *

The certificate of appointment to the Berlin Academy of the Arts is dated May 2, 1833 but was not sent to Meyerbeer until February 18, 1834. The simultaneous appointment of Mendelssohn and Meyerbeer as members of the academy created a stir. It was not until Napoleon marched into Prussia that the special laws applying to Jews were eliminated. Finally, in 1812, Jews received Prussian nationality and citizenship by virtue of the Emancipation Edict. Although many Jews had participated in the Wars of Liberation (among them Meyerbeer's brother Wilhelm), they were still not recognized as citizens. Meyerbeer often complained bitterly about the "Richesse," the term then used for anti-Semitism: "individuals can forget this word for a certain period of time (but not forever), but an assembled public can never forget it, for it takes only one to remember and all revert to their prejudices." Therefore this appointment, for which Alexander von Humbolt deserved some credit, was a source of satisfaction for Meyerbeer.

28. To the Berlin Academy of the Arts

[Milan, March 29, 1834]

Honorable sirs,

To be admitted into the respected circle of the Fatherland's Academy of the Arts is the most beautiful reward for my modest efforts. No honor has ever meant so much to me or done so much to increase my enthusiasm for the arts. Becoming a member of an art institute which commands great respect from Europe's intellectuals is flattering for any artist. This honor means that much more to me because this flattering selection was made by great and famous fellow-artists from my native city. I feel that I can be worthy of this honor only by doing what lies within my limited abilities in order to work towards achieving the goals to which this new section of the Royal Academy is dedicated and to which the other members are certainly quite devoted. As soon as possible, I shall send the brief autobiography which you require.

The letter from the honorable Royal Academy arrived very late because it was sent from Berlin to Nizza (Nice) and I had already departed for northern Italy when it arrived there. I received it only upon my arrival in Milan a few days ago. This is the only reason for the delay in my expression of gratitude which I most humbly ask the honorable members of the Royal Academy to kindly accept.

J. Meyerbeer

* * *

Meyerbeer was one of those composers who, according to old tradition, custom-tailored the roles in their operas to specific singers. He was often inspired by the timbre of a voice and he studied the peculiarities, strengths and weaknesses of his singers before beginning a new work. If an opera had not been fully cast for its premier, as in the case of l'Africaine, *the work was put aside until the desired performers had been hired.*

29. To Minna Meyerbeer in Milan

[Florence, May 1, 1834]

Dearest beloved wife,

Yesterday, I heard [Caroline] Ungher in *Parisina* by Donizetti and I shall hear her perform again today. Therefore, I could leave tomorrow except that it is Friday. I have to admit that, in this particular year, I do not want to ignore my superstitious feelings. Therefore I shall leave Saturday and shall be with you on Monday evening or Tuesday. Ungher is a very fine artist, filled with the best of dramatic intentions. If her voice had not become sharp and castrato-like, I would rather compose for her than for the extravagant Malibran. Even given the way she is, I would still very much like to see her as Valentine in Paris. Duprez is also a good singer and would be a very good Raoul. No matter how few good singers Italy has in comparison to the past, the Italians still have an infinite advantage over all other countries, without exception. The few theaters I have visited have convinced me of this once again. Every composer who writes for voice must go to Italy from time to time, not for the compositions he might hear, but to hear the Italian singers. Only by listening to great singers can a composer learn how to write singable music that flatters the human voice and I consider it a calamity that I was unable to take a more extended tour through Italy during this season. . . .

Farewell, dearest wife. May God comfort and strengthen you both in body and in spirit.

A thousand kisses to you and our dear child from your eternally devoted loyal Moor,

Giacomo

* * *

Despite his differences with Véron, Meyerbeer still hoped to produce Les Huguenots *at the Paris Opéra. Given the French copyright laws, Scribe was not able to work for another European theater and a production at the Paris Opéra Comique was not possible due to official regulations stating that only three-act operas with spoken text were allowed in that theater.*

It was in Italy that Meyerbeer, probably in collaboration with Gaetano Rossi, gave to the role of Marcel, the powerful foil and mentor of the waffling Raoul, the surly character representing "the simple but unshakable pious beliefs of a martyr." Also in Italy, he added the Lutheran chorale "A Mighty Fortress," which functions as a kind of leitmotif for Marcel and was the equivalent of a Christian "Marseillaise." This chorale was to represent "the sounds from a better world, a symbol of faith and hope." George Sand referred to Marcel as "one of the greatest dramatic figures, one of the most beautiful personifications of a religious concept to be found in the art of our time."

Scribe and Meyerbeer concluded their contract for the opéra comique entitled Le Portefaix *[The Porter] on February 1, 1831. However, Meyerbeer was not pleased with the libretto because it did not provide opportunities for effective choral scenes. As a result, he composed only a few numbers. When Meyerbeer withdrew from the contract, Scribe turned over the libretto to a third-rate composer by the name of José Melchor Gomis (1791–1836). However, the work achieved no success. (First performance: 1835.)*

30. To Eugène Scribe in Paris

[Baden-Baden, July 2, 1834]

My dear friend,

Your kind letter found me in very poor health as the result of a violent colic, an affliction from which I have been suffering ever since I became seriously ill in Nizza. For this reason, I was obliged to delay my response by a few days.

I accept with gratitude your frank and loyal statement to the effect that you are in agreement with everything I desire regarding our grand opera project and that you shall continue to keep your libretto available for me. I hope that the work itself shall be compensation for you. I also hope I am not blinded by the creator's love for his creation when I say that I feel that it is the best I have written so far; it would have a good chance of success not only at the Opéra but also at the Opéra Comique in the event that Mr. Véron does not relent and forces us to perform it there. Should this turn out to be the case, I would be very pleased if you could write a new poem for my music as you promised me in Paris, even though I already have three poems at my disposal at this time, not including *La Dame du Louvre* [The Lady of the Louvre]. According to a letter from a friend of mine in Paris, I have every reason to believe that it will not be necessary for us to choose this solution, to which I would only resort if Mr. Véron stubbornly refused to refund the breach-of-contract penalty which he never should have demanded from me in the first place. At the end of this month or the beginning of August, I must go to Paris for 15 days to undergo a delicate and difficult dental treatment and I would very much like to meet with you while I am there. During my last stay in Paris, I mentioned to you that your development of the role of Marcel did not correspond to the musical concept I had desired for the role and that there were too many numbers with no female voices. You responded that you would leave it up to me to make any changes I desired, with or without any mutual discussion of the matter. You also stated that you would allow me to make changes in the entire work provided that I request this of you only at a time when everything could be taken care of at once and when the score was complete. Very well, my friend, I acted in accordance with your wishes. In order for it to comply with my musical requirements, I have completely rewritten the role of Marcel (albeit not in German, which would have been easier for me, but in Italian because it is a language you understand). I have also found a way to add female voices to many of the numbers and I made some changes where it seemed necessary but some additional work is still needed. It is important that you review everything, make any changes you feel are necessary and give me your opinion. Only then can I tell the director of the opera that my score is finished, although for the most part it is. This should not take a great deal of your time, but your final editing is absolutely necessary because I shall not give it to the copyist until I have it back from you. This is why I very much hope that you can devote your free time to this work or that you will at least begin work on it during my brief stay in Paris. I realize that you cannot begin until I know definitively whether I will submit it to the director of the Opéra or be obliged to turn it over to the Opéra Comique. If the latter proves necessary, different changes would have to be made. Whatever effect the delay resulting from my dental treatment may have on my departure for Paris, I shall arrive by August 15 at the latest. Of course I would like to know when I shall be able to meet with you so you can then make these changes in our "Huguenots." Please write a note to Mr. Gouin to let him know your plans.

Now I shall address the second point in your letter. Concerning *Porte-Faix,* you requested that I agree to let you have control over the libretto and, given the fact that you have waited until now to make your request, you have acted as a loyal friend for you had the rights to it until January. I shall certainly regret the loss of your delightful libretto and the pieces I have already composed, but I could in no way criticize your action, my friend, because as I have already mentioned, you have demonstrated so much loyalty. There are two reasons preventing me from giving this work to the Opéra Comique in the short period of time you have requested. The first reason, as you know from our last meeting in Paris, is that after several years of silence I should not walk into the arena without a major work in my hands. Therefore, I would like to present *Porte-Faix*, which, is from a musical standpoint, on a very small scale compared to your *Valentine* [*Huguenots*], to the general public only after this major work has been performed. The second reason (which is almost more important) is that the current tenor at the Opéra Comique would not have much luck with the role of Porte-Faix given the way I have conceived the role, the dramatic situations, and the most important musical pieces. My score, thus, would be a fiasco. You are correct, my dear friend, in not wanting to wait any longer with the libretto you completed for Hérold so long ago. However, you must also understand my reasons for not wanting to perform this work until after *Valentine*, and then only with a singer like Duprez or Chollet for the role of Porte-Faix.

Well, my dear friend, do with it as you see fit. However, I am writing these words to you with a heavy heart. Because I must give you a definitive answer, I must also make my intentions clear to you. Incidentally, I am very interested in the Opéra Comique. I am happy to hear that it is in the hands of so active and intelligent a director as the present one and I am dying to write a work for this theater as soon as possible, a work in which the roles are tailor-made for the singers. This is extremely important to me and in order to realize this dream soon, I should first like to write a work in one or two acts which could then be produced immediately following *Valentine*. As soon I am back in Paris, I shall begin the search for a suitable poem. I would be very grateful if you could find something appropriate in your desk drawer.

Farewell, my dear friend. I hope to see you in Paris.

Very respectfully Yours,
Meyerbeer

*   *   *

Louis Gouin (1780–1856), a high-ranking postal official in Paris and part-owner of a vaudeville theater, had been a friend of Meyerbeer's since 1826. More than just a friend, he was Meyerbeer's closest confidant, often representing him when he was away from Paris for an extended period of time in Berlin or in some spa. Gouin supervised the performances of the Maestro's operas in his absence, especially when there were cast changes. He also supervised theater receipts, the box office and the royalties. He negotiated with opera directors, singers, artists and journalists. Meyerbeer's artistic diplomacy would not have been possible without Gouin's selfless and untiring efforts.

Here, too, Gouin's diplomatic skills succeeded in smoothing some ruffled feathers: on September 29, 1834, the contract which included the cast list was signed for the production of Les Huguenots. *Véron reimbursed Meyerbeer for the 30,000 franc fine for breach of contract.*

31. To Louis Gouin in Paris

[Paris, September 1, 1834]

My dear friend,
You are familiar with the letter I sent to Mr. Véron from Nizza in response to his letter to me. You then informed me that Mr. Véron did not wish to provide a written response and that he limited himself to the following words: "as soon as Mr. Meyerbeer has completed his score, we shall see." Therefore we are completely free to negotiate with one another. To my great artistic satisfaction, I have just completed my score which takes the form of a grand opera. I have decided to spend a few extra days in Paris (before taking a seaside vacation in Boulogne on doctor's orders) so as to offer him this new opera, if he is interested. However, I shall do this only on the explicit condition that he repay me the 30,000 franc fine for breach of contract the moment he receives the score, and that he fulfill several small requests regarding the opera (they are all of an artistic nature) and that the scheduling of rehearsals be to our mutual satisfaction. I do not think that these last two points shall be cause for any difficulties and we should be able to discuss them quite easily once the breach of contract issued has been settled. Yesterday, I was at Mr. Véron's home both to pay him a visit and to discuss this matter, but unfortunately he was out. In the event that Mr. Véron is unwilling to accept my offer under these conditions, I have wondered if it would not perhaps be as embarrassing for him to tell me so to my face as it would be for me to hear it. Therefore, I am going to seek refuge in your friendship and ask you to be the courier of my conciliatory message as well as to bring me back a definitive response so that I can take care of other matters before my departure on Thursday—the sea resort season is coming to an end.
Farewell and au revoir!

Respectfully Yours,
Meyerbeer

*　　*　　*

Alfred de Musset, born in 1810, was just 24 years old when he created a stir with his love stories set in Spain and Italy, "Contes d'Espagne et Italie" which appeared in 1829. His liaison with George Sand, who was six years his senior, and in particular their trip to Italy together in 1833, may have caused Meyerbeer to fear that the young poet now planned to collect material for some new stories.

32. To Minna Meyerbeer in Baden-Baden

[Paris, October 6, 1834]

My dearest adored wife,
I wanted to write to you yesterday and the day before, but waited because I was expecting letters from you. Indeed, three of those letters I

so desired arrived together today: one came via Boulogne, the other two directly from Paris, [Meyerbeer's error: from Berlin[although they bore different dates. I have a lot to answer, but the letters reached me too late. Therefore, I will limit myself to what is most important to me. Since the time when I had the good fortune to take your heart and hand in marriage, I can say that not only have I never suffered the torture of jealousy, but the mere fear of it seems unthinkable to me. Your gentle and pure soul, your dignified outward behavior, the strict and proper yardstick you use to measure women's values and their relationships to men, and finally the limitless love and respect of your Moor, whose love for you and the child ensure his ultimate happiness and are his raison d'être, prevent even the slightest bit of jealousy from arising within me. I have as great a faith in your virtue and loyalty as I do in all that is good and true. And yet all of this is still not sufficient for your insatiable Moor. My unhappiness would defy description if any individual, be it the most insignificant gossip monger in Baden, were to deviate from my estimation of your virtue by even the breadth of a hair. You now write to me of your many visitors, of the young people and men whom you yourself have characterized as fops and dandies, who come to meet our child. Your maternal vanity may believe this, but when young men visit a beautiful young woman, the parent will surely be the only one attributing these visits to a four-year-old child. Given the fact that you are in Baden without the company of a male relative (and your mother is not even living on your floor) I question, my dear, whether it is advisable to receive young men as visitors, especially those whom neither you nor I knew before. If you consider this to be jealousy, then it is a jealous attempt to guard the luster of your reputation which should shine for all the world the way it does in my heart. I repeat that I have rock-hard faith in your love and devotion, otherwise I would be in Baden before this letter arrives. As for Alfred de Musset, who would like to be introduced to you, he is a famous Romantic writer and an acquaintance of mine. For this reason, agree to receive him once or twice because otherwise he could be a dangerous enemy. However, graciously break off all contact with him afterwards. Someone who writes of morality with such contempt as he does is not worthy of a virtuous woman's company. Unfortunately, he is also much younger and better-looking than I.

Now that I have finished this letter and reread it, I almost want to tear it up. However, I realize that there is nothing in the letter that can hurt you. If my love for you causes me to worry too much, then my sweet Lily will forgive me for that very reason. Farewell, my dearest, and a thousand kisses to you and our beloved child from

your eternally devoted Moor,
Giacomo

* * *

It would be easy to smile at Meyerbeer's scatter-brained tendencies which even caused him to forget his wife's birthday. However, this error is understandable when one considers that, in the first decades of the 19th century, the Beer family still celebrated birthdays according to the Jewish calendar. This meant that, by our reckoning, the birthdays fell on a different date every year.

33. To Minna Meyerbeer in Baden-Baden

[Paris, November 26, 1834]

My dearest Minna,

Today I can write to you with a lighter heart than when I last wrote you. First of all, my terrible tooth aches have been cured and secondly, a problem concerning my opera, which has been troubling me night and day for the last two weeks, has been resolved. According to an article in the "Figaro," one of my most brilliant and unexpected musical effects, which was to provide a magnificent ending to the fourth act, could be found in its entirety in Halévy's new opera [*La juive* (The Jewess)]. You can imagine how upset I was. If this had been true, I would have had to cut out your favorite piece "laissez moi partir" (Raoul's "let me depart from here") along with the entire end of the act. Then there was also Véron's maliciousness towards me to worry about. If the article were not true, there was the chance that Véron would tell Halévy about it so he could include it in his new opera anyway. This would be his idea of a prank! After giving the whole matter a great deal of thought, I gathered up my courage and decided to go to Véron and tell him the entire situation and left it up to his discretion as to whether he wanted to cut out the effect, whether or not it was used in Halévy's opera. I also explained to him that under no circumstances could I forfeit this effect because it was an integral part of my work. If it were absent, what is now surprising and even frightening, would then appear insipid, a mere reminiscence.

Contrary to my fears, he reacted very well to the situation and assured me that he was unaware of the details. He also said that, if the article were true, he would do what he could to eliminate this material. Fortunately, upon closer investigation of the story, it appeared to be a rather significant departure from the truth. Therefore, the originality of my effect will not be lost.

Now let me tell you a funny story that is worthy of my charming Lily. In my contract, April 15 is designated as the deadline for submitting my score. Two nights ago, as I lay in bed thinking, it suddenly struck me like an arrow through my heart that your birthday is on April 28 and that I had to be in Paris on the 15th; how rash and thoughtless of me not to have extended the deadline a few more days. I am away from you too much as it is, and now I will not even be present for your birthday. I cursed myself the entire night and my conscience raised havoc with me because, as you know, I signed the contract some time ago. Every time I looked at your portrait, I asked your forgiveness. This morning I was so tormented by this that I asked to have a meeting with Véron. As difficult as it was to request something of Marat [Véron], I told him of my desperate plight and implored him to add a supplement to the contract so that the deadline could be postponed by 20 days, thus allowing me to be with you on your birthday in Baden. Since this arrangement also worked to his advantage (as I discovered an hour later from Duponchel), Véron agreed. The clause was formulated, inserted and he then signed it. As I was taking the pen in my hand to do the same I suddenly realized, "my God, her birthday is the eighth, not the 28th!!!" By then it was too late. Véron had already signed it and I kept quiet and signed it too so as not to make a complete fool of myself. What do you say to that? . . .

God bless you my dear, and our wonderful child.

Your ever devoted Moor,
Giacomo

*   *   *

Meyerbeer composed many songs of different types: German Lieder, Italian romances, canzonettas, French chansons and dramatic scenes. In 1850, the most important of these were compiled into a collection of 40 mélodies. Both "Le Moine" [The Monk], set to a text by Emilien Pacini, and "Rachel à Nephtali" appeared in 1834 in a collection entitled Keepsake Lyrique *published by A. Pacini in Paris. Meyerbeer dedicated these dramatic songs to Prosper Levasseur, the great French bass who made them famous in the French salons. These songs became Levasseur's favorites. The element of local color, which was taken from the world of dramatic opera, led to the creation of a new genre of song which required singers with stage experience for proper interpretation.*

34. To Wilhelm Speyer in Frankfurt

Baden, January 28, 1835

Dearest sir and friend,

If you believe that I think about you as seldom as I write, you would do me a disservice. My memories of your stimulating company in Frankfurt, the manifold demonstrations of interest, benevolence, and friendship are among the most enduring and comforting memories of my life. However, as fast as my heart beats at the thought of my friends my pen remains mired in sluggishness. I can love but cannot write; this just seems to be the unfortunate way my life is organized. And yet I so longed for news of you, my friend, that I would surely have written to you from Paris if I had not been planning to return to Germany via Frankfurt where I would have visited you during the Christmas holidays. Unfortunately, there were several circumstances which forced me to postpone my departure from Paris by a month. Since I wanted to be with my wife at the beginning of the New Year, I returned to Baden by the shortest route possible and was therefore unable to stop in Frankfurt. Please permit me to extend to you and your family my best New Year wishes which, although in written form, are no less cordial than had they been issued by me in person. I hope for your continued love and friendship for both are too dear to my heart to lose. Please allow me to enclose a small musical expression of my New Year's greetings. It is no more significant than the usual New Year's gifts and should only serve to keep me in your thoughts. They are two Romances which I recently composed in Paris and which were very popular there. This is all the more remarkable because they are very different from the sentimental, sweet Romances which are currently so popular. My Romances attempt to evoke a sense of drama and local color while remaining within the limits of this more intimate musical genre. It is my hope that the monk's struggle with temptation and repentance is clear enough to warrant no commentary. This is probably not the case in the biblical Romance "Rachel à Nephtali," in which the poet's colors are so delicately expressed that I worked with very subtle musical means. The shame felt by the young Jewess in admitting to her brother-in-law that she shares his forbidden love holds back the glow of her passion, which only breaks through in the last verse of each couplet, "Pitié, je suis ta soeur" [Oh pity, I am your sister]. I attempted to express this intense feeling by using a persistent small bass figure. In the last verse of each couplet, where the passion breaks through, this bass figure is taken over by the vocal line. I am sorry that I wrote this Romance in 2/4 instead of 4/4 time, for the movement must be slower than it appears to the eye.

I hope to be with my dear wife and child in the delightful solitude of Baden until April. I shall have to return to Paris at the end of April to begin rehearsal of my new opera. You have probably read in the French papers that my steadfast refusal to publish my score triumphed over Véron's miserly obstinacy. He agreed to repay me the 30,000 francs I had to pay him in the autumn of 1833 for breach of contract when we went to take the cure in Nizza. But I do have to put up with the fact that the opera shall not be performed this winter as I had wished (since the opera has been finished for the last five months); instead, it shall not be performed until the end of the summer. This is more suitable to Véron's interests because his two principal female dancers, Taglioni and Elssler, will be on vacation.

Well, my dear friend, I have gone on and on about myself. Therefore, please write to me of you and your delightful family, and please bring me up to date on new musical developments in Frankfurt. I would also like to know how our classical master, Spohr, is doing and what he has written lately. When you write to him again, please send my greetings. My best wishes also to the esteemed masters Ries, Schnyder, Schelble and Guhr from

your humble servant,
J. Meyerbeer

In June of 1835 rehearsals began for the premier of Les Huguenots. *Meyerbeer tirelessly rehearsed the singers in their roles individually as well as working with the ensembles and choruses. It was not only the censors who demanded extensive changes in the basic material of the work; Scribe, who supervised the rehearsals and was responsible for direction and dramatic effectiveness, had some requests and some cuts became necessary. In addition Nourrit, who sang the role of Raoul, demanded a new final duet in Act four: it became the most successful piece in the entire opera! The demands of organizing, staging and rehearsing a work of this magnitude took its toll on Meyerbeer. Exhausted and resigned, he wrote to his wife on June 18, 1835: "I am still as passionately devoted to my art as I was in the days of my youth. I still feel the urge to compose better and more significant music than I have in the past. However, I am losing the energy required to dive into the filthy sewers through which one has to swim in order to find today's theaters, audiences and critics and out of which today's successes are fished. I say this because they are all sinking deeper and deeper into the quagmire. In this insane environment, it soon will be just as embarrassing to succeed as it used to be to fail."*

35. To Minna Meyerbeer in Frankfurt

[Paris, December 24, 1835]

My most beloved wife,

I have gone many days without writing to you because the new problems confronting me have required that I make use of every minute to minimize the awkward situation in which we now find ourselves. The government has *banned* the character of Cathérine di Medici, the entire finale, as well as the scene with the monks. It may be possible to save the first two of these if some major revisions are made, which means more work for me. However, the third is *impossible* unless I rewrite half of the fourth act. You can imagine the countless meetings I have had with the Minister and the Commission. The way things stand at this point, Cathérine must be eliminated as well as the finale and even the title.

I am now busy making the necessary revisions, but time is running out. If the scene with the monks has to be changed, I will have no choice but to cancel the opera's production. Scribe has interceded on my behalf regarding this last point. You can imagine the outlandish newspaper articles and wild rumors that this controversy has caused. All of this effort and nothing but frustration! I am very grateful to Nonne and Wilhelm for being here and providing me with some measure of comfort during this difficult time. The weather is very changeable: sometimes there is a heavy frost, sometimes thawing and dampness; on the whole very unhealthy. Tomorrow or the day after, Adolph will depart, arriving there in four days. I am enclosing the "Journal des Débats" from November ninth as you requested. It is not easy to acquire individual issues. I just now received two letters from you. In one of these you ask me if you should send our child and your mother here. Surely you do not seriously wish to subject a delicate child and a fragile woman to the rigors of travel during the winter months. Even the heartiest of people fall ill when traveling during this season. Had you made this request of me in October, I would have been ever so grateful. May our gracious God keep us healthy and happy so that winter's end also brings an end to our separation.

Many greetings to your dear mother from Nonne and me. A thousand kisses to you and our child from your devoted Moor,

Giacomo

*   *   *

The first performance of Les Huguenots *on February 29, 1836 was one of the most stunning successes in the history of the Paris Opéra. Six weeks later, a reviewer for the "Revue des deux Mondes" wrote that any criticism would have to fall silent in the face of such an overwhelming success. There was spontaneous approval as well as intense debate concerning Meyerbeer's "point de vue," his esthetic point of view. The realism of the historical setting and local color were praised. It caused the audience to participate, to be caught up in this horrible event. Hector Berlioz stated that Meyerbeer had packed this opera with enough musical riches for 20 successful operas. George Sand, as previously mentioned, stressed the role of Marcel as the decisive figure in the work. The debate brought masses of people to the opera: on April 17, 1836, the box office of the Paris Opéra took in 11,300 francs, a sum never before attained. In the 64-year period between 1836 and 1900,* Les Huguenots *was the first opera ever to reach the magic number of 1000 performances.*

36. To Minna Meyerbeer in Frankfurt

[Paris, March 1, 1836]

Keeper of my soul!

I turned to you during my last moments of desperation and fear, so it is you I shall address now that the successful performance has quieted my fears. Yesterday our "Huguenots" gave the appearance of being a great success. I say "gave the appearance" because you know that the management of the theaters in Paris make a big event of their premiers so that one cannot discover the true public reaction until later. However, this is not as prevalent in the Paris Opéra as it is in other theaters. In the first act, the orgy scene, Nourrit's Romance, the chorale, the chanson and the short aria by Flécheux were all well received. The entire act produced a very warm effect. Although we had relied heavily on it and it was greeted with widespread applause, the second act really left the audience cold. On the other hand the third act, which had given us cause for concern, went over very well, especially "Rataplan," which had to be repeated, the septet from the duel, and the quarreling chorus which was brilliantly performed. The duet between Falcon and Levasseur did not make quite as

Illus. 9: Scene from *Les Huguenots*. Finale of Act V. Lithograph by
Achille Devéria (Album de l'Opera).

big an impression, although there was a lot of applause. Overall, the
opera's success is not yet definitive. The fourth act was enthusiastically
received, and the trio in the fifth act, which had not gone well during
rehearsals, went brilliantly during the performance. After the fourth act,
Nourrit and Falcon were called out; after the fifth, I was called out (but I
excused myself), and then everyone was called out. The short articles in
today's newspapers are all very favorable. What will happen in the long
run, God only knows. I am not yet completely relaxed, but I am a lot more
at ease than I was yesterday.

I bid farewell to you, my dearest, and to our child.

Your eternally devoted Moor

*   *   *

*Even before the premier, Meyerbeer had feared that sections of the opera would not
be understood and especially that the role of Marcel would be rejected as being too
modern. The intense esthetic discussions about the opera after it was performed
confirm that Meyerbeer had dared take a big step forward in the development of
opera. His comment that it was not easy to find individual issues of newspapers*

may at first seem a bit odd. However, at the time the newspapers were sold only by subscription; individual sales had not yet been introduced. Not until the end of 1847 did the Paris newspaper publisher Emile Girardin, following English custom, introduce street sales of newspapers. Charles Duponchel had taken over as director of the Opéra in August, 1835.

37. To Minna Meyerbeer in Frankfurt

[Paris, March 6, 1836]

Keeper of my soul,

I have a stupid superstition which is deeply embedded in my soul which tells me never to use the word "success" to describe an opera of mine before the third performance. However, the third performance is now over, so without exaggerating, I believe I can speak of an overwhelming success about which all of Paris is now buzzing. In the third performance, the first three acts were much better received than they had been in the first two performances. As far as the fourth and fifth acts are concerned, they could not have been received more enthusiastically than they were during the first performance. Incidentally, "Rataplan" had to be encored again yesterday; Nourrit and Falcon were called out after the fourth act, Levasseur, Nourrit and Falcon after the fifth act. The demand for stalls and boxes has been so great that there are two sentries standing at the box office every day. Whether this success shall continue can not yet be determined.

Please do not get the impression that, simply because the opera has enjoyed widespread popularity, it is not without its critics in the foyers and salons. Many people disapprove of the esthetic quality found in my compositional style. An example of this would be Levasseur's role [Marcel]. The opera is referred to as showing only skill in the first three acts, but genius only in the last two, and some consider it inferior to "Robert". However, the opera has won over countless enthusiasts who not only claim that this opera is better than "Robert", but place it on such a high level that I would blush if I were to repeat their comments. What has pleased me most of all has been that even the opera's opponents speak of it as being one of the most important works to appear in recent times, even though they are not in agreement with the direction my music is taking. I am also very satisfied with the tone of the newspapers, and not only with those which have sung my praises, but even with those which have been critical. Out of 20 to 30 newspapers, only two have been extremely critical. I have already sent you a few newspapers and shall send you nine more today. I was unable to locate any more because it is difficult to find individual issues. Some of the ones I found are only borrowed. Please, my dearest, be so good as to *keep all of the issues* as they are very important to me. If you believe that the success of my opera has won me a measure of rest, you are very much mistaken. Duponchel's indescribable stupidity and carelessness have kept me busy night and day

73

so as to ensure that every performance is not the last. He tends to nothing and his animosity towards me has been very frustrating.

Nonne and I send our greetings to your dear mother.

Your eternally devoted Moor

Tomorrow is the fourth performance and not a seat is to be had in the house.

38. To Minna Meyerbeer in Frankfurt

[Paris, March 10, 1836]

Dearest Queen of my heart,

You know from "Robert" the lengths to which one must go in Paris to *sustain* a success. Imagine a director such as the miserable Duponchel, who is completely incompetent, and you will not be surprised when I tell you that I am on my feet from six in the morning until after midnight every day dealing with matters which, in one way or another, have a major effect on the future of this opera.

Thank heavens the opera seems to have maintained its popularity. It has now been performed six times consecutively and has attracted huge crowds. They don't seem to diminish, for every day there is such a rush to the box office to rent stalls and boxes that two sentries have been posted there. The "scalpers" are still selling tickets at four times their normal price. The applause in the theater is as strong as ever. The first three acts, which were so highly criticized at the beginning of the run, are winning over new friends every day. The musical skill of the singers, orchestra and choruses is something the likes of which Paris has never heard before. With a few exceptions, the newspapers have been very supportive. Even the opponents of this opera refer to it as a very important work of art. Among the general public, there are critics of this work and of my esthetic point of view, but the vast majority of people have strongly supported it. What I find especially pleasing is that *musicians,* even the most famous ones, are the greatest enthusiasts of this opera. Whether this success shall continue certainly cannot be determined after the sixth performance. *Guillaume Tell* enjoyed 12 very successful performances, but it all came to a very sudden end. Nous verrons [We shall see]. I am sending you another packet of newspapers today, including the "Gazette de France" which is very amusing. They accused me of using my genius to glorify the Protestant religion, even though I, as a Jew, should be familiar with the intolerance and narrow-mindedness of the Protestants. Please share with Speyer the articles by Fétis in the "Temps," "Débats," and "Constitutionel" as well as any other good articles; I would be very grateful to him if he would use these as the basis for an article in one of the Frankfurt newspapers. Adieu my dearest. There were many other things I wanted to put in this letter but I had to write it amidst 1000 interruptions and now it is time for the mail to be taken.

A thousand kisses to you and our child.

Your eternally devoted Moor,
Giacomo

*   *   *

After Carl Maria von Weber's premature death on June 5, 1826, his widow asked Meyerbeer, as her husband's boyhood friend, to complete the unfinished opera entitled Die Drei Pintos *(The Three Pintos). Whether this was Weber's personal wish—as has been claimed—or one based purely on financial considerations, is unclear. Meyerbeer agreed to do it because he felt it was his duty as a friend. This proved to be a disastrous decision on his part. Time and again in the years that followed, Meyerbeer attempted to work with the few musical sketches left by Weber in order to create a meaningful entity. New librettos were written and then discarded, contracts were drawn up and then broken. It became ever more evident that, due to the differing talents and styles of the two composers, it would be impossible to complete the work. Meyerbeer was criticized by the German press and by his own family for dragging his feet and not fulfilling his duty to his friend. In order to do at least something for the family, Meyerbeer reimbursed Caroline von Weber and her two sons on several occasions for the lost royalties. When he finally returned the sketches to the family on January 27, 1852, the compensation had reached 4000 thaler which exceeded Meyerbeer's annual salary as Prussian Music Director General by 1000 thaler.*

At the end of the 1880's, Gustav Mahler used Weber's sketches for a new opera, but it was unsuccessful. Today it has been more or less forgotten. Eduard Hanslick rated Carl Maria von Weber's original sketches as "dull and conventional," thereby posthumously confirming Meyerbeer's own instinct.

39. To Minna Meyerbeer in Baden-Baden

[Paris, June 4 or 5, 1836]

My dearest wife,

I am writing you these lines to inform you that our work shall be prolonged by a few days. The response from Court Councellor Winkler from Dresden (Theodor Hell) is largely to blame. You know that he is the guardian of the Weber children and also the author of *Die Drei Pintos* which I was supposed to have finished so long ago. Since this has to be finished, I have decided of my own accord to begin serious work on it at once. This is something I would have to do sooner or later anyway. Since Weber only left enough material for two-thirds of one act, leaving nine-tenths of the work falling into my lap it will, for all intents and purposes, be a new opera. As such, I would at least like to select a good story line and perform it in Paris, or Paris and Dresden at the same time. I had Winkler read *Die Drei Pintos* for me and it is the silliest, most stupid thing in the world. Therefore, I must procure some good material from a French librettist; material which will suit the music Weber has already composed. I must also get permission from both the librettist and the management of the Opéra Comique, where the opera is to be performed, to have simultaneous performances in Paris and Dresden, or even to have the opera performed in Dresden first. This is what we are dealing with at present. I had already found a librettist and a subject for the opera but Winkler was not satisfied with the material. At any rate, this shall not delay my departure for long. If nothing is settled here I shall deal with the problem after I return to Paris.

Please forgive this chicken scratch. I am writing hastily at Crémieux's (notary) where I am having a procuration drawn up which should prevent any intrigue from developing in my absence. Rumor has it that H[alévy] and R[ossini] are planning to interfere with the success of our "Huguenots."

Farewell my dearest. I dream of nothing but you in your nightrobe with the silk bonnet on your lovely little head, at about 11 o'clock in the evening. Kiss our child for me. I am bringing wonderful things back for her.

Your eternally devoted Moor

40. To Eugène Roger de Bully, otherwise known as Roger de Beauvoir, in Paris

[Paris, June 10, 1837]

My dear Roger,

It was impossible for me to see Mr. de St. Georges yesterday. I am spending the entire day today at Versailles [festival in Versailles during which the third and fifth acts of *Robert le Diable* were performed], but tomorrow I shall definitely go to see him. I am certain that I shall be able to make him understand the situation by explaining to him the nature of the work required by Weber's sketches [Die Drei Pintos]. I shall make it clear to him that we cannot do without a collaborator who understands German perfectly and who is as good a writer as he is a musician. There are some extremely thorny problems, both in the music and in the translation of this work. A collaborative effort between three people would be very important. This is why I consider participation by Henri Blaze to be absolutely necessary.

Farewell for now. I am arranging my meeting with Mr. de St. Georges which I hope shall take place on Monday.

Many warm greetings.
Your humble servant,
Meyerbeer

*   *   *

It was not until 1839 that Gottfried Weber published an essay, mentioned by Meyerbeer, entitled "Einige deutsche Gedanken bei Gelegeneit einer französischen Oper" [Some German Thoughts on the Occasion of a French Opera]. The essay was included in "Caecilia," which was edited by Weber, and signed by someone using the pseudonym "Heinrich Paris." The author concedes that, from a musical standpoint, Les Huguenots *seems to be a very beautiful opera. However, with the subject matter pertaining to religious conflict, its performance in Germany was deemed unsuitable "due to the harm [that might be] inflicted on the uneducated members of the audience." It would be necessary "to ban the work from the stage without mercy . . . leave it to the intellectuals . . . to perform the music from the opera in their concerts and private circles." Indeed, in many areas in Germany the censors expressed opposition to the libretto of* Les Huguenots: *in Cologne, the opera was produced under the title* Margarethe von Navarra *in 1837, and in 1838 the Munich production was entitled* Anglikaner und Puritaner. *In Vienna, the opera was presented either as* Ghibellinen in Pisa *or as* Welfen und Ghibellinen *(Guelphs and Ghibellines). However, in Berlin, Meyerbeer's native city,* Les Huguenots *was completley forbidden by censors during the life of Friedrich Wilhelm III. The long-awaited Berlin premier did not take place until six years after the opera's first performance, on May 20, 1842, after Friedrich Wilhelm IV came into power.*

41. To Gottfried Weber in Darmstadt

Baden, October 20, 1837

Dear brother!

Since my last letter to you, I have not been feeling well and even had to spend two days in bed: this is the reason for the delay in the continuation of my letter; laziness was not to blame this time.

When we last saw one another, I was very disturbed to discover that you had distanced yourself from all musical activities. How could this be? You are the man who has developed the most enlightened and intelligent "theory" in recent times, who has written countless essays on every conceivable field of musical knowledge, whose "Requiem" and "Lieder" have established you as a major composer. Are you to remain silent during the prime of your life and give up the place of honor to which your spirit and your work have entitled you? Should you not be the legislator, the highest authority on music criticism in all of Germany? The one link you still have with the world of music, the journal "Caecilia," is void of any significance due to your publisher's total lack of competence. Nowadays, no journal can publish on such an irregular and arbitrary basis and still expect to have a large readership, especially not a music journal which is considered by its readers to be one of the most belletristic and intellectual of publications. Put half as much material into one issue, but make sure one issue is published every two weeks, and you shall see whether I am right or not.

And then there are your wonderful essays that you have been writing for various music journals for the last 30 years. Why have you let them fall into oblivion? Yes, that is right, oblivion! For who reads a journal except when it has first been published, and who reads it more than once? Why do you refuse to do what other great writers have done under similar circumstances? Why don't you compile all of your individual essays, edit and coordinate them, and then publish them under the title "G. Weber's Collected Writings on Music" (or some other title)? All of the critics in the music world would discuss such a publication, the general public would read what for them would be a new work, and it could finally take its rightful place in the body of musical literature instead of remaining fragments, lost to oblivion in the pages of old journals.

And why don't you have any musical circle in Darmstadt? Why aren't you the director of the opera? Have you not been offered such a position? That should not surprise me, unless it is because you yourself have not made any move in that direction. In Darmstadt, you are the only superior musical figure, and such individuals disturb other people and make them feel small. One is always grateful when these superior beings keep their mouths shut. These special people may not be loved, but one fears their intellect, their words, and their pen; and if the superior ones only demand their due, they seldom fail to attain it. You must *want* to be the director, dear brother; don't shy away from saying this to the right people and you shall surely be director. If Princess Wittgenstein (the only person at your court who comes to mind) still happens to be in Paris when I arrive there, I shall discuss with her all of the matters of which you seemingly do not wish to speak.

And finally, why have you so grossly neglected your wonderful talents as a composer? Because of pressing business matters? That is not reason enough. In our Germany, where the powers that be never support the existence of intellectuals, it has always been necessary for scholars, writers, and artists to hold some office to earn a living and yet, if they had genius, they were still capable of producing masterpieces. Of course the general public can also be a formidable barrier which one has to hurdle. We live in trying and convulsive times when the simplest of truths are no longer immutable, when criticism is so often the work of unknowledgeable laymen who use it for the promotion of personal friendship or animosity because evaluating a work of art can either deify or exterminate its creator. But if one has the firm inner conviction of having created or recognized something truly valid, then the sharpest and nastiest criticisms become less painful than expected.

Now let me respond to your letter. Many thanks, dear brother, for your friendly advice regarding the essay sent to you which was critical of *Les Huguenots*. Thank you also for the thoughtful manner in which you let me decide whether the essay should appear in "Caecilia" or not. It seems to me that, once again, your keen perception immediately recognized the most effective course of action. I agree with you completely that the essay would do less damage in "Caecilia" than in some other publication because, as you stated, by using footnotes and notes in the margin, the antidote can be placed next to the poison. (I think that such notes are more effective than a formal, but belated essay.) But who should write them, given that you are not familiar with the work? That, my dear brother, is a question which I cannot answer. In any event, it shall not be I, as you have suggested. Years ago, I swore to myself never to respond personally to attacks on my work and never under any circumstances to cause or respond to personal polemics. But since, as you state, the essay attacks the drama but barely mentions the music, I can familiarize you with the former because I am sending you a copy of it today. Whether you shall like *Les Huguenots* as a drama or consider its subject matter unsuitable for an opera I cannot say; it is my hope that you shall not find the treatment of this subject to be immoral or scandalous (as was the case with the author of that essay). It deals with a terrible fact of history, certainly well known and so often treated dramatically that the production of an opera on the same topic can hardly create any problems. It is my opinion that the Protestant religion is painted in a most noble and positive light. For the Catholics, the entire St. Bartholomew affair was no more than a political fact; history bears this out. The question of whether it is an unprecedented scandal to put religious conflicts on the stage and to go so far as to actually use a chorale in an opera is a question which was answered 25 years ago; for that was when *Die Weihe der Kraft* [The Consecration of Power] by Werner was performed in Lutheran Berlin. Luther himself was the hero of the work, his conflict with the Pope and the Emperor was the subject matter, and several chorales were sung. At that time, none of this was seen as scandalous. On the contrary, the public went back again and again to be moved and uplifted. Of course, if a chorale had in fact become an operatic aria (as the author of this essay states), that really would be scandalous. Actually, this chorale serves as a contrast to secular music and is treated in a strict church style, as if it were a voice from a better world, a symbol of hope and faith in the face of threatening danger. It rings out in moments of most glorious inspiration, weaving a thread throughout the entire opera but only comes from the lips of that individual (the servant Marcel) who, with his simple but unshakable faith, could even be considered a martyr. In view of all this, I would consider its presence in this opera as a glorification rather than a desecration of church music. As to whether my intention has succeeded, this is something that you, dear brother, cannot know because you are unfamiliar with the opera. When I visited you the time before last I had wanted to bring you a copy of the score, however, at that time you expressed so much apathy towards music that I dared not share this with you. I want you to know that the package with the name "Gottfried Weber" on it is still in my room. If it does not bore you to read through five acts of my music, just write to me and I shall send you the score.

And now, my dear friend, I think I have rambled on long enough. I have told you what was on my mind with the frankness and with the love of someone who has been your friend for the last 25 years. May this letter breathe new life into our long neglected correspondence. Boyhood friends should never be parted, lest it be by death.

Farewell and give my best wishes to your dear wife. Please believe me when I say that I am as devoted and loyal to you now as I was 25 years ago.

Meyerbeer

Illus. 10: Heinrich Heine, 1831. Portrait by Oppenheim.

*   *   *

Heinrich Heine had had a falling-out with his uncle Salomon Heine, a rich mer-
chant residing in Hamburg. As a result the uncle—although he respected his
nephew as a writer—refused to provide him with the life-long pension to which
he had earlier agreed. Heinrich Heine, therefore, went to Meyerbeer with the
request that he go to the uncle on Heinrich's behalf.

42. To Heinrich Heine in Paris

[Paris, September 23, 1838]

Dearest friend,

I hope that you will be satisfied with your ambassador. I have just
returned from a meeting with your delightful uncle and, after long negotiation, my quest was successful. You shall receive the sum you requested,
i.e., 4000 francs annually beginning on the first of January, 1839. I also
arranged that you be paid in advance on a trimester basis, so you shall

To receive a free list of our other fine titles, just complete and return this card.

Amadeus Press

Name (please print)

Address

City   State   Zip

We'd also welcome your comments on this book.

Title of Book:

BUSINESS REPLY MAIL

1st Class   Permit No. A717   Portland, OR

POSTAGE WILL BE PAID BY ADDRESSEE

TIMBER PRESS/AMADEUS PRESS
9999 S.W. Wilshire
Portland, OR 97225

receive the first payment of 1000 francs on the first of January.

Most likely I could have asked for more money but bearing in mind what you told me, I realized that this outcome is satisfactory. If you would like to know the details, please be so kind as to come to my residence tomorrow morning before 10 o'clock. Farewell my dear friend.

Your devoted
Meyerbeer

*　　*　　*

By virtue of the more generous French laws, the Jews in France were full-fledged citizens. Therefore, there was hardly any "richesse" at all. In view of this, it must have been all the more difficult and worrisome for Meyerbeer to learn from a letter sent to him by Heine—which has since been lost—of the first signs of rising anti-Semitism in the French press. The remarks refer to two articles in the "Courrier des Théâtres" dated July eighth and August third, 1839 which included the following: "la Juiverie nous enveloppe de tous côtés ... la Juiverie nous déborde ..." [The Jews surround us on all sides ... the Jews are overwhelming us]. According to the articles, it was not enough for them to have their foot in the door of almost all the theaters in Paris; they wanted to take over influential positions as well. Because Halévy held several posts, he was bitterly attacked. This was the general tone of these frighteningly ugly articles.

Heine married his sweetheart, Mathilde Marat, on August 31, 1841.

43. To Heinrich Heine in Paris

[Boulogne, August 29, 1839]

Dearest sir and friend,

My mother and I were delighted to receive your nice letter which, like everything you write, was interesting, intelligent, and witty. I would not have taken so long to thank you for it had I not been extremely incapacitated for six days by an illness which is epidemic here: intense diarrhea accompanied by very severe pain, nausea and fever; in short, a type of cholera. My poor mother also suffered from it. It was all the more unpleasant for us because we had to cut short our ocean baths which had done both my mother and myself a lot of good. However, the doctor has given us reason to hope that we can resume the cure in a few days. I passed on you greetings to Lottchen Moscheles; and she felt very flattered still to be remembered by the great German writer. She is going to Paris next month with her husband and shall be staying for six weeks. She is a charming and intelligent woman.

I am not of your opinion, dear friend, that the "richesse" is a worn-out weapon and that my enemies would not succeed by availing themselves of it. I believe that anti-Semitism is like love in the theaters and novels: no matter how often one encounters it in all shapes and sizes, it never misses its target if effectively wielded. Why? Because all people, young and old, know or have known love. Ninety-nine percent of those who read are anti-Semites. This is why they know and will come in contact with anti-Semitism, if skillfully administered. What can be done? No pommade de lion or graisse d'ours [lion pomade or bear grease], not even baptism can grow back the foreskin of which we were robbed on the eighth day of life: those who, on the ninth day, do not bleed to death from this operation shall continue to bleed an entire lifetime, even after death.

You do not realize, dear Heine, how much motherly love my dear mother has for you. I was obliged to read your charming letter to her three times and she was very sorry that she shall not see you this year because she is afraid that I will keep her here too long. Perhaps I shall still be able to convince her.

I am delighted that you found happiness in Granville. I find that this liaison has given you a more solid, domestic and even milder demeanor; as a result, we shall enjoy the products of your genius more frequently. The world of literature owes Mathilde a debt of gratitude.

Farewell, Germany's greatest writer. I am very much looking forward to embracing you again next month in Paris.

Boulogne, August 29   Your devoted
                                       Meyerbeer

My best regards to Mr. and Mrs. Laube and to Mr. Weill. Veuillez me rappeler au souvenir de l'aimable Mathilde Heine [Please remember me to dear M. H.]

*   *   *

Dr. Gustav Shilling (1803–1881), music writer and director of a music school in Stuttgart, severely criticized Meyerbeer in 1833 in his Universal Lexicon of Music (article Beer). According to him, Meyerbeer "had not produced one single work, not even one part of his complete works, worthy of a musician's respect." He went on to write that there was not one convincing moment in Robert le Diable: *"Scribe provided us with a dislocated marionette which the composer draped in a most fantastic and tasteless splendor." Now that the composer had come into his own, Shilling dedicated his writings on Basso Continuo to "Giacomo Meyerbeer, the knight . . . as a demonstration of his respect and friendship." With a libretto in hand, Schilling now wanted a share in the success of a man he had once criticized so bitterly. Meyerbeer was clever enough to comprehend the real reason for Schilling's change of heart and careful enough to write an especially polite letter aimed at turning an enemy into an ally. There is reason to doubt that Meyerbeer seriously considered collaborating with Schilling on an opera. Was he really serious about the oratorio he wanted to write while working on the new opera? There is no question that Meyerbeer was already planning his new opera* Le Prophète *(The Prophet). In August of 1838, a contract had been signed between Scribe and Meyerbeer for this new opera and Meyerbeer undertook an in-depth study of the Bible in preparation for this new work.*

44. To Gustav Schilling in Stuttgart

[Paris, October 19, 1839]

I have been in possession of your gracious letter for eight days; it was forwarded to me here. Unfortunately, I did not receive your *Generalbasslehre* [method of writing Basso Continuo], due to a misunderstanding on the part of a friend of mine in Paris who is responsible for forwarding all of my mail [Gouin]. As a result, your writings were sent to my brother in Berlin. However, I have just written him and instructed him to send them to me in Baden.

I hope you shall forgive me for not responding immediately to your kind letter and wonderful gift. Unfortunately, I have been suffering from severe abdominal pains for the last month and have not been able to write at all. Let me take this opportunity to express my deepest gratitude to you for the dedication in your book. To receive such a public display of support and respect from a man who is revered by the entire musical community in Germany is indeed very dear to my heart, and it is my fervent desire to say these words to you in person. Perhaps I shall have an opportunity to do so in the spring because I am planning an excursion with my family which shall bring us to your friendly capital. I am no less grateful for your flattering offer to write a German opera libretto for me. It is my wish and intention to compose a German opera; with whom would I rather begin such an undertaking than with a man such as you—a man whose esthetic writings have proven his deep and poetic grasp of this art form. Before I can begin such a project, however, I must meet other important earlier theatrical commitments. These consist of a major French opera for the Paris Opéra and a German opera, the first act of which is comprised of musical sketches by the late C. M. v. Weber. In accordance with his widow's request, I shall complete this opera by composing the missing acts myself. Both of these operas are coming along quite well. However, it will be at least a year before they are both completed and another year or more for the rehearsals and performances because both of the operas will be performed in several countries but cannot go into production at the same time. Only then could I begin composing your work. Would a two-and-a-half year wait before your libretto is set to music not be too long for you, especially considering how slowly I work? I am afraid that my pointing this out may have dissuaded you, but when I receive such an honorable offer from so noble a man as yourself, I consider it my duty to be absolutely frank and truthful with respect to such a flattering offer of collaboration. Please be so kind, honorable sir, as to express your views on this matter as openly as I have done and to notify me of any decision you have reached.

Let us assume for the moment that the spectre of a long wait has not completely put you off. This will give me an opportunity to respond to the suggested material (King Enzio). I do not know very much about him because, quite honestly, I am not very knowledgeable in the history of the Hohenstaufen. I seem to remember having seen Raupach's tragedy of the same name which, if I am not mistaken, was quite somber. I myself would not have chosen this material because it is so thoroughly tragic and only involves characters from the highest ranks of society; at least in Raupach's play. I feel that a pleasant German folk legend would be more suitable for a German opera. If this could not be found, there is a Biblical subject which I have considered for some time now.

However, I realize that it is not so much the subject matter that is important but how it is treated, and I have the greatest of confidence in you. Incidentally, could you please provide me with a scenario for "König Enzio" so that I could become more familiar with the subject matter . . . Before I formally close this letter, let me share with you a plan which very much requires a collaborative effort to become reality. It is a great desire of mine to write a small Biblical oratorio. Composing such a piece would only be possible while I am working on an opera because, due to the different genres, each one would provide me with a calm refuge from the other. Please give some thought as to whether you would be interested in working on this pet project of mine and what subject you would select. Recently, I was urgently requested to write a small Biblical oratorio; the request came from someone whom I could hardly turn down.

*　*　*

Conradin Kreutzer (1780–1849), composer of Das Nachtlager in Granada *(The Encampment in Granada), had directed Meyerbeer's opera* Wirt und Gast *in Stuttgart in 1813. Now he was preparing a production of* Les Huguenots *at the Kaerntnertor Theater in Vienna where it was entitled* Welfen und Ghibellinen *[Guelphs and Ghibelines], and opened on December 19, 1839. Drawn-out disputes with the censors, which Kreutzer reported to Meyerbeer in December of 1838, had delayed the production. The Empress had even written a personal letter forbidding the performance of the Luther chorale. Not until after the revolution of 1848 did the Vienna opera perform* Les Huguenots *in its original version.*

45. To Conradin Kreutzer in Vienna

[Paris, December 4, 1839]

My dearest Sir,

Your good letter did not arrive here until very late. I was in Boulogne when you addressed your letter to Paris and by the time it had been forwarded to me, I was off on an excursion along the sea coast. I have just recently returned to Paris.

Please allow me, kind sir, to apologize for the delayed response and to express my gratitude for your very interesting report. I feel happy and honored to have inspired such interest in my work in so respected a colleague because, although I have been away from Vienna for a long time, your famous name is very familiar to me. Messrs. Moscheles,

Blahetka, Heller, Panofka, and several more of our mutual acquaintances have highly commended you for your contributions and achievements whenever describing the current state of artistic affairs in Vienna to me.

Since you have always maintained such interest and support for *Les Huguenots*, please allow me to present you with an *unmutilated* copy of this opera as a small token of the composer's respect and admiration. Mr. Springer will be leaving for Vienna in a few days and I have asked him to be so kind as to deliver it to you. I hope that I have not forfeited the pleasure of receiving future letters from you on account of my long delay in responding. Dr. Bluethendorn can confirm how interested I am in your letters. In a few days I shall depart for Baden-Baden where I shall spend the entire winter. We are going there because the doctors have prescribed it for my sick wife. . . . As always, dear sir, it is with the greatest respect and admiration that I remain

Respectfully yours,
Giacomo Meyerbeer

P.S. Have your favorable predictions about less stringent censorship of the libretto for *Les Huguenots* been realized or is it still being obscured and mutilated as "Ghibellinen?"

If you should see my old friend Castelli, please give him my best regards.

*   *   *

The references to the prophet Elijah and to the consecration of the prophet Isaiah indicate that intensive preparations were underway for the new opera entitled Le Prophète. *Nowhere else, neither in his diary nor in his personal calendar, did Meyerbeer ever make reference to composing an oratorio while he was working on the new opera. In retrospect, Meyerbeer's references to this indicate that he only wished to have protracted discussions in order to avoid aggravating a former enemy by responding with a definitive "no." These references clearly concern scenes in* Le Prophète: *Meyerbeer would never have used the same material and motifs in an opera and an oratorio. As early as December, 1838 he wrote the following note in his pocket calendar in reference to the coronation scene, the consecration of the prophet: "be brief—Biblical language." There is no doubt that his precise knowledge of the Biblical passages cited is the result of this opera.*

46. To Gustav Schilling in Stuttgart

[Baden-Baden, January 28, 1840]

Above all I must ask you to forgive me for having taken so long to respond to your last letter. However, upon my return to Baden I was overwhelmed with overdue work. Then, for a month, I was so ill that I could do no work at all.

Since my recovery, I have had an opportunity to read over all of the oratorio material you have sent me and to give the entire matter some serious thought. Some of the material is excellent, but as I was reading it and looked up the corresponding passages in the Bible, I came across another passage which greatly moved me and which, if you share my feelings, I would select as my choice. The passage in question refers to the deeds of the prophet Elijah from his first appearance to his ascension. Please read (from the translation by De Wette) in the first Book of Kings, chapter XVII. Here, the prophet Elijah predicts famine and is kept alive miraculously at the brook Cherith. He was then cared for by a widow in Zerpath whose son he awoke from the dead. Please read as well chapter XVIII, where Elijah slaughters the prophets of Baal and predicts rain. In chapter XIX Elijah flees from Queen Jezebel, God appears to him, Elijah becomes his student. Verses 11, 12, 13 in this chapter are lyrical and filled with beauty. You should also read chapter two in the second Book of Kings, dealing with Elijah's ascension.

Elijah appears very suddenly in the Bible. Therefore, the work could perhaps begin when God ordains Elijah as a prophet. There are several such ordinations in the Bible containing truly lyrical elements, e.g., the ordination of Isaiah (Book of Isaiah, chapter six), which we could apply to Elijah. The only thing lacking in this marvelous material is an element of tenderness and delicacy, which could be represented by a woman's voice. If you, my dear sir, could find such an element which could weave its way through the entire work in order to counterbalance the predominantly lofty and severe aspects, then I feel we would have accomplished our goal. Perhaps the Widow of Zerpath would be a suitable character. Upon Elijah's arrival, her character could be that of a sinner who, after Elijah saves her son from a fatal illness is converted by Elijah's prayer and then becomes his lovingly devoted student, following him everywhere. Please bear in mind that this is only a quickly contrived idea, and you can certainly find a better vehicle. Amongst the material you sent to me was also Ahab's fall. Perhaps you were thinking of bringing Elijah into this passage because, if I am not mistaken, Elijah did appear before him.

If, however, you are not very enthusiastic about using Elijah, I would choose Job from the material that you sent to me, though I feel that the mere conversion would be too monotonous. We would also have to show Job during the time of his good fortune, and especially the wonderful prologue in Heaven between Jehovah and Satan. (Turn to the Book of Job, chapter two also in De Wette's translation). I now await your kind response informing me of your choice. I would be very grateful if you first outlined your approach to this work in prose, rather than immediately beginning work on the poetic text. It would also be helpful if you could indicate where the vocal numbers will occur, so that we can discuss this very important point. And one last request, honorable sir; please do not tell anyone what material we have chosen for the oratorio.

Many thanks for the receipt of your *Beatrice*. This text was set with great musical skill and knowledge of the stage. It also reads very well and completely validates your understanding of the lyric stage. I also finally received your book on thorough bass, and I read this fine and practical book very often. I hope that my response to your kind dedication shall be in your hands within six weeks.

*   *   *

On December 4, 1840, Richard Wagner sent the score of his Rienzi *to V. Lüttichau, the director of the opera in Dresden. That Wagner very much hoped for a word of recommendation from Meyerbeer can be seen in the dedication of his arrangement of the vocal score of Donizetti's opera* La Favorita *dated January 9, 1841: "Dedicated in admiration to Dr. G. Meyerbeer, Royal Prussian Music Director General. . . . Richard Wagner." There is more evidence of this in a Paris "Report by our correspondent" in the Dresden "Abendzeitung" of February 23, 1841. Here, Wagner made reference to Meyerbeer's new opera* Le Prophète *which was to be performed in Paris: "first of all, an obituary announcement! The great Paris Opèra will soon perish. She awaits salvation from the German Messiah—from Meyerbeer. If the Opèra is not saved soon, the death throes shall soon commence. . . ."*

47. To August Freiherr von Lüttichau in Dresden

[Baden, March 18, 1841]

Your Excellency will forgive me if I burden you with these lines. My memories of Your Excellency's support for me are too vivid to turn down a request to write to you on behalf of a young, interesting compatriot who, very flatteringly having placed his trust in my relationship with you, has asked me to intercede for him with this letter. Mr. Richard Wagner from Leipzig is a young composer who not only has enjoyed an extensive musical education but has great imagination and impressive general knowledge of literature. He is an individual whose talents deserve the support of the Fatherland in every respect. It is his greatest wish to perform his opera *Rienzi,* for which he wrote both text and music, at the Royal Theater in Dresden. He has played individual excerpts for me and I found them to be very imaginative and filled with dramatic power. May this young artist be so fortunate as to enjoy Your Excellency's protection, and may he be generally recognized for his remarkable talent. I appeal once again to Your Excellency's indulgence and hope to enjoy your continued good will.

Your Excellency's most
devoted servant,
Meyerbeer

* * *

In the winter of 1840–41, Meyerbeer had written only a provisional ending to his opera Le Prophète *because a performance of the work was not possible at that time due to a lack of suitable singers. At the end of May, 1841, he arrived in Berlin. Here he prepared the Berlin production of* Les Huguenots, *which had finally been approved by Friedrich Wilhelm IV. Due to his rash behavior, Spontini had lost his position as Prussian Music Director General and Meyerbeer, who is reporting to Heine about the changing mood in Berlin, had probably known for a long time that there was discussion of his becoming Spontini's successor. On September 23, Meyerbeer had departed for a three-week "cure" in Alexisbad. He did this to avoid a meeting with Mendelssohn on the occasion of a major concert and banquet in honor of both composers.*

48. To Heinrich Heine in Paris

[Alexisbad, September 28, 1841]

. . .If it is necessary to postpone the production of my opera in Paris for such a long period of time, and if I am thus obliged to be far from the artistic activities of this metropolis it would not, under the current circumstances, be such a bad idea to spend a winter in Berlin. You cannot imagine the dramatic change and new vitality now abounding in the social and intellectual environment here ever since this intelligent and truly humane King has come to power. It is remarkable to what extent previously narrow-minded attitudes concerning certain issues and individuals are disappearing. I am certain that you would share my opinion if you were here.

I informed my mother of your thoughtful wedding announcement and she has asked me to pass on her congratulations to you. You certainly have had enough time to make up your mind. Your genius resembles that of Goethe, and now your approach to marriage resembles his as well. Let us hope that you will also follow in Goethe's footsteps by living to the age of 82, which would be to the benefit of your friends and to German literature.

Farewell, dear friend. I hope to be able to embrace you once again in April when I return to Paris after more than a year of separation.

Veuillez me rappeler au souvenir de l'aimable Madame Heine en lui présentant mes félicitations les plus empressées. [Please remember me to your charming wife and express to her my warmest congratulations.]

Your devoted
Meyerbeer

On December 14, Richard Wagner received official word from Berlin that the libretto and score of his opera Der Fliengende Holländer *(The Flying Dutchman) had arrived safely and "had been particularly well recommended by Meyerbeer." Wagner expressed his belated thanks to Meyerbeer in mid-December: "I . . . sat in my little room next to my poor wife, who was plagued by me and by worries, and looked upon the fruits of last summer's anguish. These fruits, a poor little libretto and a sizable score, lay before me inquiring what was to become of them. I could think of nothing else to do other than to pack them up and send them to Count Redern along with a very humble letter. I knew that they would only gather dust there, but I could think of nothing better to do. Then a miracle occurred when I read those Heaven-sent words written by your hand: "I shall also contact Count von Redern on your behalf." . . . May God fill each day of your marvelous life with joy, and you never be burdened with worries. These are the fervent prayers of your most dedicated pupil and servant, Richard Wagner."*

Years later, Wagner condemned Meyerbeer's music in his prose work Opera and Drama *and also denounced him as a person in his essay "Das Judentum in der Musik" ("The Jews in Music").*

49. To Count Friedrich Wilhelm von Redern in Berlin

[Berlin, December 9, 1841]

Most esteemed Count,

I have taken the liberty of enclosing the score and libretto (the latter is inserted after the title page) of the opera entitled *Der Fliegende Holländer* by Richard Wagner. Two days ago, I had the privilege of discussing this interesting composer with Your Excellency. He is a man whose talents and extremely modest circumstances make him doubly deserving of access to the great court theaters which are the official protectors of German art.

Your Excellency was also kind enough to promise me that you would write him a short letter indicating receipt of the score and your intention to read through it. As I have taken the liberty of mentioning this, I also have the honor . . .

(signed) Meyerbeer

* * *

In 1842, Les Huguenots *was known throughout Europe. Its fame had even reached New Orleans, where it was performed in 1839. The Berlin premier, on May 20, 1842, was a complete success even although Ludwig Rellstab, the critic for the "Vossische Zeitung" was of a different opinion. When Friedrich Wilhelm IV awarded Meyerbeer the newly created order "Pour le mérite" it was an event which did not go unnoticed. "When a Jew, or a member of the extreme left of the French Chamber of Deputies, is made a foreign knight with voting privileges, then*

we are on the way [to equality]." These were the comments in a Frankfurt news-
paper. A bit later, in June, the King appointed Meyerbeer as Spontini's successor to
the positions of Prussian Music Director General and Director of Court Music.
This provided Meyerbeer with a long-awaited sense of satisfaction and the hope
that he would be able to establish himself in Berlin.

Raupach wrote material for a festival production with tableaux vivants
entitled Das Hoffest von Ferrara *(The Court Festival of Ferrara) which was*
performed with members of the court on February 28, 1843 as part of the carnival
festivities.

50. To Ernst Raupach in Berlin

[Schwalbach, August 31, 1842]

Esteemed sir and friend,

I received your friendly and entertaining letter 20 days ago but was
unable to answer it until today. This time it was not laziness, but illness
that inhibited my pen. Late last month I was suffering from abdominal
pains, a condition which has bothered me for years and from which the
baths in Schwalbach have always provided relief. I therefore decided
once again to return to these healing springs. Unfortunately, the air there
has been extremely unhealthy and has contributed to an epidemic of
Cholerine which inducted me into the ranks of its victims. I suffered from
this for 17 days and have only begun to recover over these last two days.
However, I am still not completely well.

Forming a first impression of the greater half of a poetic work so
dear to me under such bothersome circumstances would be a crime
against the writer and the work. For this reason, I kept my curiosity in
check until my first day without pain (yesterday) so that nothing would
stand in the way of my getting acquainted with these five new friends. I
do not dare to form an opinion after only one read-through. I am also not
yet in any condition to weigh all of the musical considerations properly,
but I do feel that the overall impression is delightful. This poem is as pure
and true an idyll as any I have ever known. There is not a verse, an
expression or word which does not contribute to its poetic mastery. Even
the shepherd's stormy heart barely ruffles the clouds in this pure ether.
One has the impression of being surrounded by blue sky and wrapped in
the peace emanating from beautiful nature and the delicate creatures of
your imagination. I only hope that my musical hues are as delicate so as
not to cover the poem's fragrance or distort the delightful coloring, while
at the same time trying to avoid being monotonous in the course of nine
pieces. It is my intention to attack this difficult task with great fervor.

On first reading, I was particularly impressed with the trio, both
from a poetic and musical standpoint. I am very anxious to start work on
it. The musical form you have suggested seems esthetically justified and
musically suited to the work, so much so, that I shall definitely make use
of it.

My doctor has given me reason to hope that I shall be able to leave for Paris in a few days. I shall spend the journey reading these poems in order to arrive at an overall musical concept. Then I shall begin composing as soon as possible. Please allow me to send you any comments or questions I may have once I have arrived in Paris. This letter was only to be an explanation and justification for the unavoidable delay in responding to your letter.

I hope that these lines find you in the best of health. Please give my best wishes to your dear wife.

Sincerely yours,
Meyerbeer

*　　*　　*

On September 5, 1842, Meyerbeer arrived in Paris.

51. To Heinrich Heine in Paris

[Paris, Fall 1842]
Do not forget that you promised to have breakfast with me at 11 o'clock. You shall be today's tastiest course for my guests.

I would appreciate it if you could come a bit earlier because I have something to tell you.

Until 11 o'clock

Your,

Tuesday   Meyerbeer

*　　*　　*

During his stay in Munich in 1812, Meyerbeer had become acquainted with Joseph Baermann (1784–1847), the very famous first clarinetist of the Munich Court theater. A clarinet quintet from this period and a cantata composed in 1816 entitled "Gli Amori di Teolinda" [Teolinda's loves] for solo soprano, clarinet, chorus and orchestra, testify to Meyerbeer's friendship with Baermann and Baermann's life-long companion Helene Harlas, one of the most important opera singers in Munich. Meyerbeer probably wrote this composition for a benefit performance given by Miss Harlas in Venice.

Berlioz' plans for a concert in Munich never materialized.

52. To Heinrich Joseph Baermann in Munich

[Paris, December, 1842]

Dearest friend and brother,

I had already written to you regarding the subject of the letter I am writing today. However, the young man to whom I entrusted it and who was to serve as my messenger has not yet departed and did not have the decency to inform me. If I had not happened to see him today in the court of the conservatory I would not have learned of this delay. As things stand, it is still not too late and I am anxious to inform you of my request. Our brilliant Berlioz, whose new and bold compositions have won your respect as you often told me during your stay in Paris, is about to begin a concert tour of Germany. I helped convince him to do this because I believe his music is far more suited to a German audience than to the public here, although his music is gaining popularity here as well.

Since Berlioz does not have a good command of German and has not had a great deal of experience in business matters, in addition to the fact that his music requires very large orchestras and choruses, it is better that he set fixed prices with the different theater directors rather than dealing himself with all the details and uncertainties of giving a concert.

Thus far, the German theater managers have shown themselves to be very gallant and loyal to him. In Frankfurt on the Main, where he will give concerts on the 25th and 29th, the theater management has placed all orchestra and singing personnel at his disposal. He is receiving a fixed sum of 1200 florins for the two concerts which will be performed in the theater and which will be comprised entirely of his music. The box office receipts from these concerts will, of course, go to the theater. He received the same favorable terms in Stuttgart; perhaps even slightly better, I believe. These concerts will be given in the first days of January and since Berlioz is also going to Vienna, he will be arriving in Munich on January seventh or eighth. Would you be so kind, dear brother, as to handle theater arrangements for his concerts? Given the fact that Munich's population is so much larger than Frankfurt's and its theater seats so many more people, I believe you could make a very advantageous arrangement for him and perhaps arrange a larger number of concerts.

Please send your response as soon as possible to the following address in Frankfurt on Main (I will be traveling there in a few days): Mr. Wilhelm Speyer ... You should make arrangements as quickly as possible with your theater director because Berlioz would probably not even stop in Munich at all if you were not able to arrange anything but would go directly to Vienna. However, I am sure that you and the rest of Munich will not tolerate being in third place behind Stuttgart and Frankfurt.

Farewell, dear brother, and send your response to Frankfurt immediately.

Your loyal friend and brother
Meyerbeer

Illus. 11: Meyerbeer ca. 1843. Lithograph by Mittag based on a drawing by Franz Krüger.

* * *

In his capacity as Prussian Music Director General, Meyerbeer repeatedly spoke out in favor of higher salaries for the orchestra and chorus. He himself received an annual salary of 3000 thaler which he did not draw when he took a leave of absence.

53. To Wilhelm Prince of Sayn and Wittgenstein in Berlin

Berlin, April 29, 1843

In Your Excellency's esteemed communication, you were kind enough to return the *Immediat Vorstellung* [petition sent to the highest authority] from the management of the Royal Music Establishment, dated the second of this month. You have been gracious enough to send me this petition so that I may become better acquainted with the situation and can

93

provide suggestions as to how the situation can be improved. I shall not hesitate to comply most humbly with Your Excellency's request.

It is quite evident that the members of the Royal Music for the most part find themselves in an extremely difficult position. Their salaries are so inadequate that they are hardly able to secure life's basic necessities. For the most part, these men have families and are without inherited means. As a result, after dedicating their lives to the painstaking process of learning and practicing so demanding an art as this, after years of service and in spite of all economies, they are unable to provide sufficient food for their families.

All of the information provided with regard to the worsening circumstances under which the orchestra members have lived over the last 25 years is completely accurate. Twenty-four years ago, the Royal Music had an annual budget of 43,785 thaler for 88 members. Today there are 104 members with a yearly budget of only 47,237 thaler— proportionally, a smaller budget than the first one. Changing times and musical trends have required a larger orchestra, but there has not been a corresponding increase in the orchestra's budget. This has not only prevented the orchestra members from securing salary increases, but in some cases has resulted in the reduction of salaries which were already insufficient. In addition, the starting salary for new members is even lower now than it used to be. Thus, many musicians who have been with the orchestra for 10, 20 or even 30 years are not receiving more than 425, 325 or even 275 thaler annually; there are 51 members who are in this situation. Even the first chair wind and string players were earning more 24 years ago than they are today. The following salary comparison bears out my point:

1819	1843
Conductor: Weber 2400 thaler	Henning 1500 thaler
Concert Master: Moeser 1200	Ries 925
First Violist: Semler 600	Gareis 500
First Oboist: Westenholz 1000	Wiepecht 600
First Bassoonist: Baermann 1200	Humann 750
etc . . .	

This problem has become even more acute for the members of the orchestra as the prices for a wide variety of commodities, especially apartments and wood, have continued to rise in the capital. There is, in fact, even more justification when one considers how much longer and more demanding the study of an instrument is now than it once was. Moreover, a musician today must have a much broader general knowledge of the arts in order to become a member of the Royal Orchestra since modern instrumental music has become so difficult. One should also take into account the demands placed on a musician in the Royal Orchestra; not only the technical difficulty of the music but also the physical demands. The technical demands of today's music and the heavier orchestration not only make the performances more demanding and tiring, but the musicians must also have three or four times as many rehearsals, and these are longer than they once were. Ballet music, which was once restricted to short, easy melodies usually performed on string instruments, has become longer, more difficult and involves more complicated instrumentation. As a result, it is on the same level of difficulty as operatic music and requires almost as many rehearsals.

In addition to the increasing demands made by the ever-changing music of today, there are still other factors which have significantly increased the workload of the orchestra members, demanding more from them than ever before. Today, there are many more opera and ballet performances in which the entire orchestra must perform than there were 24 years ago, when this was true only of a few operas by Gluck. Today, performances in both theaters are much more frequent and even the French Vaudevilles [spoken comedies with songs] require larger orchestras than the plays. Add to this the fact that the musicians in the orchestra must continuously practice their respective instruments in order to keep abreast of the ever-increasing complexities of modern music. As a result, they must devote all of their time and energy to service in the orchestra, practically making it impossible for them to give music lessons as a source of additional income. With regard to the wind players, there is still another important consideration. Given the fact that the instrumentation in today's music has become much thicker, the embouchure of the wind players degenerates at a much faster rate. Nowadays, a wind player must put down his instrument and retire six to seven years earlier than was the case 25 to 30 years ago.

Taking into account all of the above-mentioned reasons I feel justified in stating that, from both an artistic and moral standpoint, justice and necessity would be served if the financial position of these valiant musicians could be somewhat improved. This is especially appropriate when one considers that, despite their pressing food problems and demanding schedules, they perform their artistic duties with such zeal and talent that this Royal Orchestra is counted among Europe's very best. This is why I have taken the liberty, on behalf of the members of the Royal Orchestra, of appealing to Your Excellency's gracious sympathy and warm support in requesting that Your Excellency urgently submit these recommendations to His Royal Highness. I feel that the requests on the part of the orchestra are quite modest and serve as a basis for my most humble proposals. I request that the orchestra members who are now earning 400 thaler a year or less be given an annual salary increase of 100 thaler. Those earning more than 400 thaler annually should receive an increase of at least 60 thaler. This seems not only reasonable and just but becomes even more important if we are to provide talented young artists with more than the minimal existence to which they have been condemned for years as apprentices. If nothing is done, we run the risk of seeing the number of apprentices decrease rapidly. I also feel obliged to mention that, ever since the stipends approved for the apprentices in the orchestra under The Director of Court Music, Privy Counsellor Count von Redern were eliminated, a large number of the most talented among them have either gone to the provinces or to foreign lands. This became evident this past winter on the occasion of a court ball when His Majesty the King decreed that the music was to be performed exclusively by apprentices; this supreme command could not be fully obeyed. Rather, the Director of Court Music, Count von Redern, was forced to employ the services of military musicians to fill the orchestra. This description of the current state of affairs, which has been presented with all due respect, should be enough to justify the urgently needed increases in the orchestra members' salaries; it acquires even greater urgency as the result of a royal decree to increase the amount of sacred music in the Cathedral. The orchestra shall now have this additional responsibility as well, although I should like to request most humbly that these future responsibilities for the Royal Orchestra be the subject of a later report which I shall provide as soon as I have received more detailed information on the matter from Privy Counsellor von Massow.

*　　*　　*

During the night of August 18 to 19, 1843, the Berlin opera house went up in flames. Only two days later the King gave the order to rebuild. The opening of the new house was to be celebrated with a performance of a work written especially for the occasion, a Prussian opera. It is not clear who had the idea for the subject of Das Feldlager in Schlesien *(The Encampment in Silesia) which is based on an event from the Silesian War. The problem of finding a librettist was a difficult one: as a French author, Scribe was understandably excluded as the librettist for a Prussian opera, yet he was the only librettist whom Meyerbeer trusted. Through diplomacy and personal intervention, Meyerbeer arranged everything to his liking: Scribe provided the libretto and gave his written and verbal assurance that he would not reveal that he was the author (it was not discovered until recently, during the review of Meyerbeer's estate!). Meyerbeer compensated him for the lost royalties. Meyerbeer's arch enemy, the Berlin critic Ludwig Rellstab, took on the responsibility of translating the libretto and putting it into verse. He was also allowed to take credit for its authorship. This netted him considerable profits because Germany and Austria had introduced royalty payments in 1847.*

There were also difficulties in finding a singer for the leading role of Vielka: Jenny Lind, the "Swedish nightingale," for whom the role was written, did not appear at the opening performance on December seventh, 1844: Leopoldine Tuczeck, a singer popular in Berlin, had been invited instead. (The occasion also marked the gala re-opening of the opera house). Lind did not make her debut in this role until a few days later.

54. To Eugène Scribe in Berlin

[Paris, November 12, 1843]

My dear friend,

It will no doubt be easier for you to see the various details we discussed regarding the work in question when they are summarized on paper.

There is no popular chanson or patriotic song: however, there is a march which has been very popular for over one hundred years; it is called "Marsch des alten Dessauer" [Old Dessauer's March]. Dessauer was a Field Marshal under Frederick the Great's father. It would be a good idea to include this piece and have it appear throughout the opera.

In Berlin, the audiences love music accompanying spoken dialogue (as in the melodramas); you could take advantage of this in a portion of the work which is not really opera. As you had mentioned, it would be possible to do what you did in Act two of the "nonne sanglante" [sobbing nun].

In the dream, the foretelling, or the prophecy (I have mentioned all three as I do not know which vehicle you favor), it would be very effective if, before the eyes of the audience, the Berlin of one hundred years ago slowly evolved into present-day Berlin (as in "La belle au bois dormant" [Sleeping Beauty]): we could even include the opera house fire and the rebuilt theater.

With regard to the Berlin performance: the chorus there is excellent. It would be a good idea to take advantage of this and include some prominent choruses of a military and patriotic nature. These could form small independent scenes or could be inserted in other sections of the opera.

Regarding the singers, there is an excellent dramatic actress in Berlin who also sings very well (albeit material of a sentimental rather than comic nature). However, I would rather not use her. There is another who does lighter material very well (such as Domino noir, postillon [de Longjumeau], la fille du Regiment, "Diamants de la Couronne") and is very well suited to trouser roles. There is also an excellent tenor who sings all the grand opera roles, but is small of stature. He performs very well in comedies and is excellent in comic operas. Remember that he is the best singer in the company and that his role must be a musical one. We also have a young baritone who is very handsome and has a very nice voice, and another baritone who is somewhat older, but also quite good: these would be the singers for the lead parts; as far as the supporting roles are concerned, I shall leave that up to you.

Remember that Friedrich II cannot appear on stage, or at least not without making the audience wonder whether it really is he.

Should I still come tomorrow as we had arranged? Mr. Pillet told me that you had to draw up for him the plan for a major opera for Donizetti: have you had time to think about our project?

Farewell, dear friend. Unless I receive a message from you, I shall come tomorrow.

Yours,
Meyerbeer

* * *

The dating of the only proven letter to Ingres is based on an entry in Meyerbeer's appointment book dated December 7, 1843. Meyerbeer most likely came to know Ingres through the painters Heinrich and Rudolf Lehmann, students of Ingres and nephews of Meyerbeer's friend, Parisian banker Auguste Leo. Since Meyerbeer was frequently a guest in Leo's home, he probably met Ingres there repeatedly. Meyerbeer, who had a critically trained eye for visual effects, was undoubtedly interested in the work of the contemporary painter and sculptor from which he was able to draw ideas for his own work.

55. To Jean Auguste Dominique Ingres

[Paris, Dec. 5(?), 1843[

Grand and illustrious Master,

As I am obliged to leave for the country, I am afraid I will be unable to return at the time you kindly set aside for me to come to admire the products of your genius at your studio.

Illustrious master, I ask that you would be so kind as to allow me to come tomorrow morning, so that I can also bid you farewell before you leave for Liège.

Your very devoted admirer,
Meyerbeer

Tuesday

* * *

In 1844, Meyerbeer provided a loan—which was never repaid—to Heinrich Börnstein (1805–1892) who worked as a foreign correspondent in Paris for the Vienna "Allgemeine Theaterzeitung" and the "Frankfurter Conversationsblatt." He requested the loan of 3000 thaler so that he could found a journal entitled "Vorwärts" [Forward]. Meyerbeer did this because Heinrich Heine was to be one of the writers for the journal. Quite understandably, he also feared personal attacks if he refused to issue the loan. To have Meyerbeer, the millionaire, help launch the ultra-socialist "Vorwärts," published by Börnstein and Karl Marx, did not lack a touch of irony.

56. To Heinrich Börnstein in Paris

[Berlin, April 19, 1844]

Dear sir,

I need not tell or assure you of my interest in your well-being, your project, and your activities because you yourself have acknowledged this in previous letters. Therefore, you will surely believe me when I express my deep regret at not being able to fulfill your present request. At this

98

time, I do not have any sum of money at my disposal and most definitely not the large sum you require. Please remember, dear sir and friend, that when I provided you with the sum you requested in Paris I indicated to you that it would not be sufficient to found and maintain a journal as you had so hoped. I am very sorry for you that my prognosis proved to be correct. Please do not interpret this comment as an expression of ill will, dear sir, or become indignant because I am unable, on this occasion, to meet your request.

With the greatest respect and understanding.

*　*　*

For Meyerbeer, the performance of Euryanthe, *written by his friend from his student days, Carl Maria von Weber, was more than a duty. Friedrich Wilhelm IV put aside his "burning desire" to see Gluck's* Iphigenie in Aulis—*the King was a great admirer of Gluck—and approved a benefit performance which earned no less than 2000 thaler.*

57. To Friedrich Wilhelm IV of Prussia in Berlin

[Berlin, December 21, 1844]

Your Serene Highness!
Most merciful King and Sir,

After a delay of 20 years, the ashes of the great German composer, Carl Maria von Weber, have finally been buried in German soil. It is indeed sad that this pious duty was not performed sooner. A large group of friends of the arts has joined together in expressing its strong desire to erect a monument to this great German master as proof that the Fatherland's praise and admiration of Weber's music has not waned. For this purpose, a committee has been formed in Dresden, where the master was active for a long time, and has issued an appeal to all German theaters to give benefit performances in order to raise the funds necessary for the erection of this monument.

The theater in Dresden has already acted on this request. The Berlin theater has the good fortune of being the royal theater of our exalted monarch who, as a representative of the Fatherland, promotes and protects German art and science as a sacred national treasure. As such, our theater must be at the forefront of this type of national endeavor, setting an example for all of Germany.

Thus it is with great humility that I appeal to the graciousness of Your Royal Majesty, requesting that approval be given for such a performance at the Royal Opera. I also ask most humbly that I be authorized to direct Weber's masterpiece *Euryanthe* (which has not been given here in a long time) with the finest singers the world of opera has to offer (such as Madame Palm-Spatzer and Demoiselle Lind) and that this performance be given before *Iphigenia*, so that it can still benefit financially from being given at the height of the opera season and so that Berlin can set an *early* example for other theaters in Germany.

Most respectfully I remain
Your Royal Majesty's most loyal and humble servant,
Giacomo Meyerbeer

*   *   *

As a representative of French opera, Meyerbeer was chided in Germany as a deserter who was only paving the way to Berlin for such French celebrities as Berlioz. However, when he devoted himself energetically to performing the works of contemporary German composers, such as The Crusaders *by Spohr, it became clear that times had changed. Spohr's work was ridiculed as "an opera of appeasement which could be used effectively against all popular uprisings," as "a weapon against all political and revolutionary movements of the day . . . if it is German to replace all dramatic drive with a vague lyrical gush of emotions, if it is German to have no relationship between expression and thought or form and content, then Spohr's* Crusaders *is indeed a German universal opera." Criticism was leveled at the "Kotzebue-like romanticism" and sentimentality of the opera and critics found that "all of the slick civility in Spohr's music" was even more offensive than "Meyerbeer's contrived incivilities."*

58. To Friedrich Wilhelm IV of Prussia in Berlin

[Berlin, February 5, 1845]

Serene Highness
Most gracious King and Sir,

May it please Your Royal Majesty to permit my presenting an issue which, in the interest of German music, I feel obliged to address. It is my belief that the theaters of the German courts are morally obliged to perform, every year, some new operas by contemporary German composers. Such a display of respect for their work would be a source of great encouragement to German composers and would truly promote the art of music in the Fatherland. An additional point worthy of consideration is that the works of German opera composers are usually performed only in German theaters. The court theater in Dresden is setting a good example. Within the space of a year, the management of this opera house has accepted original German operas by Marschner, Spohr, Ferdinand Hiller, Hoven, Richard Wagner and Röckel, some of which have already been performed. However, the Royal Opera here lags far behind in this area, and my efforts to produce new German operas have met with no support.

Our local court theater is honored to enjoy the patronage of an exalted monarch who serves as the protector of all German endeavors in the arts and sciences. I feel that our theater, therefore, must be a leader in promoting the arts in this nation.

Thus I consider it my duty to make the following most humble request: may it please Your Royal Majesty to command that the local Royal Opera Theater perform two to three new operas by contemporary German masters annually and that, if no new operas have been written in a given year, performances be given of earlier works by these composers.

As a first worthy step in this direction, may I suggest that this opportunity be given to one of Germany's most famous senior composers, in recognition of his great contribution to music. I am referring to our splendid composer Spohr who, by virtue of the truly great works he has composed over the last thirty years, in all musical genres, by his steadfast pursuit of the true and noble, and by his courageous refusal to indulge the masses by courting the latest musical trends, has placed himself at the forefront of contemporary German music. A demonstration of respect and recognition on the part of the Berlin Royal Opera House, which has not brought any of Spohr's *newer* operas to the stage since *Jessonda,* could almost be considered a duty. Maestro Spohr recently completed a major new opera entitled *The Crusaders* which he has already performed in Kassel. It is with the deepest reverence that I appeal to Your Royal Majesty's graciousness in requesting the authorization to acquire from Kapellmeister Spohr the score of this opera for the purpose of performing it at the local court theater this coming spring.

Should it also please Your Royal Majesty to invite Kapellmeister Spohr to direct the final rehearsals and the first performance, he would certainly consider such an invitation to be an honor as it would come from an eminent Monarch who has a great love for the arts. In addition, the presence of the Master would truly be an honor for the theater and would certainly be of value for his new work.

With great respect I remain Your Royal Majesty's most loyal subject and servant

Meyerbeer

*   *   *

Louis Spohr thanked Meyerbeer and was delighted to be given the opportunity to conduct his opera in Berlin. The performance of The Crusaders *took place at the end of July, 1845. Meyerbeer noted in his diary "Spohr conducted two performances and was called up on stage twice during each of them . . . I gave a banquet in his honor at Kroll's and invited most of the singers and members of the orchestra as well as most of the important journalists." On Meyerbeer's initiative, the royal orchestra had a laurel wreath made out of gold-plated silver which he presented to Spohr in front of the orchestra along with a festive tribute.*

59. To Louis Spohr in Kassel

[Berlin, February 20, 1845]

Most respected Maestro,

As soon as I learned that you had once again graced the German stage with the fruits of your classical spirit (*The Crusaders*), I informed His Royal Majesty so as to procure this work for our theater here. His Majesty agreed to both the purchase and performance of your opera and authorized me yesterday to invite you to honor our theater by coming here to Berlin to direct the dress rehearsal and the first performance, if your schedule and circumstances permit. I have informed our general director, Mr. von Kuestner, of this because he is best able to oversee our schedules and can therefore concentrate on choosing the most appropriate time for the performance. For now I can inform you that the general director is planning to perform *Catharina Cornaro* by Maestro Lachner in April. He then plans to close the theater for the month of June. This means that the earliest available time to perform your opera would be either May or July. Therefore, dearest Maestro, I request that you inform me as soon as possible as to which of these two months would be most suitable for you; if your circumstances are such that the performance must be given at a later time, please tell me when you could come to Berlin to direct the final rehearsals and the first performance of your opera. I shall then do everything in my power to see to it that the performance is arranged for that time.

Professor Rungenhagen informed me of your letter regarding the performance of your opera here and shares my joy in the knowledge that we shall finally have the opportunity to welcome you once again to our native city and to express verbally our warmest and deepest respect for you and your music. Until such time, please allow me, esteemed Maestro, to give you written assurance of my utmost and sincere respect and admiration.

Yours very sincerely,
Meyerbeer

* * *

In 1847, Leon Pillet wrote an article in "France musicale" about Meyerbeer's first impressions of Jenny Lind's voice when he considered her suitability for the role of Bertha in Le Prophète in December of 1842: "that is not for you, it is a voice which, admittedly, is pretty, but too weak for the Paris Opéra. I shall see if I can take advantage of it in Berlin." As an excellent authority on the human voice, Meyerbeer had immediately recognized her strengths and weaknesses: he wrote the role of Vielka in his "Feldlager" for her. This role captures the entire range of expression in her voice. Although Jenny Lind had already made a successful debut in Stockholm in 1838, it was not until 1844 that she made her major breakthrough. Jenny Lind tended towards depressions and self-doubts; she was over *anxious and half sick whenever she had to debut in a new city. Her frequent moodiness presented further problems. Moreover, she was a close friend of Mendelssohn, Meyerbeer's most vigorous opponent. This was undoubtedly a strain on her relationship with Meyerbeer. The first lines of the following letter refer to this problematic relationship. In 1847, Wilhelm Beer mentioned that Jenny would probably not have any desire to sing after Mendelssohn's death and in 1849 the "Swedish nightingale" indeed renounced the stage, only five years after her triumphant Berlin debut.*

60. To Jenny Lind

[Berlin, February 28, 1845]

My dear Miss Lind,

Although I have called at your residence several times since your indisposition, I was never fortunate enough to see you, unlike several of your other friends. Therefore, I can only express in writing my congratulations and best wishes for your name day which, as Madame Reier told me, is today. I would also like you to accept these few flowers, modest and pure as you yourself.

What else can friends wish for you, a person whom heaven has so richly endowed? It has given you that smooth and lovely voice which charms and moves the heart; the flame of genius which penetrates your singing and acting; and finally, the inexpressible grace which modesty, candor and innocence lend to those whom they favor and which captivate even your enemies. One could only pray that heaven will free you from these doubts of the power of your talent; doubts which transform your days of triumph into days of anxiety. May the heavens also free you from this indecision which causes you continual anxiety and cast away all suspiciousness which makes you defiant of those in whom you inspire sympathy, for this in the end could deprive you of life's most beautiful consolation—friendship.

Whether or not heaven accords you this small supplement to your other precious qualities you, my dear Mademoiselle, will always be one of the most touching and noble apparitions I have ever met during my long artistic peregrinations, a person for whom I will always have nothing but the greatest admiration and esteem for the rest of my life.

Your very devoted,
Meyerbeer

February 28, 1845

*　　*　　*

Princess Augusta of Prussia (1811–1890), wife of Prince Wilhelm of Prussia and later empress, was not only very well educated musically, she also had a preference for French language, literature and art and was extremely interested in Meyerbeer's music.

On August 11, 1845, Queen Victoria of England (1819–1901) and her consort Prince Albert arrived for a state visit in Cologne, which at that time belonged to Prussia. On that evening, Friedrich Wilhelm IV held a great reception in her honor in Brühl Castle. During the dinner, a small concert was given under Meyerbeer's direction in which Jenny Lind was one of the performers. A full concert in honor of the two guests was given in Koblenz on August 16.

61. To Princess Augusta of Prussia in Berlin

[Cologne, circa August 20, 1845]

It is with a deep sense of joy and honor that I received, as a gift, Your Royal Highness' compositions of sacred music. These works contain the same spirit of noble simplicity, clarity and German sincerity which I found so appealing in Your Royal Highness' delightful Lieder.

While expressing my humble gratitude for Your Royal Highness' graciousness, I should also like to appeal to Your Royal Highness' good will in making the following request. Her Majesty Queen Victoria expressed to me her appreciation of the composition I wrote and performed at the court concert in honor of her arrival. Her Majesty so enjoyed the composition that I feel compelled to offer this small composition to Her Imperial Majesty as a gift. I am taking the liberty of asking for Your Royal Highness' kind protection and am enclosing this music in the modest form of its creation.

* * *

After the death of Salomon Heine (December 24, 1844), it was established that nephew Heinrich Heine's annual stipend of 4800 francs was not guaranteed in the will. As a result, the heirs, citing remarks made against the deceased, refused to continue providing it. Meyerbeer attempted to act as a go-between for Heine. On October 31, 1845, Heine wrote to his publisher Campe: "Everyone implores me to give this situation time to resolve itself and to trust in the true nature of Carl Heine which, they say, shall most certainly emerge; supposedly, I shall not have to forfeit one single penny. This is what I was told yesterday evening by the valiant Meyerbeer, who has guaranteed to compensate any deficit from his own resources . . ."

62. To Heinrich Heine in Paris

[Paris, August 31, 1845]

Dearest friend,

Allow me to provide you with a written response to the request you made yesterday that I write to Carl Heine in reference to your differences with him. Please forgive me when I say that I must refuse. When it comes to family matters of so difficult a nature as this, the involvement of a third party would be very inappropriate and an affront on my part. According to my recollection, the late Salomon Heine did indeed guarantee you a life-long stipend (however, I believe the amount was 4000 francs and not the sum of 4800 to which you referred). Since I was originally involved in realizing your request, I still have a fairly good recollection of what occurred. The kind and venerable old man said at that time that this stipend would protect you so that you would no longer have to work to support yourself in your later years.

Please allow some comments from a good friend of long standing. Carl Heine is of the kindest and most loyal character, and I have often heard him refer to you with a great deal of interest and love. I am therefore convinced that there must be a specific reason why he refuses to continue the stipend promised to you by his father. Did you perhaps insult the late Salomon Heine before his death? Or have you perhaps given your family reason to fear that you, in an outburst of clever but merciless exuberance, might at some point write an article in which you attack the memory of this truly honorable patriarch? Should this be the reason (which you could easily inquire about) then I feel if would be your duty of gratitude and piety to give your family written assurance that this shall indeed never occur.

If you do this, dear friend, I am convinced that you shall once again have the complete trust of so noble a man as Carl Heine and that he shall keep the promise made to you by his late father.

With great friendship,
Yours, Meyerbeer

*   *   *

Meyerbeer's comments on the opera project Noëma, *which was started but never completed, are an example of his close collaboration with Scribe, even during the conception of an opera. They also reflect Meyerbeer's knowledge of literature, his sense of dramatic effect and his understanding of the theater. It was characteristic of Meyerbeer that, during the early stages of planning an opera, his vivid musical imagination was oriented to the singers: he did not think about the major characters, such as Noëma or Nephtali, but rather about Madame Nau and Mr. Gardoni, the singers who were to portray these characters. In the following "comments," Meyerbeer emphasizes the importance of "couleur locale:" the first act was to be characterized by "couleur pastorale" and Biblical style. Therefore, Meyerbeer recommended that Scribe work with a Bible at his side so as to employ its language.*

63. To Eugène Scribe in Paris

[Berlin, April 21, 1846]

My dear friend,

Several days after I wrote my last letter to you, to which you have responded, I developed a very serious gall-bladder problem (possible the result of a cold). As a result, I was bed-ridden for a long period of time. I had hardly recovered when one of my children fell ill with very serious symptoms. My resulting anxiety caused me to have a relapse and I was bed-ridden once again. Thank God we have both since recovered, but for a period of 12 days I was completely inactive. This is the reason, dear friend, that I was unable to respond sooner to the plan you had sent to me.

Generally speaking, I am very pleased with it and am very grateful that it goes into so much detail. Basically, I only have a few comments to make. There is one item that I find particularly problematic: the destiny of the principal female character (Noëma), on which the entire work is based, does not inspire the slightest bit of interest. She is a fury, a shrew, for she has no excuses for her multitude of misdeeds; that she is filled with jealousy does not excuse her, for what cause does she have to be jealous? When Medea murders her children, she is still worthy of our sympathy because she was deceived. I feel that a work is seriously flawed if the protagonist fails to inspire sympathy. This becomes even more problematic when it becomes necessary to create a series of errors and evil deeds in order to gain the audience's sympathy for a character. In Paris, I was not aware of this problem because I did not have the entire outline at my disposal, but now it disturbs me a great deal. I wanted to find out if this was simply my subjective opinion, so I gave the scenario to my wife and to my brother Wilhelm to read, without giving them any of my impressions; both of them had the same impression as I. I have tried to think of any way to assist you, but this is all I have come up with: I suggest that Madame Nau [Noëma] be visiting one of her parents when Gardoni [Nephtali] is drawn to Madame Stoltz [Miriam]. He begins to fall in love with her, courts her, but does not declare his love formally. Later, when Madame Nau has returned to the family and Gardoni sees her, he falls even more deeply in love with her, which goes unnoticed by Madame Stolz. This all occurs before our story begins. However, I feel that this solution is inadequate and I fear that you will share my feelings.

Allow me, my dear friend, to ask for a favor which you have granted twice in the past while we were working on Le Prophète and L'Africaine; i.e., that we show the outline to our mutual friend, Germain Delavigne. I know that you have great confidence in his judgment and criticism. I am sure that you shall find a solution if you go to him because there is no problem that cannot be solved by your creative imagination. Please, dear friend, do not get the impression that my enthusiasm for this project has in any way been dampened. I still consider it to be extremely musical and Innovative from a dramatic standpoint. In pointing out what I consider it to be a very serious flaw, I am only obeying the unavoidable commands of my subjective feelings, but I shall submit them to your judgment which is more experienced than my own, and I yield to you in advance.

There is still another matter which I would like to bring to your attention: the work is much too long. It is particularly long for an operatic adaptation in which, as you know from experience, the individual numbers require a great deal of expansion. I could probably include a shorter number here and there, but not all too often because they not always work for me. Would the solution not be for you to shorten the libretto by eliminating some unimportant details to the extent that this is possible without detracting from the clarity of the plot? Moreover, the Biblical atmosphere of this work requires a certain musical simplicity which must pervade the entire first act and the first half of the third. This doubles the risk of producing an opera of excessive length.

Finally, my dear friend, I have some comments regarding musical details in the three acts. Although these are not extensive, I still feel too weak to continue this letter today. Tomorrow, my friend, you shall receive the remainder of my comments. I shall also arrange the deadline for the delivery of the libretto and the several acts in keeping with the suggestion in your letter.

Farewell, my dear friend and may this letter find you and Madame Scribe, to whom I send my warmest greetings, in the best of health

Cordially yours,
Meyerbeer

* * *

On February 19, 1846, Meyerbeer noted in his diary: "visit from Lassalle, who used a very flowery but transparent allegory to inform me that Heine was going to write material critical of me. The true reason for this animosity is that, before my departure from Paris, I refused to loan him the 1000 francs he demanded, after having loaned him many thousands over the years, of which not one penny was ever repaid." A few days later, on February 27, Heine wrote to Lassalle: "it is time for you to put the thumb screws on the bear (a pun on Meyerbeer's original family name, Beer). Take whatever steps are necessary to make the bear dance to our tune. He must write to Carl [Heine] immediately, in confidence . . ." On March seventh, Heine repeated his demands: ". . . see to it that he writes a strongly-worded letter to Carl Heine . . ." Meyerbeer did not comply immediately, but did yield on Lassalle's insistence. Carl Heine answered Meyerbeer immediately with a bitter letter of refusal.

64. To Carl Heine in Hamburg

[Berlin, June 14, 1846]

My dearest sir,

Two different sentiments have compelled me to write this letter, and it is my hope that you will forgive me if it appears to be indiscreet. The first sentiment is the great respect I have for your honorable and benevolent character and for the memory of your unforgettable father. The second sentiment is based on my long-standing friendship with Heinrich Heine and on the admiration I have for this great poetic genius of whom our German Fatherland is so proud!

Through Mr. Lassalle, a friend of Heine's who corresponds regularly with him, I have recently learned that Heine's health, which has long been precarious, has continued to decline over the last few months. This serious deterioration of his health has been hastened by the anxiety and moral agitation he feels as a result of his insecure financial future. He has stated that this situation has arisen because you will guarantee him neither the full amount of his previous pension, nor the continued payment of it for the remainder of his life. As an outsider, I would never interfere in this family matter were I not able to provide some information regarding the convictions which motivated your late lamented father at the time he granted Heine this pension. I am in this position for it was I who initiated the granting of this pension by your ever so kind father.

When the venerable old man came to Paris for your wedding celebration, Heinrich Heine was receiving temporary subsidies, but had not been given a regular pension. At that time, I took the liberty of bringing this matter to your father's attention and this wonderful old gentleman, who demonstrated genuine good-will in memory of his friendship with my dear parents, often discussed this matter with me in great detail. Based on these encounters, I can say with all certainty that your father considered Heinrich Heine's pension to be for the duration of his life. This is supported by the phrase your father used when announcing this benevolent act. His words were the following: "now at least you shall not have to depend on writing books to earn your keep in your later years."

Many sources have indicated to me how diligently you, honorable sir, have endeavored to fulfill every desire and benevolent intention expressed by the noble deceased. Thus I consider it my duty under the current circumstances to humbly bring this information to your attention in the hope that you shall not only consider this a reflection of my friendship with Heinrich Heine, but also an indication of my deep respect for you and the memory of your unforgettable father.

In expression of this hope,
M.B.

* * *

In 1827, the censors banned a performance of Michael Beer's Struensee *in Berlin because, according to the law of the day, the depiction of any member or ancestor of the royal family on the stage was forbidden. In addition, the Danish ambassador to Prussia had voted against the performance on orders from his King. It was not until 1846 that the laws were liberalized because they were "too great an impediment to the free expression and promotion of dramatic writing." In particular, the old law made the depiction of historic events from the nation's own past all but impossible. Given the turbulence on the political horizon, the demand for patriotic plays increased. This paved the way for a performance of* Struensee. *The King of Hanover gave his approval (a princess of his house was an important character in the play) and there was now ample justification to prefer this work to the one by*

Laube. Any other choice would have been an affront to Amalia Beer, who was greatly respected by the court, and to the court music director general.

"*The performance of* Struensee *was magnificent and in every respect superb," reported Alexander von Humbolt to his King after the premier on September 19, 1846, "and the Berlin audience, which usually sits stoically waiting to pass final judgment, was very satisfied and stimulated."*

65. To Louis Gouin in Paris

[Berlin, September 19, 1846]

My dearest friend,

You must be quite surprised not to have received any letters from me over the last two months. However, this time the delay was not due to my laziness, but to another reason which I would like to explain to you. Seven weeks ago, my King requested that I compose music for the tragedy *Struensee*, written by my deceased brother Michael. It has never been performed because the censors banned it 15 years ago but the King has now lifted this ban. He stated to me that he wanted to see the performance before his departure for Silesia which had been set for the beginning of September. Therefore, I had to work continuously because I had to write a great deal of music for this play: an overture, four large entr'actes, marches, choruses, melodramatic scenes, etc. As soon as I had completed the music, I had to begin rehearsals which were doubly difficult for me because, as you will understand, my love for my poor brother obliged me not only to supervise the musical rehearsals, but the rehearsals for the actors in the tragedy as well. Everything is finally completed; we had the last dress rehearsal yesterday evening and the play (assuming no unforeseen problems) shall have its first performance tonight.

Without exaggerating, my dear friend, I can swear to you that I have had so much to do these last seven weeks that I was unable to find one single free hour to write you a letter. It got to the point where my daughter Blanca had to assume the responsibility of writing to my wife who is still in Switzerland, but will return next week. I am using the day of the premier—the first free day I have had in seven weeks—in order to at least explain to you the reason for my silence so that you do not believe it was due to my old laziness. This is the only reason for today's short letter, for I have neither the intention nor the energy to respond to your letters today; in particular, I am unable to address the difficult questions they contain. You know me well enough to understand that the day of the premier is a day filled with anxiety for me. This time my anxiety is doubly intense because there is a writer (Mr. Laube) who belongs to the "Young Germany" group, a disquieting and extremely rebellious society. He recently wrote a play on the same subject of *Struensee*; he and his gang are furious that my brother's play was chosen for performance instead of his own, and I have every reason to believe that he has planned some great ruckus for this evening's performance. I am sure you understand how pained I would be on account of my dear mother and the memory of my dear brother, if a malicious prank against this tragedy resulted in its failure. I assure you that it is a very noble and poetic creation. Moreover, my music would become tangled in this fiasco if something were to happen. Let us pray to God that none of this will happen. Please say a prayer for the success of the play and my music when you receive this letter. I can count on this, can I not? I know what interest you have demonstrated in everything that affects me as a person and as an artist. I shall write to you again the day after tomorrow because tomorrow I must go see the doctor for medical treatment. You must know that I have been quite ill for the last two months, but despite my condition, I was able to take on the job, and I had the strength to complete it exactly on schedule.

Farewell, my dear friend, and please give my greetings to your entire family.

Your
Giacomo

* * *

In January 1846, Louis (Ludwig) Brandus (1816–1887) and his brother Gemmy (1823–1873) took over Maurice Schlesinger's music and publishing business which, from that point on, published almost all of Meyerbeer's works. Shortly thereafter, they published a collection of 32 songs by Meyerbeer who now hoped that his Struensee overture would help him conquer the concert hall since it had been very well received at the premier due to its great dimensions and distinctive character. Although an arrangement of the play's music with explanatory text was never made, the overture to Struensee did find its way into the concert hall.

66. To Louis Brandus in Paris

Berlin, November 13, 1846

Dear sir,

Please forgive me for responding to your letter in French although your letter to me was written in German; it is because I would like my friend, Mr. Gouin, to see this letter and the two of you to discuss its contents. In your letter, you have requested that I sell you the French publishing rights to the music I composed for the tragedy *Struensee*. Mr. Schlesinger has most likely informed you as to the number and character of pieces contained in the score. I must add that many people have indicated to me that this music (taken in its entirety) would be very suitable for concert hall performance. This could be done by linking the pieces together with a text which would explain the poetic content of each piece. There is a writer here who is currently working on a similar project. There is not the slightest doubt that, as you stated in your letter, the most promising avenue for me as a composer and most profitable for the publisher would be if the French public were to hear the music in the setting for which it was composed, i.e., in the theater, during the tragedy to which the music is intimately bound. However, your theaters of tragedy, the French ones as well as the Odéon, do not have a good orchestra or chorus at their disposal. As for the Théâtre Montpensier, it has not yet opened and it would be wise in any event to find out what arrangements were being made for an orchestra and chorus. If this material were good, if a man of great talent such as A. Dumas were to rework the tragedy (as it is now, it does not correspond to the style of the French stage), and if I were to like the revision, I would agree to write new pieces to be added to the ones I have already completed, if this is required by the new structure of the work. I am going into detail because you seem to be interested in this combination and I, too, feel that it has a good chance of success.

Under no circumstances shall I be able to delay publication of this music in Germany once it has been printed because theaters have already started to ask for it frequently. In the meantime, you could engrave and print the music (so as to guarantee your copyright), but you cannot publish the music immediately if you wish the performance in the Théâtre Montpensier to be successful from a musical and dramatic standpoint; you could publish the music immediately if you do not expect a strong dramatic performance. Concerning the financial arrangements: I shall give you the exclusive publication rights for France *and England* (to the extent that the laws of both countries permit me to do so) for a fee of 3000 francs, half of which is payable immediately and the other half in six months.

Please accept this expression of
my utmost respect,
Meyerbeer

*   *   *

As early as September 1846, the Berlin gazettes were discussing whether Meyerbeer would submit a new request for a leave of absence because he could no longer stand by and watch the deterioration of the Royal Opera: "The extent to which the Royal Opera has deteriorated under its enthusiastically praised central administration [i.e., under the general management of Theodor von Küstner] has become painfully obvious ... Never has the state of the Royal Opera been more neglected and utterly miserable than it is now!" As general music director, Meyerbeer had to answer to Küstner; they had many differences of opinion regarding the approval of additional personnel and the hiring of prominent singers. Adalbert von Ladenberg and Wilhelm Beer collaborated with Meyerbeer on the composition of the following "so-called" letter—one of many to be found in Meyerbeer's correspondence—which seemed as if were intended for publication. This explains the formal tone of the letter, addressed to Alexander Humboldt, one of Meyerbeer's friends.

Several days later, Meyerbeer addressed an almost identical letter to Friedrich Wilhelm IV who responded to Humboldt immediately: "I am returning the letter from our wonderful Giacomo. I am fully prepared, in the hope that better times are ahead, to extend his leave of absence indefinitely . . ." The King's only request was that Meyerbeer continue to direct the court concerts.

67. To Alexander von Humboldt in Berlin

[Berlin, November 23, 1846]

You Excellency,

Before I was called back to the Fatherland, Your Excellency extended to me so many memorable proofs of your kindness that I feel encouraged to seek your enlightened views on a matter that is as important to me as it is delicate. Your Excellency is aware of the very difficult circumstances surrounding the painful decision I felt obliged to make repeatedly in 1845 humbly requesting that I be dismissed from the King's service. By virture of His Majesty's graciousness, which shall forever remain imprinted upon my heart, the following oral decree was issued on my behalf on October 8, 1845:

> The reasons which resulted in my earlier refusal to grant your request for dismissal have not lessened in importance for me; therefore I cannot grant your most recent request of the same nature. Instead I hope that, by reorganizing the theater administration, all further collisions between the general music director and the general manager shall be avoided, thereby eliminating the reason for your dismissal request. In recognition of the fact that you have demonstrated service above and beyond your duty by extending your stay in Berlin and dedicating yourself to the activities of the opera, I have approved a leave of absence for one year with full salary. However, I reserve the right to employ your services for the musical performances at court.

This one-year leave of absence which was so graciously granted to me has now come to an end and I must decide whether I shall resume my position in the service of the Royal Opera as I have done in the past, on December 13. I would not hesitate to do this with great enthusiasm, were it not for the fact that the reorganization of the theater management which His Majesty has planned has not yet become reality.

I still have the same perspective on this matter as I did last year when, with a heavy heart, I made the decision to ask my most gracious King, whom I served with great pride, to relieve me of my duties. Therefore, given the current state of affairs in the theater, my past experience has clearly shown me that it would be utterly impossible for me to serve my King effectively or to do justice to the art of music and the general public. I find myself once again in the very painful position of humbly requesting that I be completely relieved of serving His Highness. My request to dissolve this union, which has kept me so firmly linked to my most gracious King, is all the more painful for me given the tremendous respect and deep sense of gratitude I feel for His Royal Highness. I have been blessed with his continuous demonstrations of his kindness: it is with the deepest sense of humility that I have often, indeed very recently, been favored by His Royal Majesty with words of appreciation for my modest talents. Our King, by virtue of his inexhaustible benevolence, has struck a chord still deeper in my heart. My love for my dear eighty-year-old mother and for my late brother has indeed been exalted by our gracious King, for it was through His Majesty's direct intervention and on his orders that my brother's tragedy *Struensee* was brought to the Berlin stage. The King's graciousness mixed the tears shed by an elderly mother for the untimely loss of a son with tears of joy for the triumphant production for which His Royal Majesty was fully responsible. Your Excellency will certainly understand how painful it is for me to request this break, especially when the heart speaks so loudly. However, I see no other alternative than perhaps an *indefinite extension of my leave of absence*. If Your Excellency is of the opinion that it could indeed be the intention of His Royal Majesty to grant me such a leave, then I would continue to perform my duties as director of court music as I have done in the past. This indefinite leave of absence would come to an end if, at some point in the future, the circumstances at the theater are such that it will be possible for me to resume my position there, or if His Royal Majesty should later decide to grant my request for dismissal. In any case, circumstances being what they are, it is impossible for me to accept a salary for services I have not had the privilege of rendering. Therefore, I respectfully request that His Royal Majesty withhold my salary for the duration of my leave of absence. It is also my hope that His Majesty will not think it ungracious of me if, for the previously stated reason, I decide to turn over my salary from this year's absence to the members of the Royal Orchestra and theater chorus. I do this because, with the exception of the music for *Struensee,* I have performed no services in this past year.

After having provided Your Excellency with this detailed statement of my position in this matter, please allow me to pose the following most humble question: Would it be best to pursue the above approach or some other, if I am to make this appeal without forfeiting the good will of His Royal Majesty while at the same time satisfying the obligations my honor and my art impose upon me?

In unwavering respect and devotion, I remain

Your Excellency's most humble servant,

Meyerbeer

P.S. May I appeal to Your Excellency's indulgence in requesting that I receive a response to my letter as soon as possible? I must still request of His Royal Majesty that I also be granted a two-month leave of absence from my services as director of court music, effective December first. This would allow me to travel to Vienna to rehearse and perform my opera *Das Feldlager* in which Miss Jenny Lind will appear.

* * *

Meyerbeer arrived in Vienna on December 10, 1846. Countless tiring rehearsals of Vielka, a revised version of Das Feldlager in Schlesien, were necessary: according to the newpapers Pokorny, the theater director, was at his wit's end regarding the strictness and unwavering punctuality on which Meyerbeer insisted while working. The besieged Maestro also had to find the additional musicians necessary for the enlarged orchestra and choruses. At the request of the protagonist, he was also obliged to rewrite material and even to compose new music. However, all of this activity at the "Theater an der Wien" merely served to heighten expectations: Mr. Kriehuber, a famous master of his craft, was sent to sketch Meyerbeer. He was cut in topaz, celebrated in society with wreaths, songs, and poems. Everyone fell victim to "Jenny Lind fever" and nibbled "Jenny Lind ices." An elaborate prelude preceded the performance, which was finally given on February 18 to a standing-room-only house.

68. To Amalia Beer in Berlin

[Vienna, February 5, 1847]

My dearest Nonne,

Though I cannot be with you in person on the festive day when Blanca delivers this letter to you, I shall certainly be with you in spirit, my dearest Nonne. I kiss and embrace you and thank almighty God for keeping you so physically fit and alert to this present day. I also pray that he shall continue to keep you healthy, happy, and satisfied and that he shall keep you with us for many more years to come. Amen. You, dearest Nonne, are the guardian angel, the guiding spirit of our family. As long as the Almighty keeps you among us, our family shall continue to do well. May it at least be long enough for you to have the children of my little Cornelia on your lap. And why should this not come to pass? Just yesterday Salomon von Rothschild was telling me that his mother, who is now 97, is as fit, spry, and energetic as a young woman. May God grant the same to you and much more, from the bottom of my soul, Amen and Maseltov [Yiddish for may it bring luck].

If the first performance of my "Feldlager" could have been given three days before your birthday, nothing would have prevented me from leaving the opera to its fate so as to be with you, dear Nonne, for the big family celebration of your 80th birthday. However, in spite of all my activity and iron-fisted drive, I was not able to make that a reality. I do not think I shall be able to leave before Sunday the 13th. Now I have been asked on several occasions to do a production of Les Huguenots at the court theater. The theater is currently doing an abridged and mutilated version of it, but they want me to restore it to the original version and to direct some rehearsals and the performance. I am also supposed to rehearse and conduct a Concert spirituel performance of music from Struensee. Whether I actually will do all these things I do not know, for I am worn down to the bone by the demanding rehearsals for "Feldlager" and am craving some rest. The day before yesterday there was another pleasant and cordial celebration held in my honor. This time it was given by the Merchants' Society.

It goes without saying that, as I sit at my lonely little table, I shall certainly propose a toast to your health on your birthday. When the family is gathered on that very festive and happy day, please do not forget the absent Giacomo who would so much like to be with you to give you a congratulatory kiss on the lips.

Farewell for now, my dearest Nonne.

Your loyal son,
Giacomo

*   *   *

Despite the revisions, Vielka *remained a Prussian opera. The only possible stand to take was that of the outsider, of the non-Prussian. Such was the reaction expressed by one Viennese critic: "from the very beginning, we are unable to identify with the spirit of nationalism which pervades the opera and makes it a true opera of the people." "Meyerbeer," wrote another critic, "had the courage to emancipate the lyrical shallowness of our operas from their melting sentimentality, these syrupy effusions of two and three voices . . . this self-centered revelling and delight taken by a soul in love, swimming in raspberry vinegar . . . Meyerbeer is the Abbé de l'Epée for the musical masses; he teaches them to feel, articulate, speak, thrill, excite, conquer, and rejoice. . . ."*

69. To Amalia Beer in Berlin

[Vienna, March 28, 1847]

My dearest Nonne,

I have not written to you very often because I, whose laziness makes writing a letter such a difficult task, had instructed Wilhelm to inform you of everything worth raving about. However, today I must write to you myself, first of all to tell you that the director of the Prague theater wrote that our dear Michael's *Struensee* had enjoyed great success in Prague. All the performers had two curtain calls at the end of the performance and the overture had to be played twice, etc. etc. On the day that a second performance was announced, all the stalls were sold out at once. If only Michael had been able to experience the triumph of his wonderful play!

In addition, I can report to you that the 13th and final performance of *Vielka* (final because the theater remains closed during the entire Holy Week and, after Easter, Miss Lind will sing Norma only one more time, as a benefit performance, then she leaves for London) was greeted by a large audience with such wild enthusiasm that it defies description. After the overture was finished and the curtain went up, the audience applauded and wildly shouted "da capo" for so long that the curtain had to be lowered again and the overture had to be repeated. In addition, during the evening performance, five numbers had to be repeated, and a certain section of the flute piece, which got no reaction in Berlin, Miss Lind had to sing four times in a row. Yes, four times! I was called out on stage eight times and when I appeared after the second act, a laurel wreath was thrown down to me (this had already happened in the first performance) *from the imperial box*. I have been told that it was thrown by Archduke Albrecht. The performance was a benefit for Staudigl and he doubled the prices that had already been raised. This meant that a stall sold for 4 guilders and a 4 person box for 30 guilders. Nevertheless, on the day of the performance there was not a single ticket to be had.

In a few days I shall depart, my dear Nonne, and since you are so against my traveling via Breslau, I shall travel via Prague and Dresden. By the way: the overture to *Struensee* has also been very popular here. In the philharmonic concert, concert spirituel, even in the concerts by Strauss, in short, wherever it was performed in Vienna, the orchestra was obliged to do an encore of it. Well my dear Nonne, I think that this is gossip enough for one letter. Please pass this information on to Wilhelm who shall certainly be glad to hear it. Farewell my dearest Nonne. Give my best to Doris, Georg, Julius and our dear old lady. Also to Mr. Burguis.

Your loyal,
Giacomo

* * *

In May, 1847 the London audiences gave Jenny Lind a triumphant reception, on the occasion of her debut as Alice in Meyerbeer's opera Robert le Diable. *At the end of the performance the enthusiasm reached such a feverish pitch that it thundered through the house for 20 minutes.*

However, at the beginning of July, Meyerbeer received an alarming bit of news from London: Miss Lind had inserted the flute piece from Vielka *into a performance of* The Barber of Seville. *This bravura aria had been composed especially for her; with its breathtaking coloraturas Lind demonstrated her great abilities. Meyerbeer did not dare to criticize "dear Jenny," not even so much as to admit to the oversensitive singer that he had been told about the performance. He decided—very characteristically—to pursue a diplomatic approach by making a carefully formulated request to avoid a repetition of this performance.*

Vielka *was not performed in London. To do this it would have been necessary to adapt the "Prussian fairy tale" for an English audience.*

70. To Jenny Lind in London

[Franzensbad, July 24, 1847]

My dearest Miss Lind,
The kind and friendly letter you addressed to me in Berlin just

arrived here in Franzensbad, where I have been residing for the last four weeks, hoping that the mineral springs would conquer the nasty cough which bothered me so much in Vienna. On the journey here, it turned into a cold and fever which kept me in bed for three weeks. Only now am I beginning to recover.

It will be a pleasure for me, my dearest Miss Lind, to arrange for voice, two flutes, and pianoforte and to send it to you the flute trio from *Vielka*, for performance in your concerts in the provincial cities of England. My only request, dear Jenny, is that you do *not sing this music in London*, so that, if *Vielka* should be performed in London in the future, this music will not already have been heard, thereby losing the advantage of novelty. If I had the score with me, I would complete this little project posthaste, but this is not the case. I shall leave for Berlin on August 10: once there, it shall only be a few days before it is finished and sent off to you. You can certainly plan on having it in your hands by August 20. Since, as you stated in your letter, the concerts in the provinces do not begin until the end of August, this music shall arrive in time.

The reports of your staggering successes in the British capital have made the rounds in all of the European papers; I, as one of your enthusiastic admirers and trusted friends, was delighted but not surprised. You remember that I always assured you (back when you were afraid of going to Berlin, then Vienna, then London, Paris and Italy) that wherever there are listeners with feeling hearts and a sense for the truly beautiful and noble, your success was guaranteed, that you had no reason to fear comparison to any living artist of prominence in the world because you entrance both the heart and soul.

You have seen, dear Jenny, that you have fulfilled my prophecies from one capital to the next. You have left your friends with only two other things for which to hope: your continued good health, so as to celebrate many more triumphs in the years to come, and a happy disposition so as to enjoy your success.

*   *   *

Franz Grillparzer (1791–1872) made a rather grumpy entry in his diary in reference to a dinner at Amalia Beer's house during the spring of 1836 in Paris. Once again, the rather unsociable poet was not very receptive to Meyerbeer's obliging invitation and Alexander von Humboldt's conversations. "He made nothing but kind and clever remarks," he noted in his diary, "but there is no intellectual atmosphere. One does not feel the presence of a great man."

In 1833, Grillparzer had written a review of Robert le Diable *that was never published. Later, he placed* Les Huguenots *above "Robert:" he wrote that* Robert le Diable *"did on the whole have more beautiful moments, but nothing on the consistently high level of the last two or even three acts of* Les Huguenots.*"*

71. To Franz Grillparzer in Berlin

[Berlin, September 25, 1847]

Dearest Sir,

This morning I learned of your arrival in Berlin from the newspapers. I would have immediately rushed over to see you, were I not leaving for Potsdam for a few hours. I shall come by tomorrow morning to greet you, but first I must pass on a request from my mother (who had the pleasure of seeing you in Paris). She requests the privilege of your company tomorrow afternoon (at four o'clock) for lunch. It will be an intimate group, but the good Alexander von Humboldt will be there; someone I am sure you would like to see. In the hope that you shall accept this invitation, I shall have the honor of calling for you at three-thirty tomorrow with my carriage, as my mother lives far from your hotel *Zum Kronprinzen* (in the Tiergarten).

Please permit me, esteemed sir, to express my respect and devotion.

Your
Meyerbeer

*   *   *

After the contract had been signed on March 11, 1848 for the Paris performance of Le Prophète, *binding contractual arrangements had to be reached with the singers: on the same day, Meyerbeer wrote a letter to Louis Viardot in London to clarify as yet unresolved matters regarding the hiring of his wife, Pauline Viardot-Garcia. The new directors, Duponchel and Roqueplan, had agreed to hire her as long as she did not demand a salary in excess of 75,000 francs annually. Even at that time, the directors of opera houses outbid one another for the prima donnas, with some singers receiving twice the salary of a government minister, even in Germany. However, the question of Viardot-Garcia's employment was the decisive key to the success or failure of this opera because she was to be Fides. This was also significant because it was the first time in the history of opera a mezzo soprano (or high alto) was to sing the leading role.*

The performance of Les Huguenots *in London, in the presence of Queen Victoria and her consort, Prince Albert, was a major triumph for Meyerbeer: one London article reported that Meyerbeer was finally being treated justly in England, adding that this score was treated with respect and was not massacred, i.e. shortened, altered, and poorly performed, as had been the case with* Robert le Diable.

72. To Louis Gouin in Paris

Ischl, August 11, 1848

My dear and wonderful friend.

My children and I spent a few days up in the mountains. Upon my return yesterday, I found your letters of July 30 and August 3. After reading what you wrote about Duponchel's good arrangements regarding the singers that I had suggested, I shall not waste a minute and shall get a letter out today. However, please inform Mr. Duponchel that it will take three weeks before he can know the result of this demarche. Yesterday I received a letter from Mr. Viardot in London. He wrote that *Les Huguenots* had been very successful in London. He also informed me that Roger has assured him that he shall not wait for the premier of *Le Prophète* to debut at the Opera. Instead, he wishes to debut with Madame Viardot in November in the role of Raoul in *Les Huguenots*. I am very happy for our opera directors and for myself, but most of all *for the opera itself;* one that our directors neglected for so long, after it had been subjected to such terrible treatment by Pillet. This also pleases me because I can study Roger's voice much more effectively when he is singing my own music. It is my guess that the directors have not yet learned of Roger's decision and I think you should make them aware of it. Would you, dear friend, be so kind as give them this good news. Farewell, dear friend. I am ending the letter so quickly so I can write to our soprano at once.

Let us pray that I am succesful. This would be excellent for *Le Prophète,* but better yet for our directors.

Cordially yours,
Meyerbeer

*   *   *

After a vacation in Bad Gastein and Ischl, Meyerbeer returned to Paris in September to begin rehearsals of Le Prophète. *The delay in starting the rehearsals and the resulting postponement of the performance created some controversy. This led to new negotiations because the contracts of the two protagonists, Roger and Pauline Viardot-Garcia, had been terminated.*

After breaking with Meyerbeer, Heine resumed his relationship with the composer at the beginning of the year. In a review of Miss Lind's debut published in the "Allgemeine Zeitung" (Augsburg) in 1847, Heine had exposed Meyerbeer to ridicule. Despite this fact, the composer could not spurn Heine's requests.

Meyerbeer composed a cantata for the silver anniversary of the King of Prussia. It was a hymn of celebration entitled "Du, Du der über Raum und Zeit" (Thou, beyond time and space). Based on a text by Karl Winkler, it was composed for solos and a cappella chorus and was performed on November 29, 1848 in Berlin.

73. To Amalia Beer in Berlin

Dearest beloved Nonne,

Today Gouin presented me with the very beautiful overcoat you gave me as a birthday gift. It is a very elegant piece of clothing which shall stand me in very good stead this winter; I thank you, dearest Nonne, from the bottom of my heart. With great sorrow I learned from Mr. Burguis' previous letter that you have been suffering from arthritis in your knee. I was all the happier to learn from Wilhelm's letter that you are now feeling better (*knock on wood*) ...

Heine, the writer, is in very poor health. His entire body is so lame that he can no longer move. He has also been subjected to the most terrible cramps. When I left Paris six months ago, he extorted 500 francs from me and I gave him another 500 now, upon my return. This is a lot of money by today's standards, especially when it is given to someone who has been so ungrateful. However, I could not supress my sympathy for his appalling state. Benny Goldschmidt saw him yesterday and he told me Heine had stated to him that the only thing in his life he bitterly regretted was having changed his religion. He also said that, if he survived, he would become so pious as to eat only kosher food.

Could you please be so good, dearest Nonne, as to tell Wilhelm that I still have not received the poem from Winkler for the King's silver anniversary. Could you also pass on to Wilhelm the following notes regarding *Le Prophète*. According to my contract, rehearsals for *Le Prophète* should have started on October first. However, that miserable, spineless Duponchel calculated incorrectly when planning the schedule for the new opera *Jeanne la Folle* [Jean the Madwoman] which is supposed to be performed before my opera. The result of this is that this opera, which should have gone into performance on September 15, is so far behind schedule that the rehearsals shall not be completed until November second at the earliest! So I must wait until then before beginning rehearsals for my opera, thereby losing a whole month. Thus my opera will be performed a month later than scheduled; from February 15 it has now been pushed back to March 15. If I had decided not to tolerate this and had taken Duponchel to court, he would have been obliged to adhere to the terms of the contract. However, that would have made a very nasty impression because it would have meant telling another composer, whose opera was ready for performance, that he would not be able to perform his opera because his rehearsals were a month behind schedule. In addition, Scribe is the librettist for *Jeanne la Folle* [music by Clapisson] and he asked me to wait. Since I made him wait so long with *Le Prophète,* I could not refuse him this request. Therefore, I am waiting calmly until November second ...

Farewell, my dearest Nonne. May this letter find you in the best of health and state of mind. Give my best to Wilhelm and all the others.

Your devoted son,
Giacomo

74. To Amalia Beer in Berlin

Paris, February 6, 1849

My dearest Nonne,

This is the third time that I have not been able to be with you to celebrate your birthday. Once again, I shall not be able to kiss you and give you my very best wishes. However, even though I am not there in body, my heart and soul are with you on this happiest of days. It is a day which has blessed us with the best and most gentle of mothers who also is a tireless noble benefactress for the suffering and needy. May God keep you strong in body and spirit for many years to come, and may all of us give you nothing but happiness. Amen: let it be so.

My cough, thank God, has been much better recently (knock on wood). However, now I very frequently have pains on my right side, in my back and shoulders. This, too, has been much better during the last week. Thus far, I am very happy with the way the rehearsals are going (again, knock on wood). All the singers and chorus members are making a great effort and are aglow with ambition. They also seem to be happy with the music. The individual coaching has ended and the singers and chorus members have memorized the five acts. Yesterday I began the quartet rehearsals. May God bless and protect this work. On the day of the premier, I ask you to bless me and *Le Prophète,* for who, my dearest beloved Nonne, should have more credit with our dear God than such a fine and noble woman as yourself.

Farewell, dearest Nonne. May this letter find you in the best of health and spirits, and may God grant us a happy reunion once I have completed my difficult work here.

Your loyal son,
Giacomo

* * *

Meyerbeer was considered an excellent conductor, which Berlioz also acknowledged. As such, he considered it in his own interest to rehearse and conduct his works personally when they were performed in Europe's major opera houses. This was also considered a polite gesture vis a vis the audience. Only in Paris was Meyerbeer not allowed to conduct his own works. The demand for perfection in Paris may have been the reason for this Solomonic decision: it relieved the opera house director of having to decide which of the composers was also a good conductor. Perhaps the director did not wish to reduce the regular conductor to the role of conducting only routine performances, given the many premiers in Paris which, unlike Germany, had a very centralized cultural life. However, Meyerbeer did conduct most of the rehearsals and familiarized Girard with his concepts. Narcisse Girard (1797–1860), also a professor of Violin at the Conservatoire, proved to be a reliable conveyor of Meyerbeer's musical wishes. This was demonstrated on the evening of the premier.

The letter to Girard, which is representative of many other letters of grati-

tude, demonstrates that Meyerbeer was aware that the success of a work depended on the good will of all participants and performers.

75. To Narcisse Girard in Paris

Paris, April 14, 1849

On the evening before the premier of *Le Prophète,* please allow me to voice through you my deepest gratitude to the artists of the opera orchestra for the tireless dedication they have demonstrated throughout this long and difficult rehearsal period. I am also very grateful for the loyal and artistic manner in which they united their efforts to overcome magnificently all of the difficulties associated with rehearsing so difficult and complicated a work. Thanks to their spirit of cooperation I can hope that my modest work shall be performed with the perfection for which the Opéra has long been famous and which has elicited the admiration of the musical world. Never would I have considered robbing myself of the joy of personally expressing my deepest gratitude to the members of the orchestra, but I was most anxious to give more weight to my expression of gratitude by allowing it to come from your lips, dear Sir. For it is you, the respected and masterful conductor of the orchestra, who has contributed so much to the success of this opera. This was not simply the result of your conscientiousness and the extreme care with which you conducted the orchestra, but can also be attributed to your vast experience and critical acumen. It is my greatest hope that your excellent direction shall, for many years to come, continue to provide secure and infallible guidance for the members of this orchestra as they pursue their noble mission.

Your very humble and grateful,
G. Meyerbeer

*   *   *

The premier of Le Prophète *took place on April 16. The success was unprecedented—over the first ten days of performances, the opera took in the unheard-of sum of 9000 to 10,000 francs per performance. Meyerbeer received from his publisher the highest sum of money ever paid for the purchase of a score: 19,000 francs for the publishing rights in France, 17,000 francs for the English rights and 8000 francs for the German rights—a total of 44,000 francs. Meyerbeer's skaters' ballet, known as* Les Patineurs *[The Skaters] in modern ballet literature, created quite a sensation; the view of the picturesque winter landscape before the gates of Münster and the gliding movements of the skaters fascinated the Parisians. The Grisettes and Lorettes, the seamstresses and the elegant ladies accompanied by their beaus who entertained themselves in the upper balconies all broke out in cheers for the "Redowa," the most beloved and fashionable dance of the day in Paris. The ice skates were actually roller skates, which had been invented in Paris in 1790, but which had been considered a useless curiosity;*

Illus. 12: *Le Prophète,* Act IV—Exorcism Scene with Gustave Roger and Pauline Viardot. From *L'Illustration, Journal universel,* Paris, 1849.

however, with the onset of the opera, the merchants did a booming business with "Prophet Skates!"

At the end of the opera, the prophet blows himself up along with his mother and the imperial soldiers who had broken into the palace. All of the prophet's splendor comes to an end in a giant conflagration. Meyerbeer had not represented the fire in his music; instead, it merely expressed the general tumultuousness of the scene. The fire was used only as a visual stage effect unlike the final scene of Wagner's Walküre, *in which the magic flames were also represented musically. Meyerbeer is objective enough to admit this artistic shortcoming as well as his music's weakened effectiveness at this point in the opera.*

76. To Amalia Beer in Berlin

[Paris, April 16, 1849]

Dearest beloved Nonne,

At the prescribed moment, I read with great reverence and emotion the motherly blessing you included in your letter. I fervently kissed your

Illus. 13: A dancer, after rehearsing the *Skating Ballet*. "The composer: please don't let anything transpire." [A pun: "transpire" also means "perspire." The puppet which Meyerbeer holds under his arm is *Le Prophète*.-Ed.] *Illustration*, April 1849.

sweet name and carried the letter close to my heart until the end of the performance. God heard your prayers, dearest Nonne, because, as far as one can tell by the first performance, *Le Prophète* (cross your fingers and knock on wood) is a brilliant success. Many people have said that this opera stands head and shoulders above "Robert" and *Les Huguenots*. The reception was *very enthusiastic*. Roger had already been called out on stage after the second act, Madame Viardot after the fourth act, and everyone was called out at the end of the opera. The audience did not relent until I decided, albeit reluctantly, to walk out on stage. Shouts of "Meyerbeer" would not cease. Judging from the applause, the entire opera was well received, with the exception of four or five pieces. The following pieces made the greatest impression: in the first act it was the great ensemble number with the Anabaptist sermon and a two-part romance sung with utmost perfection by Mademoiselle Castellan and Madame Viardot. In the second act, it was the telling of the dream and a romance sung charmingly by Roger. There was also a simple adagio sung by Viardot with such exquisite perfection and tragic feeling that the audience demanded two encores. Then came the major piece of the act, a male quartet in which Roger gave a moving performance both as a singer and actor (this piece concluded the act). After his stirring performance, he was

Illus. 14: The corps de ballet rehearsing on skates. Nevertheless, Mr. Roqueplan is sure that at the performance everything will "roll right along." [Again a pun, "Comme sur les roulettes" also being an idiom meaning "like clockwork."-Ed.] *Illustration*, April 1849.

called back out on stage. The highlights of the third act were the buffo trio for three men's voices and the ballet divertissement which was charmingly staged. This time my ballet music is said to have gone over very well and the Gallop and Redowa were particularly popular.

The second scene of the fourth act takes place in the church and lasts 22 minutes, although it only contains the triumphal march and the Finale. This scene is the high point of the opera, both musically and dramatically. You can imagine how anxious I was to see how it would be received. By the grace of God, the response exceeded my expectations; the audience cried during this scene as they would have done during a tragedy. I am greatly indebted to Viardot for the success of this scene for she reached unprecedented tragic heights both as a singer and as an actress. Roger was also magnificent in the scene in which he denies his mother. Both received thunderous applause. During rehearsals there was general concern as to whether a fifth act would even be possible after the fourth. Nevertheless, Miss Viardot's big aria in the fifth act made such a stunning impression that she was greeted with four rounds of applause the likes of which I have experienced only in Vienna. The response was so overwhelming that the performers had to pause before beginning the duet. And here too, the duet between Viardot and Roger created an exceptionally intense tragic effect. After this, the musical effect wanes somewhat. It was only the magnificent fire scene at the end of the opera which came to my rescue and kept the audience's enthusiasm until the very end. Everything I have recounted to you here, dear Nonne, is only the response to the first performance. Very often the excitement generated by the first performance is not maintained in those which follow. Let us pray that this shall not be the case for *Le Prophète*.

Farewell, dear Nonne: please pass on the contents of this letter to Minna and Wilhelm. I shall write more after the second performance. Today in "Débats and "Constitutionel," there already were some very favorable comments regarding the first performance.

Your loyal son,
Giacomo

*   *   *

Meyerbeer was very concerned that the growing political unrest in Germany could also reach Berlin. On April 28, 1849, Friedrich Wilhelm IV declined to be considered for the post of German emperor and in so doing also rejected the bicameral parliamentary system. At the beginning of May there were revolts in Dresden which were put down by Prussian troops. By mid-May, many Berliners flocked to Dresden for what Minna Meyerbeer referred to as a "pleasure trip." Their purpose was to inspect what was left of the barricades. "It was said that, for four to five days, no seats were available on the trains."

Due to the events of the day, Meyerbeer's opera Ein Feldlager in Schlesien *(Encampment in Silesia) received an unexpected political interpretation. The slogan "our blood for our King!" (after the capture of Frederick the Great) and the chorus entitled "A Prussian Heart Beats with Courage in the Face of Death and Danger" were greeted with an explosion of jubilant applause during every performance and had to be repeated. From that point on, "Feldlager" was frequently given on the occasion of patriotic events and state visits.*

77. To Minna Meyerbeer in Berlin

Paris, May 4, 1849

My dearest wife,

The hunch I expressed in a letter to our dear Nonne two days ago has now been fully confirmed. Last night I received the following letter from the Minister of the Interior:

> Dear Sir, By virtue of a decision based on my proposal, the President of the Republic has appointed you Commander of the Legion of Honor. It is a privilege for me to inform you of this demonstration of great esteem on the part of the government. The Chancellor of the Order will have the Diploma of Appointment sent to you immediately.

The remainder of the letter contains the usual closing lines. Today, already, my appointment is included in the official section of Le Moniteur. What I find most gratifying about this is the fact that absolutely no steps were taken on my part to initiate this action, nor are any of my aquaintances connected with the present government. Therefore, I feel I can interpret this appointment as an expression of public support. Despite the fact that the elections for the new parliament are approaching, with countless election meetings and a resulting drop in theater receipts, attendance for the seventh performance of Le Prophète was very good: the proceeds from this performance amounted to 9600 francs and the response to the performance was very good. Today was to be the eighth performance, but unfortunately Roger has taken ill. Please do not forget to pass on all of this information to our dear Nonne, who is very interested in these developments.

I am very saddened by the news coming from Berlin and dread the dark days which appear to be fast approaching. I pray to God that I am mistaken and that all shall end in peace and unity. May these lines find you, my dearest, and our beloved children in the very best of health.

Your adoring husband,
Giacomo

* * *

In January of 1850, Meyerbeer directed the rehearsals for Le Prophète *in Dresden but departed for Vienna immediately after the premier on January 30. A great deal of hard work was required in Vienna to rehearse this difficult opera. On February 28, the day of the premier, people were already standing in line for tickets by early morning. Around noon, such a large crowd had gathered in front of the opera house that the military had to be called in to maintain order. In the end, people paid scalpers up to 100 gilders for a seat! That evening's performance was a tremendous success for the ensemble. Meyerbeer was wildly acclaimed and crowned with a golden laurel wreath.*

Meyerbeer, who was deeply religious and even superstitious, always had his mother bless him before important occasions or journeys. This blessing is called "benchen" in the Jewish vernacular. When away at premiers in foreign cities, he always had his mother send him her written blessing.

78. To Amalia Beer in Berlin

Vienna, February 6, 1850

My dearest Nonne,

Once again I shall not be with you on your birthday. Although I shall not be there in person, I shall be with you in heart and spirit on February 10, dearest Nonne. Wherever I am on that day my thoughts shall be of you, and I shall thank the heavens for giving me such a dear, sweet mother. I shall also pray that God allow you to remain among us and to enjoy perfect health and happiness for another 100 years. You are the guardian angel of the entire family; as long as the good Lord sees fit to keep you among us it is my firm belief that our entire family shall enjoy good fortune. I have no doubt of this because such a virtuous and devout woman as yourself surely commands the attention of the Creator who looks into the hearts of people and weighs the value of their prayers. On the occasion of your birthday this year, I pray to heaven that Wilhelm shall soon be restored to permanent good health. If only Wilhelm would decide to go to his regular doctor exclusively instead of seeking advice from other doctors at the same time. This is not good because it confuses the patient and robs him of the trust that is so important for successful treatment. May the Lord bless him and may his treatment be successful.

As I was writing you this letter, dearest Nonne, I received a letter from Marseille informing me that Le Prophète was performed there for the first time on January 25 and was received with great enthusiasm.

Here in Vienna, the theater staff has demonstrated the greatest devotion and enthusiasm for this work. Without my having to ask, the new director (Hollbein) had an entire row of seats removed so that the orchestra could be enlarged to strengthen the performance of Le Prophète. He also wants to enlarge the chorus in the opera. Since I have only been here for two days and have only rehearsed with a few of the singers individually, I am unable to say at present whether the overall production will be a good one or when the opera will be performed, but I hope that it shall be ready by the end of this month.

And now, dearest Nonne, let me wish you health and happines with all my heart, on the occasion of your birthday, which is more a day of celebration and joy for us than it is for you. May God keep you in the very best of health until your 100th birthday, and may He continue to bless you with your keen sense for all that is good, noble, and beautiful. And finally, may your children and grandchildren bring you nothing but joy. Amen! Let it be so.

Please give Wilhelm my warmest greetings.

Your loyal son,
Giacomo

P.S. The letter containing your blessing which you sent to me in Paris was also next to my heart during the premier in Dresden. Once again, this dear talisman exercised its blessed power.

* * *

The business councillor and banker Wilhelm Beer (1797–1850) was a second lieutenant in the Wars of Liberation and had been a senior member of the Association of Berlin Merchants since 1836. His further activities included being a member of both the board of directors for the Potsdam-Magdeburg railroad company and the central committee of the Prussian Bank as well as being a Berlin civic commissioner and member of the Prussian House. He was also a respected scientist: in 1824, after years of observations made from an observatory on the

Illus. 15: The Beer Villa with Wilhelm Beer's private observatory in the Berlin Tiergarten. From 1855 to 1857 Naval Cadet Institute of the Prussian Navy. Water color, approx. 1856 (Naval School Flensburg-Mürwik).

roof of the Beer villa in the Tiergarten section of Berlin, he and Johann Heinrich Mädler published the first lunar map. Meyerbeer lost a true brother in Wilhelm Beer; one who furthered his work in an unselfish manner, always ready to give advice. Occasionally, he attempted to spread his brother's fame by writing articles, especially about concerts at court to which journalists had no access.

79. To Karl Kaskel in Dresden

Berlin, March 28, 1850

Dearest Brother,

I know how much you loved my dear Wilhelm, and he counted you among his closest and dearest friends. Unfortunately, he is no more. Yesterday evening at 5:30 P.M., he passed away quietly and without struggle: the fever which had persisted for the last four weeks finally exhausted all his strength. No words can express what I have lost in him. In addition to this irreplaceable loss I am very worried about how my dear 83-year-old mother shall take the shock of having to bury a third son. May God bless and protect you from such misfortune, my dear friend and brother.

Your loyal,
Meyerbeer

*　　*　　*

On April 28, 1850, Le Prophète *premiered in Berlin under Meyerbeer's direction. The opera played to overflowing houses 11 times in one month, despite extremely high ticket prices, yet public reaction was mixed. The majority of the Berlin critics especially—now as always in the past—gave the opera unfavorable reviews. Meyerbeer spent most of that summer in Berlin fulfilling his responsibilities as General Music Director of the opera and as director of court music. On August 18 he departed for Spa to take a cure, remaining there until September 24. On September 25 he returned once again to Paris.*

80. To Amalia Beer in Berlin

Paris, October 10, 1850

My dearest Nonne,

For the last few days I have been unable to write to you because I was exceptionally busy. *Le Prophète,* which was not be presented again until Miss Viardot returns to the stage, had to be performed after all for administrative reasons. It seems that Miss Alboni did not make enough money in her other roles. It was necessary to recast some of the roles because several of the artists had already departed. Therefore, in the interest of the work, I took charge of the rehearsals and had no free time at all. *Le Prophète* finally went into performance again on Wednesday (with Miss Alboni). Public demand was so large that the box office took in 10,742 francs. The performance went very well and was exceptionally well received. As an actress, Alboni does not even begin to compare with Viardot. As a result of her natural apathy, she lacks the necessary fire in the exciting moments of the opera. However, in all sections of the opera requiring motherly tenderness or melancholic grief, she sang beautifully. In such moments, her wonderful voice can shine brilliantly because the entire role appears to be written exactly for her voice range. She was very well received by the audience. Although *Le Prophète* was performed only this past Wednesday, it was performed again last night and it once again brought in close to 10,000 francs. There will be another performance tomorrow, bringing the total to 76 performances. . . . An hour from now, an agent from the management of the royal theater in Madrid shall visit me. A new royal theater by the name of "Teatro del Oriente" will open there next month, beginning with an Italian opera (Alboni and Gardoni are going there). *Le Prophète* shall also be performed there. According to

Der Einzug des **Propheten** in Berlin.

Illus. 16: Caricature of the 1850 premier of *Le Prophète* in Berlin, by Wilhelm Scholz. The head of the donkey is a likeness of the manager Karl Theodor von Küstner (*Fliegende Blätter*, 1850).

what I have secretly learned, this agent is going to ask me under what conditions I would consider going to Madrid to direct the rehearsals and conduct the first three performances of *Le Prophète*. I have learned that, if I were to agree to go to Madrid, the Queen of Spain would send me a written invitation. If I had received such an invitation years ago while my dear brother Wilhelm was still alive, I might have accepted, for it is certainly a great honor. However now, my dearest Nonne, it is my duty to be with you as often as possible. My business here shall be completed in a few days and with God's help I shall be returning to Berlin in a week at the latest. May this letter find you in the best of health.

Your loyal son,
Giacomo

*   *   *

Only a few of Meyerbeer's letters to his three daughters Blanca, Cäcilie and Cornelie have been preserved. They provide proof of his tender affection, but also of his gentle strictness. The teaching of modesty and thrift, something for which

131

Meyerbeer was praised time and again, was very important to him. Even later, when his daughters were almost adults, he tried to teach them the value of things which should be worked for, earned, and kept. Presents were always lovingly selected in accordance with the daughters' wishes, but these gifts were never lavish, as one might expect for the children of a wealthy man. As this letter shows, attending a theater performance or taking an ice in a cafe were not everyday events for the young Cornelie, who later developed considerable skill at the piano. She also enjoyed occasional lessons from Joachim Raff who wrote some compositions for her.

81. To Cornelie Meyerbeer in Bad Ischl

[Prague, May 27, 1851]

My dearest daughter Cornelie,

I know how much you like to sleep late in the morning and how difficult it is for you to get up. This is why I was especially pleased, my dear child, that you had asked to be awakened at five o'clock in order to say goodbye to me at five-thirty before I left on my journey. I believe that your most pleasant reward would be to learn that you have made your father very happy, which I indeed was.

On my journey here, I learned that a high-wire act is performing at the Carl theater in Leopoldstadt and that they are supposed to do extraordinary things. Since I would like to return the happiness you gave me this morning, you may go to this performance with Henri, after having a dish of ice cream at Dehne's. Show this letter to your dear mother; I am sure that she will give you her permission and advance you the necessary money. I will then reimburse the money when you all return to Berlin. I will tell Nonne what a good girl you have been: I will also give little Mathilde your letter, along with a couple of pretty writing books, a ruler, and some sweets, all *in your name* and as *your* gifts.

Goodbye, my dear child. Be a good girl and obey your mother. Be loving to your sisters and practice hard at the piano in Ischl.

Your loving father,
Meyerbeer

Prague, May 27, 1851

*   *   *

Adolphe Sax (1814–1894) was certainly the most creative, talented, and important instrument maker of his time: the bass clarinet, cylinder trumpet and the saxophone, which was named after him and celebrated in Paris as a "veritable création de génie, were all examples of his ingenuity. Meyerbeer was very interested in his work and was on friendly terms with the instrument maker. He was also one of the first composers to use these new instruments in his scores. When Sax later ran into financial difficulties, Meyerbeer attempted to save him from bankruptcy by paying him a large sum of money.

82. To Adolphe Sax in Paris

[Berlin, June 16, 1851]

My dear Mr. Sax,

You have always been so helpful and kind to me that I have assured a friend of mine that you would be good enough to give me your opinion on a difficult matter relating to a subject on which you can competently speak. The problem is as follows: musical works of Johann Sebastian Bach are currently being edited in Leipzig. The works in question are those which have remained in manuscript form to this day. This project is under the artistic direction of the very knowledgeable Professor Dehn, librarian for the Royal Library in Berlin. I am writing you this letter on his request.

I am sure you know that, during the period when these compositions were written, i.e. about 130 years ago, trumpets did not yet have valves or keys. Trumpeters not only depended on manual dexterity to execute the most difficult passages, but also used mouth pieces which made it much easier to play the natural trumpet in the high register than is possible today. In the enclosed excerpt from a Bach concerto, the line written in red ink must be played on an F trumpet. This is impossible for the natural F trumpets of our day. Since the director of the edition would like to be as true to the original as possible while at the same time using our modern instruments, he would like to know if there are trumpets or cornets à piston with exchangeable parts which could be used when performing these very difficult passages. If you were to inform me that such instruments do exist, a note could then be made to that effect in the printed score. If I am not mistaken, you invented small E-flat cornets which offer a wide range of possibilities in the high register. However, I am not certain enough to swear that this is the case. Would you be so kind as to look at this passage and send me your opinion in a letter? I know that you are very busy, but I shall appeal to your kindness in asking that you send a response as soon as possible as the edition is almost completed. Please excuse, good sir, that a foreign hand is guiding my pen, for a small indisposition obliges me to take to my bed.

* * *

For a long time the drafts for the "vecchia Africana," the old "Africaine" (African woman), had been tied up in bundles put away in a closet. Meyerbeer began the composition in 1837, but stopped working on the opera when Cornélie Falcon, who was to play the female lead, left the Paris Opéra. He was also dissatisfied with the libretto because there was still no material dealing with the Vasco da Gama story. In 1842, Meyerbeer admitted to his friend Gouin: "Just between us, the music and libretto for L'Africaine are inferior to Le Prophète which is the best score I have ever written." Three years later, when there was once again discussion as to which opera should be presented first, Meyerbeer stated the following:

Illus. 17: Eugène Scribe. Photo by Nadar, ca. 1850.

"My faith in the music of Le Prophète *is every bit as great as my lack thereof in the music of* L'Africaine, *and since I have not produced any work for quite some time, I think it would be a good idea to present my strongest work in Paris." However, in 1851 the work was still in its beginning stages, even though Scribe had delivered a new scenario on December 1.*

Meyerbeer, though the most successful operatic composer of his day, continued to have scruples. He was forever anxious to repeat or exceed his brilliant international successes of the past by producing a new work. This prompted him not only to work with great care, but sometimes drove him to take measures that were overly cautious.

83. To Eugène Scribe in Paris

Minden (in transit) October 27, 1851

My dear friend,

As the result of an illness which has sapped most of my strength, I have been forced to take this journey at a slower pace. Therefore, I am now sitting in the train thinking about our new *L'Africaine* and the last meeting we had on this matter. I do not know if I am misguided, but I think I have an idea for a good and clear opening scene which would also provide a wonderful musical introduction. It would be a festive council scene of the Portugese admiralty before which Vasco presents his plans for the discovery of India and makes an appeal for ships and troops. The head of the council would be Vasco's rival, the future husband of Ines. As in all meetings, the members of the council do not agree. Each supports his own views, but finally the cabal against Vasco prevails. They say that his projects cannot be carried out, are nothing but fantasies. The grand inquisitor, who is present at all council meetings, criticizes Vasco's view of the heretical country. Vasco has an outburst of rage, issues threats, is relieved of his office and banished. He leaves in a rage exclaiming that he shall take it upon himself to secure and equip a ship in order to prove that he was not mistaken. The scene then changes to a slave market. The first act consists of only two scenes, but they are very important ones. They are sufficient because the new work must be one third shorter than the original version. If it were necessary for the story line to be understandable to have the two lovers meet in the first act, you could insert an additional scene in recitative immediately after the curtain rises. Ines, who has learned from her father of the council's make-up and of Vascos's poor prospects, gives her beloved a sign indicating that he must be on his guard. In this scene, you could have her provide all the information the audience needs to know. I am presenting you with this idea just as it occurred to me, my dear friend. Treat it as a man of your experience sees fit, but I am counting on your earnest promise that you shall attempt to design a new foundation for this work; one with a historical and noble backdrop, complete with characters which are more interesting and more sharply defined than Fernand, Inez and Salvator were before; they did not evoke the slightest bit of interest. In particular, Vasco must have a heroic and chivalrous character. Please do not settle for making small, "touch-up" adjustments in the work, dear friend, and do not give a thought to saving the music I composed for the old work. We do not need to retain one single piece from the original. I myself shall approach the work on the new "Africaine" with great enthusiasm if it interests and stimulates me. And rest assured that I shall finish the musical composition in less time than it took me to complete the old work, although that is more or less completed. As you know, I cannot see my way to performing it.

Please allow me to remind you that you agreed to make the new version shorter than the original in order to provide more time for the ballet. You also promised to send me a detailed and complete scenario so that I can familiarize myself with it and decide whether or not this opera shall be performed. I believe, my dear friend, that since you have once more warmed up to this project, you should now seize the opportunity to construct a new plan and to commit your scenario to paper before you are confronted with other projects which shall dampen your interest in this one and prevent you from moving forward. Once we are in agreement on the scenario I shall no longer pressure you about the time needed to write the actual text.

There is one more matter: I know how important it is for you to remain in Nice to regain your health. I, too, am ill at this time, as you know. However, it has always been my experience that an illness passes quickly when I make a concerted effort to return to my work. I am sending this letter via my dear friend Gouin to whom you can say anything you wish in response to this letter. If you would like to respond to me directly, here is my address in Berlin ... With regard to our opéra comique, I have postponed the beginning of rehearsals to the time you suggested at our last meeting, i.e., next autumn.

* * *

In one of his "Vertrauten Briefe" (intimate letters) to August Lewald, Heinrich Heine described an occasion when he found Meyerbeer "eating a sparse meal [consisting entirely] of dried cod ... like his outward appearance, Meyerbeer's pleasures are also the essence of modesty. It is only when he has guests that a good meal is served ... for others he is the essence of generosity ..."

Meyerbeer was taught by his parents and his grandparents to preserve inherited wealth and to increase it for his heirs. Only education and wealth assured a non-converted Jew the desired emancipation and a respected position in society. Meyerbeer always knew how to look after his interests. Even as a youth he was not frivolous when it came to financial matters, as can be seen in his early diaries. Meyerbeer signed contracts with publishers and opera directors only after consulting a notary so as to protect himself against all eventualities. It was his common practice to have his money invested by a trusted financial manager, yet he always kept tabs on his financial situation. There are many indications, such as this letter, that Meyerbeer closely followed the stock market of his day and made his own investment proposals. He is distinguished by being meticulous both in art and in life; to quote Heine: "It seems as though the word "care" was invented for him."

84. To Herrmann Sillem & Co.

Messrs. Herrmann Sillem & Co. in London

Berlin, November 25, 1851

I am thinking of buying, for the sum of 5000 dollars, bonds with a six percent yield which are issued by the free states of North America. They are issued to the bearer and include coupons (not those issued by the individual states, but rather those guaranteed by the entire United States [United States bonds]). These bonds do not become payable until 1868.

I would be grateful if you could tell me whether bonds in this amount with the attached interest coupons can be bought in London at this time and at what price. (I know that the course was 111½–112.) Also, kindly advise how much Sterling I would have to remit to you, were I to make this purchase. Of course if a purchase amounting to exactly 5000 dollars were not possible, I would like to make one or more purchases in approximately the same amount. I would be very grateful if you would be so good as to send me a sample invoice for such an amount, including all details (e.g., your commission, a safe way of mailing, and the cost for sending me the papers here in Berlin etc.) so that I can then decide whether or not I want to make this purchase.

In order to calculate exactly how high the return will be on the money invested in these government bonds, I would also like to know the rate at which the interest coupons are usually converted at the London Stock Exchange.

And finally, would you be so kind as to tell me whether, in the year and a half since I last received the interest on the Mexican bonds I have with you, there have been any new dividends, and if not, whether there are likely to be any in the future.

Respectfully yours,
G. Meyerbeer

Pariser Platz No. 6 A
in Berlin

*　　*　　*

In the Fall of 1851, Meyerbeer suffered for a long time from effects of "sporadic bouts of cholera." What really prevented him from doing serious work on his score were the many tasks and distractions in Berlin. Hardly an evening went by that he was not at the opera or attending a concert. Courtesy calls and the many dinners and soirées were part of everyday life. Meyerbeer was frequently invited to dine with the King, with the Princes Karl, Wilhelm, or Albrecht, with the various ambassadors he met at court, and with members of the aristocracy. Artists who were passing through presented themselves, often in the hope that they would be engaged for one of the attractive court concerts, all of which were programmed and prepared exclusively by Meyerbeer. The larger festive court concerts with the orchestra and the cathedral choir required many rehearsals. For more intimate chamber concerts, the Maestro himself accompanied his soloists on the piano. In keeping with the custom of the time, the programs were colorfully varied and demonstrate Meyerbeer's comprehensive knowledge of the repertoire. He knew how to fulfill the wishes of his monarch who was a Gluck addict. He also occasionally provided the royal guests with a surprise. As an example, during the last Halali (horn call) of the Hunt Overture by Méhul ("La chasse du jeune Henri") he once added 12 horn players who suddenly appeared in the gallery of the hall. Meyerbeer noted proudly in his diary that, during the dinner afterwards, the King had words of praise and gratitude for him.

85. To Louis Gouin in Paris

Berlin, January 30, 1852

My dear and wonderful friend,

Scribe has finally sent me all five acts of the revised version of *L'Africaine*. Though it took him very long to complete the project, he did devote a great deal of time and effort to it. I shared some of my thoughts with him regarding the first two acts he has already sent me. He responded indicating that he felt my comments were justified and he immediately reworked the first two acts. He did this in such a way that the entire opera now has an entirely different foundation. I believe that we now have the right focus. However, there are still some major inconsistencies and shortcomings, above all regarding the excessive length of the opera. Scribe and I shall still have to exchange many letters before he can start writing the libretto, but that does not matter. The important point is that the new fable is a moving subject which is both clear and interesting. It also has a grandiose historical backdrop, musical situations and a new and brilliant type of staging. I also wrote to Scribe informing him that I no longer wanted him to look for a new opera subject and that I accept this new version of *L'Africaine* as my next work for the Paris Opéra, on the condition that we are in agreement on all of the difficulties and comments I have submitted to him regarding the details of this new version. It is important for us to be in agreement on these points before Scribe begins work on the libretto. I have great expectations for the work in this new form, and with God's help I believe that it can be a great and lasting success at the Opera.

With regard to specifying when I could submit this score to the Opéra, I cannot make any decision until I have received the complete libretto in verse. Only then shall I know how many pieces from my original score are to be kept and how many additional ones will have to be composed. After all, if Mr. Roqueplan knows that it will take several months from this point in time, then this should be sufficient for him because, in my last letter, we agreed that he would go to another composer for the next major opera after *Le Juif Errant* [The Wandering Jew; Halévy] to find an opera for the end of next autumn. I was pleased to read in the Belgian newspapers that Mr. Roqueplan had not expected me to make this decision and had already signed a contract with Mr. Verdi for a major opera after *Le Juif Errant*. I approve of this wholeheartedly. An opera in five acts cannot be improvised, and Mr. Roqueplan is fully justified in securing a major work from a famous master. I also approve of the fine revival of the masterpiece *Guillaume Tell* [William Tell; Rossini] with a chorus which was three times as large as the original one. I think this speaks very well of the Opéra, especially if this does not remain the exception and if the enlarged cast can be employed in all works of the repertoire, including new operas.

Farewell, my dear and wonderful friend. Please share the contents of this letter with our kind director and tell him how happy I was to hear that his concession has been renewed for another ten years and that the government has come to his assistance by paying the debts which were really the result of Leon Pillet's management. I hope to give him at least one work while he still has the concession.

Your devoted
Meyerbeer

*   *   *

The most popular pieces from Meyerbeer's opera were published—in keeping with the great demand and the custom of the day—in countless arrangements for small and large orchestras, for military and dance bands. Famous virtuosos and composers wrote arrangements for piano and other instruments: paraphrases, potpourris, marches or waltzes were arranged by Adolphe Adam, Frederick Chopin, Carl Czerny, Anton Diabelli, Henri Herz, Friedrich Kalkbrenner, Joseph Lanner, Johann Strauss, Gioacchino Rossini, and Franz Liszt. Liszt may have paraded his virtuosic abilities in his paraphrases on Robert le Diable *and* Les Huguenots *and in the dramatic romance entitled* Le Moine *(The Monk), but the fantasy and fugue for organ based on Meyerbeer's chorale entitled "Ad nos, ad salutarem undam" stands out from the lighter salon compositions. This work, which is mentioned in the following letter, is more substantial than the "occasional" compositions by virtue of the instrument and because of the serious treatment of the subject, although virtuosity is not completely absent. The diversity in the thematic variations and the large dimensions of this first work in a series of great organ compositions by Liszt lift it above the category of "arrangement:" it is a piece of music which stands on its own, using Meyerbeer's theme as a point of departure only.*

86. To Franz Liszt in Weimar

[Berlin, February 8, 1852]

My dear and illustrious colleague,

Mr. Schlesinger has informed me of a letter you wrote indicating that you had written a major piano composition based on the anabaptist chorus from *Le Prophète,* that it was your intention to dedicate this composition to me when the piece is published, and that you would contact me before the work was published. I do not want to await the arrival of this letter to express to you how pleased I am that you would think one of my pieces worthy of use as a motif for one of your piano compositions. It is most certainly destined to be performed throughout Europe and shall amaze those fortunate enough to hear your magnificent and poetic performances. I am even more honored by the friendly gesture you have made in wishing to dedicate this piece to me. It is already a great honor to see one's name appear with yours, but it is even more flattering to me if this is a testimony to our friendship.

Incidentally, some people believe and some critics have even written that I used a period chorale for the Anabaptist chorus just as I did for the Lutheran chorale in *Les Huguenots*. Since I usually do not contest what has been erroneously written about me in newspapers, I said nothing when this error appeared, but I feel it is very important for you, honored colleague, to know that what was written in the papers is not true. The Anabaptists' song, whether good or bad, is my own composition. I attempted to give it the flavor of a chorale of the period, but that is all.

The Marquis de la Ferrière had the privilege of hearing your most recent compositions including the piano concerto, some overtures, and your music to "Prometheus," all of which he recounted to me very enthusiastically. This makes me regret even more that I was unable to attend your concert last summer. I have frequently been tempted to go to Weimar to partake of this pleasure, but I was critically ill this past summer and have still not recovered to the point where I could undertake a journey of that length in winter weather. It would be much longer than a trip to Dresden, which is the only journey I have dared make since falling ill. Had I not been ill, I would have come to Weimar to see the performance of *Benvenuto Cellini* by our illustrious friend Berlioz, especially since he was conducting this masterful work himself. Please shake his hand in my name.

I have not had the honor of meeting Princess von Wittgenstein personally, but from all I have heard from those who do know her, she is a woman of great spirit, character and intelligence and possesses great poetic imagination. Therefore, I deeply regret having been deprived of the opportunity to make her acquaintance. Until such time that I have the honor of being introduced to her by you, would you be so kind as to extend my homage and most humble best wishes to her.

Please allow me, dear and honored colleague, this expression of my deepest devotion.

Your admirer,
G. Meyerbeer

Berlin, February 8, 1852

87. To Louis Gouin in Paris

Berlin, May 30, 1852

My dear and esteemed friend,

I received your kind letter dated the 24th; as always, it was a source of great joy for me and makes me wish that you would write to me more frequently. I would now like to respond to all the items in your letter.

You wrote that Mr. Nestor [Roqueplan] intends to design a new set for the interior of the church in act five of [*Les Huguenots*]. Please tell him that I have have been informed and that I am all the more happy about this decision because the effect of the trio in the fifth act suffered greatly from the stupidity of the set and staging in Paris, whereas this scene had an extraordinary impact throughout Germany due to the sets which were designed in Berlin. It is not the set design alone which creates the great effect, but rather it is the design of the interior of the church which exerts on the staging a realistic effect that evokes fear and trembling. If Nestor so desires, I can have a detailed sketch made of this set (of the rest, nothing can be used in Paris) and send it to him in Paris. However, we must find out what he intends to do as soon as possible so as not to lose any time. Please feel free to obtain his response verbally so he does not have to write to me himself. I am always very embarrassed to write to him myself because he writes so exceptionally well and will get together with his friends to make fun of the errors in my French.

Scribe was in Berlin for three days and returned to Séricourt yesterday [his country residence near Paris]. We spent the entire time together working and discussing our differing opinions on the new plan for *L'Africaine*. We now agree on all issues. I am now busy revising my notes and shall send them to Séricourt in a few days. He has promised me that he will then begin putting the work into verse and will have it completed in a few months. This would then allow me to begin composition of the new work on August 15. I say "new work" because all that remains of my original score is half of the third act and two-thirds of the fifth. Everything else must be composed anew. However, this makes no difference to me because I am so impressed with this new libretto that I shall tackle the composition with great joy and ambition.

The cantata ["Maria und ihr Genius"; Maria and her Guardian Spirit] which I composed for the silver anniversary of Prince Karl, the King's brother, and which was performed on the 26th in his palace, was very successful, I believe. My audience consisted of nothing but crowned heads. The Emperor and Empress of Russia attended, along with the King and Queen of Prussia, the Archduke of Weimar and son, the Archduke of Oldenburg and son, the Archduchess of Mecklenburg, the Princes of the Netherlands as well as our own royal princes. This illustrious audience was very receptive.

I believe I forgot to write you that Madame Lagrun performed the roles of Valentine and Alice in Dresden to a very warm reception. I feel that Nestor would be doing something beneficial both for his administration and these two works if he would let her sing in them as soon as the new opera has to be interrupted by the departure of Roger.

Farewell, dear friend.

Most cordially yours,
Meyerbeer

* * *

The 91st Psalm, one of Meyerbeer's most impressive sacred works, was premiered by the Berlin cathedral choir on May eighth in Potsdam. It was performed during a festive religious service in the Friedenskirche (church of peace) in the presence of King Friedrich Wilhelm IV of Prussia and his royal guest, Leopold I of Belgium.

On the following day, a gala performance of Le Prophète *was given at the Berlin opera, to honor the Belgian visitor. Meyerbeer composed the Psalm within a few days; the preliminary sketches are dated March eighth. On March 14 Meyerbeer wrote in his diary: "have completed (but not yet written down) everything up to the closing fughetta." This and other references clearly demonstrate that Meyerbeer composed to a large extent in his head even large movements and sections of works. At times he also sought inspiration while improvising at the piano. He made his corrections while writing out the music, sometimes not until the rehearsals. A movement of the 91st Psalm had to be rewritten after the choir rehearsed it because it did not suit the singers' vocal range.*

Johanna Wagner, the adopted daughter of Richard Wagner's brother Albert, had been a celebrated member of the Berlin opera since 1850 and had achieved great success as Fides in Le Prophète. *She undoubtedly hoped that, with Meyerbeer's help she would now be able to conquer Paris. On December sixth, 1852, Albert Wagner wrote to Meyerbeer: "it is easy to understand that making a Parisian debut in a new opera by the famous Meyerbeer is quite different from doing the same in a new opera by any other composer."*

In May 1852, L'Africaine *was still only in the planning stages. For the entire year, Meyerbeer was busy completing and revising his new opera* L'Étoile du Nord *(The North Star) which, for the most part, was completed in January of 1853. Not until January 16 did Scribe submit the first three acts of the completed libretto for* L'Africaine. *After returning to Berlin, Meyerbeer began work on the new opera on February 13. However, in March his work was interrupted by the commission for the 91st Psalm. As director of court music, it was Meyerbeer's natural and honorable duty to compose a torchlight dance for the marriage of Princess Anna of Prussia. In April Meyerbeer began to revise* L'Étoile du Nord *for the rehearsals, which took up all of his time in the following months until its premier in February 1854. Work on* L'Africaine *thus was interrupted again.*

88. To Louis Gouin in Paris

Berlin, March 24, 1853

My esteemed and dear friend,

You must be quite surprised by my long silence for it has been more than a month since I last wrote you. The reason is as follows: on the first of this month, the King commissioned me to set the 91st Psalm to music. He wants it to be performed during a solemn service at the cathedral at the beginning of next month. As this is a very large composition, I had to put all other projects aside to complete this by the requested deadline. I finally finished and submitted my score this very morning and despite the haste with which I had to write this piece, I dare say that it came off well and I don't have anything of which to be ashamed. The first thing I am doing with my newly recovered free time is to write to you, dear friend, to explain the reason for my silence. Eight days ago I also received a letter from Mr. Deligny on behalf of Mr. Roqueplan. I have not been able to answer him until now for the same reason which has prevented me from writing to you. Please tell Mr. Roqueplan that I am sorry for this involuntary delay, and please be so kind as to commuicate the following lines to him. In sending me the letter that Miss Wagner had written to him, Mr. Roqueplan had Mr. Deligny ask me what the response to her letter should be. This is what transpired between Miss Wagner and me. Miss Wagner came with her father to show me the number of engagements she had been offered by several German theater directors for next fall and winter; she also showed me the letter from the theater director here asking her to state whether she wanted to take the extended leave she had reserved for herself in the event that I was to present *L'Africaine* next winter. She made me see what an immense loss it would be for her if I were not to present *L'Africaine* next winter. If she had been informed of my decision too late, she would have lost the performance offers she is now getting in Germany because she was determined to sing in Paris only if she were not to debut in *L'Africaine,* as stated in her contract.

My intention had been to wait another month to six weeks before making a decision as to when I will give *L'Africaine:* however, whenever I studied the new libretto for *L'Africaine,* and as I composed the music for it, I came to realize that I would be able to use very little of my original score because not only had the plot been changed, but the personality of several characters was completely different from the original version. Therefore, the music had to be completely different from what I had originally used. I realized that nothing would remain of the original score except the fifth act and that it would be impossible for me to complete four new acts for next winter considering I just received them on February third. Taking all this into consideration, I told Miss Wagner that I would not be able to complete *L'Africaine* in time to present it next winter, but I also added the following: "if, despite this situation, you would like to sing at the Paris Opéra in other works next winter, and are concerned that this would offend me and make me change my mind about giving you the role of *L'Africaine,* you are mistaken. I give you my word that I would still give you this role regardless of whether you had first sung in other works at the Opéra." To this she responded, as before, that her mind was unchanged, and since I had told her that *L'Africaine* could not be completed by next winter, she would not go there either, just as her contract entitled her to do. I have not told Mr. Roqueplan about this, first of all because until today I literally have not been able to find one hour to write, and second and most important, because the contemptuous and offensive manner in which Mr. Roqueplan treats my operas at his theater has led me to believe that he is not the slightest bit interested in receiving a new work from me. In the letter I received from you yesterday you wrote that he had protested this accusation of antipathy for me and my works. So much the better; let us hope that, in the future, the facts will justify his protests. I would be only too happy to believe that our director is motivated by feelings for me that are just as positive as mine are for him. I hope to give him proof of this by means of the zeal and, I dare say, enthusiasm I am putting into the composition of the new *L'Africaine.* I may not finish quickly what I want to do conscientiously, but in any case, I will

143

not undertake the compostion of any other major work until this one is completed. Since this one cannot be ready by next winter, I would at least like it to be ready by the fall of 1854. I have great confidence in this work in its new form and, God willing, I hope it will bring in money for Mr. Roqueplan and some honor to me. Farewell, my dear friend, and give my compliments to Mr. Roqueplan.

Your devoted
Meyerbeer

*   *   *

As a contributor to such publications as the "Revue et Gazette musicale" and the "Revue des deux mondes," Pietro (Pierre, Paul) Scudo was among the serious and respected music critics in Paris. He came to Paris when he was young and received his training from Choron at the very respected "Institution royale de musique classique. . . ." Before he took up writing he had been an opera singer, clarinetist, and voice teacher. Meyerbeer met Scudo on April 9, 1849 during a dinner and press conference given for journalists by Roqueplan, the director of the Opéra, shortly before the premier of Le Prophète. *"Chose singulière" [remarkable event] were the words Scudo used to describe Meyerbeer's new operatic success, calling the scene with Fides in act four "certainement l'une des créations les plus saisissantes du génie de M. Meyerbeer" [certainly was one of the most gripping creations from the genius of Mr. Meyerbeer]. In his biography of Meyerbeer, Johann Weber wrote that Scudo had referred to Meyerbeer as "le grand maître de la décadence de l'opéra" [the grand master of opera's decadence].*

It is not clear whether Scudo accepted the loan mentioned in the following letter. In the following years, 1857 and 1858, Meyerbeer did make payments, as he did for so many others who requested loans from him.

89. To Louis Gouin

Berlin, April 23, 1853

My esteemed and dear friend,

I just received your dear letter. Thank you very much for having visited the honorable Mr. Scudo on my behalf and for giving me news of the state of his health. I was unaware that his health had taken such a dramatic turn for the worse and that he would need such a long recovery period. This must be very annoying for him: since he was not able to leave his residence, he could not attend the first performances of operas and concerts and therefore was unable to write reviews of these events. He will not be able to give any voice lessons either. This will perhaps create some temporary difficulties for him for which I am sorry, because he is not only a writer of great talent and value but also a very respected figure. I would be very pleased if he would allow me to assist him during his momentary difficulties because I am very fond of him both as a man and as a writer. I know that he is very sensitive about his independence and has very strict principles when it comes to honor. I would never think of offering him a gift but if, now that he is unable to work and earn an income, he would accept a loan of a thousand francs which he could then repay when he has had the time and good health to recover what his illness has caused him to lose, I believe that even the most scrupulous conscience could not object. I would be very happy if he would do me the honor of giving me preference among his many friends. I ask, dear friend, that you act as my cashier for this transaction because you still have a thousand francs of mine.

Farewell, dear and honorable friend.

Your very devoted friend,
Meyerbeer

*   *   *

Joseph Bacher, the son of a Viennese banker and a great admirer of Meyerbeer, zealously represented the interests of the maestro in Vienna. He negotiated with theater directors and journalists, supervised the singers and kept them in good spirits and, by virtue of his many contacts, had influence on the administration of the city. All of his efforts failed, however, when confronted with the censors; people in Vienna were aware that one spark would be enough to ignite the flames of revolt in the Austrian provinces of northern Italy. Social history depicted as vividly as it was in Le Prophète *seemed too dangerous to the censors. It was not until 1855 that* Le Prophète *was performed in Milan.*

90. To Dr. Joseph Bacher in Vienna

Berlin, May 29, 1853

Honorable sir and friend,

I just now received your friendly letter announcing your arrival in Vienna. I hope that you are once again in good health, for you informed me earlier that this would be a prerequisite for your departure from Paris. The enclosed letter is one Ricordi sent to me from Milan. I cannot deny how pleased I was to read in Ricordi's letter that Le Prophète is to be performed on the major stages in Italy. For the same reason, I was very sorry to read that the censors in Milan have banned the scheduled performances of Le Prophète for Milan and Trieste as well as for all other cities in the Austrian provinces of Italy. Given the fact that performances of Le Prophète have not only been permitted and given in Vienna, but also in Bohemia, Hungary, Galicia, and Moravia, this ban defies explanation. If you could use your contacts in Vienna to see that this ban is lifted, I would be extremely grateful. If this is not possible for Lombardy and Venice, then please try to obtain an exception and get the ban lifted for Trieste. I would be greatly in your debt if you could accomplish this because the theater and audiences in Trieste have always been very receptive and kind to me in the past.

I would be very interested in hearing news from you regarding the state of the German opera house at the beginning of the season under the new director [Franz v. Holbein]. As you well know, I am very interested in the state of music and theater in Vienna, and in its rich artistic life.

Should you have occasion to see the dear and kind court councillor, Mr. v. Remont, please extend to him my best regards.

With the warmest of greetings to your wonderful family, I remain . . .

* * *

Princess Anna, a daughter of Prince Karl of Prussia, was married to the Prince of Hesse in May of 1853.

Meyerbeer composed a total of four of the torchlight dances that were traditional for wedding celebrations in the Prussian royal house. These dances marked both the end and the highpoint of the festivities: after the "Zeremonientafel," the festive banquet, the bridal couple and guests positioned themselves to dance the magnificent Polonaise. The ministers and court officials led the procession with burning candles in hand to pay homage to the royal couple.

91. To Princes Anna of Hesse, née Princess of Prussia, in Berlin

Berlin, July 3, 1853

Most serene royal Princess,

Having the privilege of composing the torchlight dance for the marriage festivities of Your Royal Highness was one of the most beautiful and rewarding duties of my position as director of court music. I was also filled with joy upon learning from Marquis Lucchesini that Your Highness was pleased with my modest composition. My happiness was all the greater when taking into account the effusion of musical talent demonstrated by Your Highness, thereby making your critical artistic assessment of my work all the more precious to me. I trust that Your Highness will understand my intense desire to enable my modest composition to live on longer in your memory than is possible during the fleeting moments of a performance. I appeal to the graciousness of Your Royal Highness in making the bold request that I be allowed, in all humility, to present Your Royal Highness with a copy which has just appeared in print. I make this offer as an expression of my steadfast devotion and deepest admiration.

Illus. 18: Meyerbeer approx. 1854. From a lost oil painting by Jäger.

*   *   *

Louis Véron (1798–1867), who took over the management of the Paris Opéra in 1831, had been accused by the press of having the millionaire Meyerbeer pay for the organ in the fifth act of Robert le Diable. *When Véron was writing his memoirs, he requested a written statement from Meyerbeer in reference to this accusation. He then reprinted that statement verbatim in his autobiography. Véron had indeed worked very hard at that time to enlarge the orchestra and chorus as well as the number of extras. He was able to win the participation of students from the Conservatoire and by hiring a "professeur de danse et pantomime" in addi-*

tion to the ballet director, he created the groundwork for the dramatic integration of ballet into the plot of an opera. Under his management, new costumes and sets were mandatory for new productions; no expense was to be spared when it came to pomp and splendor so as to attract the bourgeois public . . .

92. To Louis Véron in Paris

Paris, February 9, 1854

Dear sir,

It has always been a steadfast principle of mine never to respond to false rumors concerning me. However, I must admit that my conscience has often troubled me for not having bent this rule in cases where the false rumors did not concern me alone, i.e., in a situation in which reference is made to one of my works as a means of hurting someone for whom I myself have nothing but praise and who deserves to be rewarded for his services. I am referring to the false rumors which have appeared in many newspapers stating that you permitted the production of *Robert le Diable* against your better judgment and only on the condition that I myself pay for the organ to be used in the fifth act. My conscience has often tortured me for never having spoken out against these untruths, but time went on; the years passed and I was afraid that it was too late to revive these events from the past.

However, you, my dear sir, have now presented me with this opportunity in that you are publishing your memoirs which shall perhaps contain a few lines dedicated to a work which became a great success under your excellent management. I would like to take this opportunity to state that all of the above-mentioned rumors are completely false. It was you who acquired and paid for the organ, as you did for everything required for the staging of *Robert le Diable.* I would also like to state that you went well beyond what was normally expected of a manager in your dealings with the authors and the public.

I shall never forget the service you rendered me in recasting the role of Bertram. Poor judgment caused me to give the role to the otherwise very talented Dabadie and I did not have the courage to take the role away from him. Fortunately, you had the courage which I myself lacked; the negotiations were successful and the role was given to Levasseur. You also managed to persuade Massol, an outstanding performer, to accept the very small role of troop herald. Every evening, you enlisted the services of the students from the Conservatoire to strengthen the chorus. Finally, you spared no expense with regard to the sets, costumes and props. I recall these matters, insofar as this is still possible, only to confirm and acknowledge your steadfast and active contribution to the success of *Robert le Diable.* I regret that I am unable to recall as vividly the countless details to which you attended or the thoughtful favors you extended for the benefit of both the author and the work. For these I owe you an even greater debt of gratitude than I do to the public.

Please accept this expression of my utmost respect.

G. Meyerbeer

*　*　*

On October 8, 1853, after the debut of Marie Cabel at the Théâtre Lyrique in Paris, Meyerbeer noted in his diary: "a brilliant talent, especially for brilliant coloratura singing." He would have liked very much to engage her for his opera L'Étoile du Nord, *however the die had already been cast: rehearsals for this opera had already begun. Meyerbeer then hoped to give renewed life to the opera after the summer break by recasting the leading role. The rumor that Perrin had also assumed the management of the Théâtre Lyrique proved false and as a result, Cabel could not sing at the Opéra Comique, i.e., in Meyerbeer's opera. Meyerbeer was determined to win Cabel for a leading role. Since as a lyric coloratura soprano she was not suited to the leading roles of his grand opera, he offered to compose an opera especially for her. This was quite an offer for Cabel and is a clear example of how strongly Meyerbeer was influenced by the vocal characteristics and abilities of his singers. Meyerbeer even went a step further, thereby reinforcing this observation: when Eugene Scribe, Meyerbeer's librettist of long standing, protested the fact that Meyerbeer wanted to put aside* L'Africaine, *Meyerbeer bought his consent for the respectable sum of 10,000 francs. He then put his score for* L'Africaine *aside once again and composed* Le Pardon de Ploërmel *(Dinorah), literally tailoring the leading role to Cabel who possessed the superb dramatic qualities required for this role. Her debut in the "Shadow Aria"[Ombre légère], with its highly virtuosic dialogue between soprano and solo flute, is still considered a touchstone for coloratura sopranos.*

The delay in publishing the score may have been due to financial difficulties on the part of the publisher: barely four weeks after writing this letter, on August 14, 1854, Meyerbeer received notice that Brandus was unable to pay and wanted to withdraw from the project. The crisis, however, was averted with assistance from Meyerbeer, among others.

93. To Louis Brandus

Paris [recte: Berlin], July 18,
1854

Honorable sir,

I am responding to your esteemed letters of the 15th and 16th. If Perrin really did obtain the Théâtre Lyrique as well, this would be a disaster for composers and singers alike. If he does wish to have Miss Cabel sing only at the Théâtre Lyrique, it means the ruin of the Opéra Comique in general and of *L'Étoile du Nord* in particular. His interests, however, would not be served at all well were he to prevent Cabel from singing at the Opéra Comique because, if she has a full house there, she can bring in 6000 francs while she can only earn 4000 francs for the Théâtre Lyrique. It is, of course, quite possible that he does not want her to sing in *L'Étoile du Nord* and is using this as a pretext.

I would be very grateful if, as soon as possible, you would write to Miss Cabel, stating that you had heard that she had been engaged by

Perrin, that you know that I would very much like her to sing the role of Cathérine in L'Étoile du Nord, and that you are in a position to promise her that, if she made her debut at the Opéra Comique in this role I would then, immediately thereafter, write a new opéra comique in which she would have the leading role. I would even present that opéra comique before L'Africaine. Tell her that you would like to know whether she would have anything against making her debut in L'Étoile, whether there is anything in her current contract which would prevent her from doing this and, finally, whether her contract gives Perrin the right to have her sing only at the Théâtre Lyrique. Please try to get this information from her as soon as possible because only after receiving it will we be able to deal with Perrin for he will never tell us the truth. Finally, it is of the utmost importance that I know as soon as possible whether or not Miss Cabel will sing in "Étoile" because if she does, I really will drop everything so as to compose a new comic opera as soon as possible. If she will not, then I will put this aside and accept a commission for another location and a completely different, non-dramatic piece of music which I have been asked to write. Therefore, I very anxiously await your kind response. When you speak with Perrin about this, after having received Miss Cabel's response, could you please point out to him how much consideration I have always shown for him. If, during contract negotiations, I had insisted on having Ugalde, he would undoubtedly have engaged her but, because she demanded 50,000 francs, I decided against her in order to save him the expense. In order to reduce his costs for the military music, I willingly eliminated 20 of the players called for in the contract. As a result, I scored the music for two theater orchestras instead of three which, by the time of the 60th performance, already represented a savings of 12,000 francs. Finally, the possibility of obtaining a new comic opera from me (which I definitely will not compose if he does not allow Cabel to sing in "Étoile") should also encourage him to meet my request. Do make it a point to see Mr. Gouin because he and Perrin had a conversation, the contents of which you should obtain from him.

And now to some other comments. Perrin promised me that he would not give "Étoile" until September if the box office receipts fell below 4000 francs. This has already occurred three times. Remind him of this; if he now beats this work to death when, after a short break, he could take in large receipts in September, he is not only hurting me but himself as well. Make this point very clear to him.

I have to return the letter from Chorlei with the request that you translate these hieroglyphics. I cannot read one syllable of it, but it is very important that I know its contents.

In the letter I received today, you wrote that I should have received the introduction to the second act [of L'Étoile du Nord]. So far, I have received from Sax neither it nor the score of the military music for the second finale which, you informed me a week ago, had been sent. Nor have I received one line of proofs from you after having returned to you the two duets from the finale of the first act.

Nabob [by Halévy] was performed in Geneva six months after its premier, so the score must have been engraved two months before. On the other hand, five months after the first performance of "Étoile," I have only the proofs for the first act. This demonstrates to me how unimportant this work must be to you; I, however, depend very much upon its distribution to the theaters and am severely hurt by this delay in publication.

Since, as you wrote, Marx's orchestra in A . . . is so good, you can permit him to play the overture to "Étoile."

In great haste as the train is departing, I respectfully remain

Sincerely yours,
Meyerbeer

* * *

Meyerbeer's letter to Rosine Stoltz (1815–1903), primadonna of the Paris Opéra, still demonstrates a traditional approach to composition which was thought to have disappeared by that time. Yet there were composers who, like Meyerbeer, were still mindful of the vocal characteristics of their singers when composing a work. These composers did not yet place the integrity of a composition above all other considerations. There were many changes and additions; new arias were written and other arias substituted for particular singers and occasions for benefit concerts and performances. These have been preserved in printed or manuscript form and remind us of a completely different way of thinking, as can be seen very clearly in the following letter.

94. To Rosine Stoltz

[Berlin, December 19, 1854]

Madame,

Mr. Gouin sent me the brief and kind letter you addressed to me. In it you expressed the desire to cut the middle section of the allegro from Fides' aria in act five ("Sainte Phalange"). I have no objection to this, nor would I object to your cutting the entire allegro of the aria (from "comme un éclair") if you think it advisable. You would then sing only the first cavatina in E-flat minor. The range of the allegro in this aria is a bit high for a contralto and I understand why this could present a problem for you. I always believe that a role must lie well within the singer's vocal range for it to be effective. Therefore, should you find that some notes are not within your good range, it would be advisable to change them though it is important that you do this in such a way that the character of Cantilena is not changed in the process. I am sure that your talent and good taste will enable you to avoid this pitfall. I know from reading the newspapers that your performance of this role in Turin was a great success.

Please accept this expression of my deepest admiration and respect.

Your devoted
Meyerbeer

151

* * *

Das Feldlager in Schlesien *was written for a special occasion yet Meyerbeer, ever since its first performance, wished to bring it out in Paris. By rewriting it, and creating a new plot he hoped to be able to save many of the effective pieces from the original score, in particular the virtuoso flute aria. In addition Scribe, the real author of "Feldlager," was to be compensated for lost royalties. Scribe skillfully changed the milieu of the opera: the story of* L'Étoile du Nord *takes place in a village on the Gulf of Finland. Instead of Frederick the Great, it was the Russian Czar Peter who learned to play the flute. The gypsy milieu and military scenes of "Feldlager" were kept so that a large portion of the original music could be used in the new score. The premier of the opera took place on February 16, 1854 at the Paris Opéra Comique. It was attended by the Emperor and Empress and was a great success. Within a year the opera was performed in Stuttgart, Brussels, Toulouse, Lyon, Lille, and Dresden. The 100th performance of* l'Étoile du Nord *took place on the first anniversary of the premier, February 16, 1855.*

95. To Bonard

Berlin, December 22, 1854

I hereby authorize Mr. Bonard, lawyer and legal advisor for the French embassy, Chancery Lane 56, to pursue the legal means necessary to ensure that the London courts forbid the Drury Lane theater to perform my opera *l'Étoile du Nord,* which I composed for the Imperial Théâtre de l'opéra comique in Paris. This is in consideration of the agreements signed by France and England guaranteeing each country's dramatists and composers rights of ownership of works written for the French or English theater. I am the sole owner of my score, though the Beale music publishing house in London has bought the rights to publish vocal selections of this opera with piano accompaniment. I have reserved ownership rights with regard to performance of this work in English theaters. In addition, I have a contract with my French publisher, Mr. Brandus in Paris, who has engraved the entire score. According to this contract, the publisher is not allowed to sell one single copy of this score without my permission. Mr. Brandus is prepared to give written confirmation that he did not sell a copy of my score to the Drury Lane Theater. Therefore, the Drury Lane Theater cannot have acquired my score by legal means.

Some time ago, I received a letter from London (which I have enclosed) written by Mr. Reynoldsen on behalf of the Drury Lane Theater, inviting me to come to London to direct the rehearsals and first performances of my opera when it was scheduled for performance in his theater. For this, I was offered a certain sum of money. I responded to Mr. Reynoldsen indicating that I had already made other arrangements for performances of my works in England and therefore did not wish my work to be performed by the Drury Lane Theater; I sent my response from Berlin by registered mail and have retained the receipt which I will make available to you should it become necessary.

152

Illus. 19: *L'étoile du Nord,* Stuttgart, 1854. Anonymous woodcut in the
Illustrierte Zeitung, vol. 23, Leipzig, 1854.

96. To Pietro Romani

Berlin, May 21, 1855

My dear Maestro,

I received a letter from Mr. Guidi in Florence informing me that there are plans to perform my new opera *L'Étoile du Nord* at the Teatro della Pergola next autumn. I was truly delighted to receive this piece of news. The genre of opera semiseria and buffo mixed with elements of tragedy is no longer very common in Italy. To a certain extent *L'Étoile du Nord,* which is of this variety, is more difficult to stage than my other works. For its first presentation in Italy, *L'Étoile du Nord* will require a director blessed with such marvelous talents as you, my dear friend, possess. It will require the delicacy and skill you demonstrated so brilliantly during the rehearsals for "Crociato," "Robert," and "Prophète." You can rest assured that it was a great pleasure for me to grant the Teatro della Pergola permission to perform my opera.

Please allow me, my dear maestro, to make a few important comments regarding the distribution of roles. The casting of the two principal

153

Illus. 20: Portrait of Homage, ca. 1855.

roles for the most part determines the success of the opera. These two roles are Catherina and Czar Peter. The role of Catherina requires a soprano acuto [a slim soprano], one who must be very agile and who must have style and expressiveness so that she can sing both the buffo material and the serious scenes. She must also be a good actress. In short, it is a role demanding dramatic and vocal qualities like those for the *Daughter of the Regiment* and *La Sonnambula*. The role of Czar Peter also requires someone who can act as well as he can sing. This role is written for a Basse-taille (high bass) but I have added a supplement at the end of the score where I have arranged it for baritone. In that case, it must be a very low baritone. Among the Italian singers I think Mr. Belletti, who performed at the last carnival in Turin, would be an excellent choice. The role of Gritzendo must be given to a good buffo comico caricato [a very coarse, comic buffo]. It is more important that he be a good actor than a good singer.

I predict that casting the two canteen women is going to present a problem due to the traditional Italian approach to ensembles. They have only one scene, but this scene is of such significance that it greatly contributed to the success of the opera in Paris. Their buffo duet and sextet are too important to be given to second-rate singers. These roles require "petites prime donne" [soubrettes] who are also called "comprimarie." They must be young, lively and good buffo actresses.

The role of the tenor Danilowitz, as it currently appears in the score, is not of any great importance but if you want him to sing the two new arias I added for the production in Dresden [for Joseph Tichatschek], then you must find a good tenor "mezzo carattere" [lyric tenor]. These are optional arias; if you do not have a good tenor on hand I do not believe it is worth trying to find one. It would be better to omit these two arias and apply the effort and money you would have had to spend on this tenor to the roles of Catherina and Peter, i.e., on the primadonna and the baritone.

Please accept, my dear maestro, this expression of my deepest admiration.

Yours sincerely
Meyerbeer
P.S. I need not stress, my dear maestro, that I am available for any further information you may require.

* * *

In France, theaters were restricted to performing only certain types of works. Thus, the Paris Opéra Comique was allowed to perform only three-act works with spoken dialogue. Meyerbeer had to comply with this requirement when composing L'Étoile du Nord, *but for performances outside France he chose to write a new version with recitatives.*

97. To Franz Baron von Dingelstedt

[Vienna, January 5, 1856]

Most esteemed General Director,
I have waited until now to respond to your kind letter so that I could hear for myself whether the change from dialogues to recitatives, which I

composed last summer for the performance of *L'Étoile du Nord* at the Italian Opera in London, would also be suitable for the German stage. After hearing the Vienna production (which uses recitatives), I am definitely in favor of using them instead of the dialogue, not only because the majority of German singers speak opera dialogue very stiffly and awkwardly, but also because the opera benefits from this musically. Should you, esteemed sir, also wish to use the recitatives instead of dialogue in your theater, you can obtain the recitatives in Vienna from the theater agent Holding. He supplies the theaters with copies of the recitatives upon request. Since the opera is too long for performance in Germany and must therefore be shortened, I believe that the cuts I made for the production in Vienna would be the most suitable. I have the honor of including a list of these cuts at the end of this letter.

The role of Czar Peter was originally written for a bass; however, I have arranged it for a slightly higher vocal range so that it could be sung by Faure (the second singer to perform the role in Paris). I believe that this second version (which has also been engraved as a supplement) is more suitable for Mr. Kindermann's vocal range than the first. Therefore, I have the honor of enclosing this transposition along with a German translation of the staging instructions. I am also enclosing the libretto and recitatives from the Vienna production.

The role of Danilowitz is too small for a real primo tenore. Therefore I added an arioso for Mr. Tichatscheck in the third act for the Dresden production of the opera. This arioso was also sung by Gardoni in London and Ander in Vienna. Should you desire to use the same arioso for Mr. Auerbach, you can find the score at Schlesinger's music store in Berlin, where the piece was published.

You ask, esteemed sir, whether I have any comments or wishes with regard to the music and staging? In a house where everything is in the hands of such extremely talented and intelligent men as yourself and Maestro Lachner, any type of commentary would be superfluous.

Please allow me, sir, this expression of my sincere devotion.

Meyerbeer.

*   *   *

Meyerbeer had been in Vienna since the end of October 1855 to rehearse L'Étoile du Nord: *it opened on December 29th. On January 7, 1856, he departed for Italy with the still unfinished score of his new opera* Dinorah *in his luggage. His first stop was Venice, where he took advantage of the mild climate to recover from a long chronic cold. He then went on to Mantua, Parma, Brescia, Verona, Florence and Genoa, among other cities. He was inspired by hearing old and new works and by Italian vocal artistry.*

Meyerbeer was specially interested in Verdi's operas, as is shown by his attendance at the following performances:

Jan. 11, 1856: La Traviata, *Venice*
Jan. 21: I Masnaderi, *Brescia*

Feb. 1: Rigoletto, *Venice*
    Il Trovatore, *Venice*
March 2: La Traviata, *Siena*
March 3: I due Foscari, *Florence*
March 6: Macbeth, *Genoa*
March 9: Nabucco, *Genoa*
March 24: Nabucco, *Venice*

His letter of gratitude to Ander is also directed to the people of Vienna for the continued popularity his operas enjoyed there. On April 14, 1856, Meyerbeer noted in his diary: "even during the most recent German opera season, my works were performed more frequently than those of any other composer. Of 173 opera performances, 45 were performances of my operas. There were 15 performances of L'Étoile du Nord, *12 of* Le Prophète, *11 of* Les Huguenots *and 7 of* Robert le Diable."

98. To Aloys Ander

[Vienna, January 6, 1856]

Most esteemed sir,

I cannot leave Vienna without repeating to you once again how greatly indebted I am to you for kindly taking on the role of Danilowitz in *L'Étoile du Nord.* In comparison with your other roles, this one has so few musical numbers that it would be justifiable for a tenor of your stature to consider the role too small. However, you have demonstrated that, for a great artist, there are no small roles. By virtue of your masterful performance, in particular of the arioso in the third act, you gave the role a significance it did not have previously, by which you contributed greatly to the success of the opera.

In expressing my gratitude for the great service you rendered to the opera and to me, I would also like to ask you to continue to lend your talents to this role. Your making the modest role of Danilowitz a permanent part of your repertoire will transform it in the eyes of the public into a major operatic role.

Please allow me, esteemed sir, this expression of my utmost respect.

Your devoted
Meyerbeer

*   *   *

99. To Giovanni Battista Velluti

Venice, April 25, 1856

My dear illustrious friend,

Day after day I have hesitated to accept your invitation to come to your country residence because I first wanted to completely cure my stubborn cough. Once recovered, I would be able to fully enjoy an outing to the retreat of the immortal artist who bears the name of Velutti. Unfortunately, I am still not completely recovered and, as the result of a letter I have just now received, am obligated to depart for Berlin immediately. I will therefore once again be robbed of the opportunity of seeing you, my illustrious friend. Still, let me at least take this opportunity to tell you how delighted I was to see you again in Venice after so many years of separation. You, my illustrious friend, are one of the greatest singers your so richly blessed fatherland has produced. I love you as someone of great and noble character; I am proud and happy to have your friendship which is an honor for me. I hope that it will endure, as does my deep and life-long gratitude to you for your admirable creation of the role in "Crociato." I am indebted to you for the success this work was fortunate enough to enjoy.

Farewell, my dear and illustrious friend. As soon as I have arrived in Berlin I will send you a lithograph of my poor, dear mother who so loved and admired you.

> Your most devoted friend and
> admirer,
> Meyerbeer

*   *   *

On February 23, 1856, Meyerbeer noted in his diary: "I read in the theater journal that Heinrich Heine died on the 17th. May his ashes rest in peace. I forgive him in my heart for the ingratitude he demonstrated towards me as well as for his many malicious references to me in his writings." There was still material by Heine which had not yet been published. Meyerbeer learned from Duisberg, who was handling Heine's estate for Mathilde Heine, that the writer had withheld several poems concerning him. Meyerbeer then attempted to prevent publication of these discriminatory and abusive poems. In June, 1857, Mathilde Heine demanded 3000 francs from Meyerbeer to prevent the inclusion of these poems in a planned new edition of Heine's works. After much negotiation, Meyerbeer and Mathilde Heine reached an agreement on February 20, 1858: he paid Heine's widow 4500 francs to halt the printing of the poems "Der Prophet," "Der Wanzerig," "Puppentheater," and "Die Menge thut's." Just the same, they were published by Strodtmann in 1869 after Meyerbeer's death.

100. To Louis Brandus

Berlin, March 29, 1857

Esteemed sir,

I received your esteemed letter two days ago and I agree with you completely regarding the importance you place on the H[eine] memoirs. Unfortunately, all kinds of lies and slander can be expected from this type of character. In the knowledge of one's own respectability one can ignore such things, but when they are uttered by so beloved and popular an author as H[eine], they achieve an unfortunate significance, especially if they appear in a work published posthumously. Therefore, I would be very grateful if, in the event that there are attacks against me in this work, they could be excluded by the editors (who always exercise their own judgment in such instances). Right now, the first and most important objective would be for you to find out who the editors of the German and French editions will be. I read in a German newspaper that Mr. Duisberg has been employed by Heine's widow to organize and edit these memoirs. Is this true? Recently I heard that Heine's widow was living with a man of letters by the name of Julliat: could he perhaps be the publisher of the *French* memoirs? Perhaps your brother would know whether this newspaper article was true or not, since he often has dealings with Duesberg. In any event, I would be very grateful if you could inform me as soon as possible of everything you learn about all this, especially since I am not sure that I will be able to come to Paris in May. I may not be able to leave Berlin until June or July . . . I would be greatly indebted to you if you would read the Feuilleton musical of the Assemblée nationale, which is published every week (on Tuesday, I believe), and send me anything that contains references to me.

Please remember me to your wife and accept this expression of my utmost respect.

Meyerbeer

*   *   *

As a publisher, Louis Brandus had won Meyerbeer's respect. After the death of Louis Gouin in 1856, he also earned Meyerbeer's personal trust and even his friendship. As Gouin had done in the past, Brandus now devoted all his energies, both in word and deed, to Meyerbeer's service. He negotiated with impresarios, singers or journalists and kept Meyerbeer abreast of events in Paris when the composer was away.

Since Meyerbeer always composed his roles with certain singers in mind, the anxiety in the following letter is understandable: it was not until December 9, 1857 that a new opera entitled Le Carnival de Venise by Ambroise Thomas, was performed at the Paris Opéra Comique with Madame Cabel in the leading role. Meyerbeer, however, had also planned to engage her as Dinorah in his own opera.

101. To Louis Brandus

Berlin, April 30, 1857

Esteemed sir,

I have received your kind letter of the 13th of this month. I am very grateful to you for the interesting information regarding H[eine]'s memoirs and posthumous poetry. I feel that your views on this situation and the steps you plan to take to resolve it are most effective. It would be good if you would let me know in particular what material concerning me

D[uisberg] has thus far discovered in the estate, i.e., which poems contain references to me and what kind of references they are.

Why is it that Madame Cabel has not yet sung in the new opera written for her by Thomas which, I believe, has been in rehearsal for a number of months now? Since Madame Cabel will not return to Paris until August, I wonder when this opera is to be performed? If I were to decide to present my opera in Perrin's theater and not in any other (a decision I have yet to make), it would be performed very late in the year if the opera by Thomas were rehearsed first. Still, I do not wish to create difficulties for a fellow composer.

What you and your brother mentioned concerning Calzado's proposal is worthy of consideration and is indeed very important for me. In its current form, "Crociato" would have little or no chance of pleasing today's audiences, due to the music as well as the unpalatable libretto. On the other hand, the music does contain elements that might please if a new libretto were written by a good Parisian dramatist. The good pieces in "Crociato" could then be retained and I would compose new music for the remainder of the opera. An interesting work might result; it could be very well suited to the Italian theater. This would require a great deal of work on my part because even the numbers retained from the original would have to be adapted to the new libretto and to the requirements of today's singers, and the recitatives would have to be completely rewritten. I would not be adverse to doing this because Gye made such a request last year for Covent Garden, but it would be very difficult to accomplish in this season because I will be very busy with the rehearsals of my opera comique. It might be conceivable for the beginning of the 1858 season. In the next few days, I shall write to your brother who wrote to me on behalf of Calzados. In my reply I shall state when and under what conditions I would do it (they are considerably more reasonable than Calzados' very generous offer). I will instruct your brother to inform you of the contents of my letter beforehand.

I have read in the papers that Madame Lauters will sing the role of Alice in "Robert". I would be very grateful if you could tell me candidly how she executed this role and if her performance was well received by the audience. Since she must sing one of the two leading roles in my L'Africaine', I would of course be pleased if her performance in "Robert" were successful. I am afraid that the current directors, who were very hostile towards me in the matter of Madame Borghi Mamo in Le Prophète, will therefore refuse to support Miss Lauters in "Robert."

If you can provide Mme. Lauters with any assistance in this matter, please do so. If you know her personally, tell her that I would much rather see her as Valentine in Les Huguenots than as Alice because the character of the music for the role of Valentine is much more in keeping with that of L'Africaine.

I also read in the newspapers that the tenor Giulini and Miss Spezia are now singing for Lumley. Giulini has already enjoyed great success singing Les Huguenots in Milan both this year and last, as did Spezia. You might point that out to Lumley.

Please accept this expression of my utmost respect.
Meyerbeer

* * *

In 1851, James Étienne Pasdeloup (1819–1887) founded a "Société des jeunes artistes du Conservatoire" which was basically a student orchestra. He and the orchestra gave symphony concerts in the "Salle Herz." During a performance of the overture to Struensee, *the young men played in an obviously half-hearted manner. Meyerbeer noted in his diary that it "was given a cool reception." Its performance at the dance music concerts of the "Concerts de Paris" was better received, he added, contrary to expectations. The overture became so popular that it had been performed daily for two weeks.*

The Wallfahrt nach Ploërmel *[The Pilgrimage to Ploërmel], originally entitled* Das Verfluchte Tal *(The Cursed Valley) takes its material from a Provençal legend.*

102. To Louis Brandus

Nice, December 13, 1857

Esteemed sir,

I was glad to receive both of your letters and would like to thank you for the many pieces of interesting information which they contain. You were right in having Mr. D[uisberg] visit Madame H[eine]. If would be a good idea if D. could arrange a seemingly chance encounter between you and M[adame] H[eine] because I think you would be able to communicate more effectively with her than with her lawyer. I would very much like to see this problem resolved. I have already made so many concessions in this matter that I would be prepared to pay the last portion of the disputed sum (if you conclude that there is absolutely no other option). In that case, I would like you to have Mr. Gautier once more read through the contract and have the clauses contained therein made even more explicit, so as to avoid the possibility of any future perfidy.

Your expressed intention to supervise the Pasdeloup performance of the *Struensee* overture, and what this performance entails, pleases me greatly. I would be very grateful if you would provide me with an objective and unflattering report on the success of the performance as well as any reviews in the press, both good and bad ones.

I have received a letter from a poor man by the name Galant who, according to his letter, lives at No. 3 Rue Mornay (9th arrondissement). He requests my support and describes his miserable circumstances. Since he says in his letter that he is a Berliner, I authorize you to give him ten francs from my account . . .

I was very surprised to learn from your letter that Roqueplan has asked you if you thought it made any difference whether the story of my new opera took place in Brittany or somewhere else. I think it would be a good idea for you to tell him the following: I informed Meyerbeer of your question because I did not feel that he would be indifferent to the idea of changing the locale of his new opera, which is in Brittany. He responded indicating that both the local color of the libretto and of the music are rooted in this region. Therefore, for the sake of consistency, the locale could not be changed. It is a good idea to make him aware of this *now*. I really do not understand what prompted him to ask this question.

In your letter, you asked me if I had a subscription to "Le Figaro." I do, but I do not have it forwarded to me here in Nice. Was it the Figaro article about my apartment in the Gouin house that prompted this inquiry? That article was reprinted in the newspaper in Nice, which is where I read it . . .

Hoping that this letter finds you in the best of health and that I will receive news from you again soon, I remain, with the greatest of respect, your devoted

Meyerbeer

*　*　*

Meyerbeer's opera Le Pardon de Ploërmel *[Ploërmel's Pardon], also entitled* Dinorah, *was premiered by the Paris Opéra Comique on April fourth, 1859. By July of the same year the Italian version had already been performed in London at the Covent Garden Theater, followed by the English version in October. In 1859 there were also performances in Koburg, The Hague, Brussels and Stuttgart, followed in 1860 by performances in Geneva, Dresden, Gotha, Rostock, Augsburg, Hamburg and Gent. Theaters competed among themselves for the new opera, even though the role of Dinorah made extraordinary demands on the singer. The*

Illus. 21: Caricature by Wilhelm Busch for *Dinorah*, Act II: The shadow dance (Fliegende Blätter 1860).

Illus. 22: Minna Meyerbeer, née Mosson. Oil painting by Meyerbeer's son-in-law, Gustav Richter, ca. 1860 (original owned by the family).

famous "Shadow Aria," a typical mad scene so beloved in opera, is one of dizzying virtuosity. Making the onset of Dinorah's madness and subsequent recovery believable requires a superb actress who also had to look the role.

The popularity of the opera is documented in the amusing verses and illustrations in Wilhelm Busch's "Dinorerl oder die Wallfahrt in Hemdärmeln" [Little Dinorah, or the Pilgrimage in Shirtsleeves], complete with a delightful caricature of the shadow dance in the "Fliegende Blätter." These illustrations were among the first, still unsigned, works by Busch, who went on to become very famous.

103. To Minna Meyerbeer

[Paris, April 5, 1859]

Dearest beloved wife,

Since I am completely exhausted both physically and mentally, please forgive me if I write only a brief letter to tell you that my opera was finally launched yesterday. Given the manner in which premiers are

163

orchestrated in Paris, it is impossible to know whether the success of a work is real or fabricated when it is performed for the first time. If I am to believe what I have seen and the assurances given by the many people who have visited and congratulated me, *Le Pardon de Ploërmel* was indeed a *great success* (knock on wood!). At the beginning, the overture unleashed a storm of applause which did not abate for the entire evening. After the second act, the Emperor and Empress, who were both present, called me to their box to express their approval and satisfaction. At the end of the opera I was called out on stage and, although I had decided not to appear because I find that sort of thing so comical, I finally had to make an appearance because the storm of applause did not cease. The Emperor and Empress did not leave their box so as to continue applauding me, which they did very obviously when I appeared. I pray to God that the coming performances may confirm the success of the first. More tomorrow, my dearest beloved wife, and please give a kiss to our beloved children from your

> loyal and devoted husband,
> Giacomo
> Paris, April 5, 1859

*   *   *

Meyerbeer and Liszt met in January of 1860 on the occasion of a large dinner given at the residence of Count Redern in Berlin. "Liszt was very friendly and even visited me although I had been told that he had indirectly attacked me in his essay on 'The music of the Gypsies'," noted Meyerbeer in his diary. Meyerbeer had received information about this article and Liszt's criticisms "about Jews and Jewish music" on November third.

From September 29 to October 26, 1859, Meyerbeer composed the "Schiller-marsch" and a "Festkantate" for the celebration of Schiller's 100th birthday on November 10, 1859. Over 4000 people attended the festival performance in the Cirque des Champs Elysées which was conducted by Jean-Etienne Pasdeloup and also included the "Festgesang an die Künstler" [festive hymn to artists] by Mendelssohn, the last movement of Beethoven's Ninth Symphony, and Weber's Oberon overture. "My Festive March was greeted with great applause and had to be repeated. My cantata was also well received, but not nearly as well as the March," confided Meyerbeer to his diary on November 10.

104. To Franz Liszt

Berlin, February 1860

My dear and illustrious Master,

I have received your kind letter in which you honored me by requesting the score of the March I composed for the Schiller celebration in order to have it performed in Weimar for Their Royal Highnesses at a court concert conducted by you. I have no need to tell you how happy and proud I would be to know that my March was to be performed before such an august audience and under the direction of such an illustrious master as yourself. I shall hasten to send you the score as soon as I can do so. Right now it is in the hands of Mr. Kullack who is arranging it for piano for the publisher M. Schlesinger. As soon as he has finished the arrangement, I must have a copy made for the Queen of England, in accordance with the orders of Her Royal Highness the Princess Fréderic Guillaume. When this is completed, I will have the honor of sending you the score at once.

In the meantime, dear and illustrious master, please accept this expression of my utmost respect and admiration.

Your devoted
Meyerbeer

*   *   *

Soon after his return to Berlin in mid-January of 1860 Meyerbeer, in his capacity as director of royal court music, conducted a brilliant orchestra concert at the residence of Prince Wilhelm, the Prince Regent. Among the pieces performed was his "Schillermarsch." Prince Wilhelm had assumed the Prussian regency in 1858 in the place of his brother, Friedrich Wilhelm IV, who was afflicted by severe mental illness. Therefore, his wife, Augusta, had at that time already held the highest position in the land. For some thirty years, since her marriage in 1829, Meyerbeer had enjoyed her warm support at the court. Since the performance of the march had been very well received, as Meyerbeer clearly states in his diary, he took it upon himself to dedicate the march to the Princess because she, a born Princess of Saxony-Weimar, had since her earliest youth been very fond of Goethe and Schiller.

105. To Princess Augusta of Prussia

[Berlin, June 5, 1860]

Most serene and gracious Princess,

Your Royal Highness graciously allowed me to dedicate my "Festmarsch" to you. This work was composed for the celebration conducted in Paris on the occasion of Schiller's 100th birthday.

Your Royal Highness' gracious permission made me all the happier because it was in Your Royal Highness' enlightened parental home, with its strong promotion of German art and science, that the great writer whom I, with my modest talents, strove on this occasion to glorify, found the support which helped him overcome life's afflictions.

In view of this demonstration of Your Royal Highness' kindness, may I now respectfully request that Your Royal Highness graciously permit me to lay the score and the piano reduction of this march at your feet.

With deepest respect I remain

Your Royal Highness' most
humble servant,
G. Meyerbeer
Berlin, June 5, 1860

*   *   *

In 1857, Franz Baron von Dingelstedt assumed the direction of the court theater in Weimar. Weimar was an intellectual center: Schiller and Goethe at one time had attracted scholars and artists to the court of the Grand Duchy. However, the financial resources of this small Thuringian residence were limited, which meant that there was a lack of first-class singers. It is to Dingelstedt's credit that he accepted Meyerbeer's objections to a performance of his opera in Weimar and abandoned his plans.

Dingelstedt's wife, Jenny Lutzer, had been a brilliant coloratura soprano in the 1840's and was loved and respected in Vienna. In 1847, the title role in Vielka, *the revision of* Ein Feldlager in Schlesien, *was designed with her in mind because it seemed questionable at first whether Jenny Lind would sing in Vienna, a city she very much feared. On the advice of her husband, who wanted to avoid any comparison with Jenny Lind, Jenny Lutzer declined the offer.*

106. To Franz Baron von Dingelstedt

Berlin, June 28, 1860

Honored General Director,

I received your esteemed letter upon my return from a short journey. You ask me whether, and under what conditions, I would be willing to provide you with a score to *Dinorah,* so that you could produce it in the coming winter season.

Above all, esteemed sir and friend, allow me to thank you for this new confirmation of your support for me and my operas. By virtue of the manner in which you handled the production of my earlier operas in Munich and Weimar you have clearly proven that, under your careful direction, *Dinorah* would be in very good hands indeed. If I express some doubts regarding the advisability of performing *Dinorah* in Weimar, it is only due to the special nature of the work. Unlike my other operas, *Dinorah* does not have several leading roles, nor does it benefit from the strong support of a chorus. In addition, the background of this opera is only a simple rustic setting. There are really only three roles in this opera, the most important of which by far is that of Dinorah. It is the cornerstone of the entire opera and without a good Dinorah, the opera cannot be a success. Given the complex nature of this role, it presents a host of unusual difficulties, for it requires a fine coloratura singer in the first half of the opera and a dramatic singer and good actress for the rest. Based on what I have heard about the the personnel of the Weimar Opera, the only singer who seems suitable for the role would be Mrs. von Milde. However, she does not appear to be available, since you did not include her name in the cast list. This is why I do not think a production of *Dinorah* would be appropriate at this time.

That your esteemed wife (my unforgettable Isabelle and Margarethe) still has fond memories of me, as you wrote, fills me with joy and pride, and I would be grateful if you could express these words to her on my behalf.

*　　*　　*

Henri Blaze de Bury, writer and contributor to several newspapers, had intensively studied Goethe's life and works and also translated Faust *before he began work on* La Jeunesse de Goethe *[Goethe's Youth], a play for which Meyerbeer was to compose some incidental music. Meyerbeer began composing on July 31, 1860. In September, an agreement was reached for the completion of the score by May 1861. On December 19, Meyerbeer noted the following: "Have completed score for* La Jeunesse de Goethe." *There was still some work to be done on the instrumentation because of uncertainty regarding the orchestra in the Odéon, a Paris theater.*

107. To Henri Blaze de Bury

[Berlin, January 28, 1861]

My dear friend,

Your letter of January 20, which was not postmarked in Paris until the 25th, arrived here this morning and I hasten to answer it immediately. The music for the act you requested was completed weeks ago. I had been waiting with this piece of news until I heard from you as to the arrangements you promised to make to secure a theater. Now I read in your letter that the theater is the Odéon. If you find the required singers among your company, feel that you can stage the fourth act, and have been guaranteed the means to meet the musical requirements I mentioned in my letter to you, then I think this theater is a good choice, particularly with a director such as Mr. de le Rounat, who is said to be daring and intelligent. You also indicated in your letter that Mr. de la Rounat has already scheduled an engagement with Madame Ristori for April, the month agreed upon for the delivery of the score, and that, as a result, he has suggested that the work not be performed until the spring of 1862. As far as my musical obligations are concerned, I will definitely be free at that time. The new opera I am preparing will not be performed until the coming winter, therefore I do not foresee any difficulties at this

Illus. 23: Giacomo Meyerbeer. Photograph by Numa Blanc, Paris, 1861.

time. As head of a family, I hesitate to make a definite commitment for something which will occur 14 months from now. Without having a permanent residence in France and given the uncertainty of the times in which we now live, who knows what could happen by then to keep me here.

If we want to wait until October first to sign the contract for April 1862, as suggested by Mr. de la Rounat, then he can be sure to receive the work seven months thereafter. From our standpoint, this would mean that delivery would not be postponed for such a long time. I do believe you when you say that Mr. de la Rounat is interested in the work, so this should present no obstacles.

Now let us talk a little about our work. The scene which prompted most of my reservations and which I suggested be changed (Faust's scene in the cathedral) was the most successful of all and I hope that you are pleased with it. I see no need for any other changes, neither for the other scenes nor the melodramas which I executed according to your suggestions.

There is only one piece which disturbs me from a musical perspective, which is why I am hesitant to continue working on it; this is the ballad of the Erl King. Schubert's music for this ballad has become so popular the world over that I do not think the public would accept another musical setting of these words. I myself am so influenced by his music that I have been unable to write any satisfactory music. Therefore I would like to retain Schubert's melodic line by using it as a basis for the chorus of the Erl King's daughters. Schubert's melody would be divided among the three speaking roles, and (this can be done) the piano accompaniment would be arranged for orchestra.

There are two possible approaches: one would be to have the father and son speak to each other, melodramatically, while Schubert's melody is given to the orchestra. The Erl King and his daughters would be the only characters who actually sing. The other approach would be to have singers take the roles of father and son as well. Please write me as to which of these two approaches you prefer. From a purely musical standpoint it would be more effective if father, son and Erl King sang, but I will go along with whatever you decide. Please let me know also whether you have inserted a chorus of students in the first act, as you planned. If so, please send me a copy immediately because I would rather compose the music now while the other music is still fresh in my head than wait until I have become distanced from it due to other projects. Please remember me to Madame de Bury and my charming Jetta, and please do me the favor of responding quickly with information in this matter.

* * *

In March of 1861, Friedrich Baron von Flotow (1812–1883) was in Berlin for the performance of the music he composed for Shakespeare's A Winter's Tale. *He met with Meyerbeer on several occasions. After the second performance, Meyerbeer noted in his diary: "very interesting performance; very skillful adaptation [by Dingelstedt], very interesting, beautifully orchestrated music..."*

108. To Friedrich Baron von Flotow

Berlin, April 30, 1861

Esteemed Maestro and sir,

I am doubly happy that you were pleased with the photograph I sent you of myself because it also gave me the pleasure of receiving your kind letter. I was delighted to read that I enjoy the support of the famous Maestro who, by virtue of his lovely, universally appealing compositions and personal kindness, has long commanded my utmost admiration. I still have but one wish: that I might have the pleasure of receiving your photograph. This would be a lasting and pleasant souvenir of our recent encounter.

* * *

Meyerbeer objected to a performance of La Jeunesse de Goethe *scheduled for the spring of 1862 because he had already planned a trip to London in April to see the World's Fair. He had been asked to compose a festive overture for the exposition's opening ceremonies. However, his duties as Director of Court Music obliged him to remain in Berlin during 1862. In addition, Meyerbeer, who at this point was in his seventies and frequently in poor health, did not muster the energy to travel to Paris for rehearsals of the music he composed for* La Jeunesse de Goethe. *When he did return to Paris in September, 1863 to prepare the production of* L'Africaine, *he devoted all of his energy to this new work. According to Blaze de Bury,* La Jeunesse de Goethe *was finally to be performed after the premier of* L'Africaine. *Meyerbeer's death ended Bury's hopes, and Meyerbeer's manuscript is lost, along with portions of his other unpublished works.*

109. To Louis Brandus

Berlin, September 29, 1861

You will no doubt note from the contents of the enclosed letter that it is written for a specific purpose, and I ask that you be so kind as to read it to Mr. Blaze de Bury. Yesterday I received a letter from him in which he wrote that the Odéon would remain open throughout the summer, instead of closing on the first of June as it usually does, if I decided to come to present his work there. This would then allow our work a long performance schedule. He also sent me a large scene with the students in the first act which he wants me to set to music and which has the dimensions of a finale. He also indicated that he would like to have music for the end of the act. His remarks also seem to indicate that he wants music for the other acts, and he closes with the words "and now, my friend, let us go to work."

Despite the sorry state of my health when last you saw me, I was able to carry out my duties for the court concerts in Königsberg and Berlin as well as for the concert for the London exposition in the Crystal Palace. However, it would be impossible for me to write new compositions for Henri Blaze this winter. Nor am I obliged in any way to do so. As you know, the promise I made to compose music for the third act was kept long ago. I must admit that, even if I were not to compose any new pieces, I would still not wish to subject myself to the stress of traveling to Paris to direct the rehearsals on account of my poor health. From an artistic standpoint, it would normally make no difference to me whether the work was performed in April or the coming autumn. However, I feel the need for an extended rest before devoting myself to the great effort which rehearsing a new work always requires. For this reason I would prefer the work to be performed next October rather than next spring. It would be your task, esteemed sir, to make Henri Blaze come to the same conclusion—that a fall performance would be more advantageous to him than presenting the work in the summer. I am well aware that he cannot force me to do anything. Given the fact that I like him, and in view of our long-standing friendship, I took on the large task of composing music for the third act. Still, I do not wish to anger him by suggesting this postponement. I trust that you can expedite this matter, and I respectfully request that you inform me of the result of your encounter with him . . .

*   *   *

On July 13, while spending a few days in Wiesbaden before going for his cure in Schwalbach, Meyerbeer noted in his diary: "read in the Cologne newspaper a poem entitled "A Song of the Blind Hessian." It made such an impression on me that, within an hour, I set it for tenor and men's chorus, without instrumental accompaniment and without using a piano. Only the fourth verse, which is to have a different melody, remains to be composed." This, too, was written within a few days.

110. To Carl Altmueller

Berlin, November 5, 1862

Esteemed sir,
    A fortunate happenstance recently provided me with the opportunity to read your zestful and very patriotic "Song of the Blind Hessian." I was so stimulated by it that I immediately set it to music as a choral piece for men's voices. It is a privilege for me to present you with the enclosed manuscript copy of the product of our combined efforts as it will not appear in print for several weeks to come. Please accept this as a friendly souvenir of our small collaboration, esteemed sir, and be assured of my utmost admiration.

Yours respectfully,
G. Meyerbeer

*   *   *

As we know from Meyerbeer's diary, on the morning of the festival performance of his "Schillermarsch" and "Festkantate" to celebrate Schiller's 100th birthday on November 10, 1859, he visited Joseph d'Ortigue. On the evening of the 11th, he wrote in his diary: "Evening: worked on Cantique." Encouraged by the great success of his Schiller compositions, Meyerbeer probably took immediate action on a suggestion put to him by d'Ortigue who, as an expert in the history of sacred music, may have directed Meyerbeer's attention to a text by Corneille (the epic "L'Imitation de Jésus Christ." completed in 1656) based on a book by Thomas à Kempis. The unusual scoring for six solo voices and organ/harmonium suggests a specific purpose for the performance. D'Ortigue undoubtedly wanted a composi-

171

tion for "La Maîtrise," a journal he founded. Meyerbeer was encouraged by the rapid progress of his composition; on November 12, during a visit to the journal's publisher, Jacques Léopold Heugel, Meyerbeer promised him the composition for publication and, one day later, the work (which Meyerbeer dedicated to d'Ortigue) was completed.

Ludwig Rellstab provided the German translation in February, 1860.

111. To Louis Brandus

Frankfurt on Main, June 12, 1863

Esteemed sir,

I arrived here two days ago on my way to Schwalbach. Unfortunately the weather was so rainy and stormy that I did not dare to continue my journey to Schwalbach for fear of catching cold and delaying the start of my cure. Today the weather seems to be clearing up and if it continues to do so, with God's help I will leave tomorrow for Schwalbach. Since I asked you to send your letters *to Schwalbach,* I do not yet know if Benedict is willing to meet the conditions I set, which you kindly conveyed to him, regarding permission to perform the cantique "Aspiration." Since the concert is to be on the 24th and time, therefore, is running out, I am telling you what I have done *in the event that Benedict accepts my conditions.* On closer observation, I noticed that, if I had composed the harmonium part under the vocal parts more like a brilliant obbligato, the vocal parts and the solemn mood which the entire piece should express would have suffered greatly; therefore I refrained from doing so. However, in order to give more importance to the harmonium part I composed an extended prelude for the harmonium (in the style of the entire piece) which is directly followed by the first recitative ("Ineffable Splendor"). I am enclosing the prelude in this letter.

I have also changed the vocal parts in the third recitative so that the three bass soloists will sing together in three-part harmony at least once. I have also enclosed this change. Since I have only the *French* edition of the "Cantique," every reference to page and measure numbers is based on that edition.

Would you please be so good as to inform Mr. Engel and Mr. Benedict of these changes (the latter because he must conduct the rehearsals). In particular, please explain to Mr. Engel why I was able to expand the harmonium part only by adding a prelude. Would you also be so kind as to send my manuscript to one of your brother's proofreaders so that if there is something that is unclear you will still have time to request clarification from Schwalbach. Still, I hope that Engel and Benedict will be able to read and understand everything. The first recitative must be sung by Mr. Obin, the second by Mr. Faure, and the third by Mr. Sauntley.

This evening, an Italian opera company is giving a debut performance of [Donizetti's] *Lucrezia Borgia* in which the tenor Bignardi is singing. Recently he had great success in Oporto with "Huguenots" and "Robert." I will attend tonight's performance. Please send your reply to Schwalbach.

Respectfully,
Meyerbeer
P.S. How was the performance
of [Gounod's] *Faust* in Her
Majesty's Theater [London]?

* * *

In March of 1860 Meyerbeer resumed work on Vasco da Gama *which was the new name he had given to* L'Africaine; *progress on this work was briefly interrupted in October while Meyerbeer worked on the music for* La Jeunesse de Goethe. *However, the unexpected occurred once again: on January 1, 1861 Friedrich Wilhelm IV died in Berlin. Meyerbeer was then commissioned to compose a coronation march and festive hymn for the coronation of the new ruler. Little time passed before Meyerbeer received the shocking news that Eugene Scribe, his librettist and collaborator of long standing, had died suddenly and unexpectedly on February 21, 1861. Who was now to make the libretto changes and cuts which always proved necessary during the composition of the music and even while a work was being staged? Until the point, Scribe had always been available to provide the benefits of his rich experience and infallible sense for theatrical effect. Who could possibly replace him? In addition, Meyerbeer was plagued with uncertainty regarding the casting of his opera. As a result, work on* L'Africaine *progressed slowly.*

112. To Louis Brandus

Schwalbach, August third,
1863

Honorable sir,

Although I have been in possession of your three esteemed letters for several days now, I have been unable to answer them because the cure I am taking has been very strenuous . . . As a result of my congestion the doctor was forced to prescribe a three-day interruption of cure. I will take advantage of this to reply to your three letters. I was truly *disappointed* to read that the hopes Villaret had aroused in *Guillaume Tell* [Rossini] were dashed in *Vêpres Siciliennes* [Verdi] and that, in your opinion, I would not be able to use him for my new opera. Based on everything I read about his performance of Arnold in "Tell," I had hoped that he would be able to play the role of Vasco. It is the most important tenor role I have ever composed, and the success of the opera depends to a *large extent* on the performance of this role. Geymard, who is old, fat, and worn out, is not at all suitable as the young heroic cavalier.

The cure I am presently taking will be completed on the 24th instead of the 21st, due to the three-day break. I shall then go to Baden where Naudin will be singing in the Italian opera. I would like to hear him in order to find out if he would be suitable for the role of Vasco. I am sure you remember my having told you in Berlin that I was informed by a very competent German, who had heard Naudin sing Raoul in *Les Huguenots* in Italy, that he had the most polished and graceful tenor voice of our day as well as possessing great passion and energy. Well, we shall see whether he impresses me the same way. At any rate, this recommendation is important enough for me to go hear him and to consider whether he is suitable for the role. Despite this excursion to Baden, I can still be in Paris in early September to hear Lucca's debut which, as you indicated in your letter, will take place at that time.

I must also implore you *not to mention to anyone* that I am going to Baden to hear Naudin. Naudin himself would most likely bring out the brass band in order to stir up some publicity and Bagier, the director of the Italian opera [in Paris], who did not hire Naudin due to a salary dispute, would then hire him at any cost so as to take him away from the French opera. I myself would then be cut to pieces by the French opera personnel and their journalist allies. Do not even mention this to Perrin, for although it would be in his interest to keep this quiet in order not to increase Naudin's pretensions, he would be required to discuss it in the State Ministry and, as you know, those gentlemen are not good at keeping secrets. Besides, I do not yet know if Naudin is suitable and if it turns out that he is not, any preliminary discussion of this matter would have been a waste of time . . .

Have you told Perrin that there are two leading roles for women in my opera and that *both* are in the tradition of Falcon, hence not of the *chanteuse légère* variety? If Miss Tietjens or Miss Lucca were to be so successful in Paris that I could entrust them with *L'Africaine,* then Miss Sax could sing the other role. If neither Tietjens nor Lucca were to enjoy a major success, or I felt that Miss Sax (whom, as you know, I have not yet met) was more suitable for this type of role, then we would still have to find a singer for the other female role because I do not believe the Opéra has anyone. Miss Barbot may be the only possible candidate, although I am not overly enthusiastic about her abilities . . .

Have you sent my new Prelude for "Aspiration" to Engel in time? Has he received it and already made use of it? I ask because I have not yet received a single word of gratitude from him for my troubles. This is difficult to explain if he has received the piece, given how polite he usually is.

I would be very grateful if you could find out (without letting on that the inquiry comes from me) if Henri Blaze is still in Paris or, if not, whether he is in Germany or simply in the country, and when he is expected to return.

Please accept this expression of my utmost respect.

Meyerbeer

* * *

Meyerbeer was a man with religious principles, but was not an orthodox zealot. Prayer was a daily requirement for him. His diary contains eloquent testimony of his subjugation to the almighty God.

However, Meyerbeer's deep religious beliefs along with his very superstitious nature made for a very puzzling sort of cohabitation. He feared Fridays, considering Friday an unlucky day; as a result, he avoided making important decisions, signing contracts, or concluding trips on Fridays.

Being Jewish, for him, was both a trauma and a duty. For religious reasons, Meyerbeer felt obliged to perform a daily good deed. There are countless examples of situations in which Meyerbeer provided spontaneous assistance to those in need. His mother taught him to be charitable and to help relieve society's woes. At important moments of his life Meyerbeer always beseeched his mother for her blessing. His closeness to her was a key element of his life.

The personal prayer he wrote down as part of his daily routine a few months prior to his death is both an intimate and unusual testament to Meyerbeer's fervent dialogue with God. It is an expression of religious faith which provides greater insight into the real man.

113. Daily Prayer

Paris, December 8, 1863

Almighty and merciful God! Have mercy on the souls of my beloved parents and brothers! Accept them into your heavenly paradise: give them everlasting peace and salvation and allow my dear mother to be the guardian angel of her entire family, protecting all of us just as she so gladly did in this life.

Dearest, most devout and beloved mother, send down your blessing to my beloved wife Minna, my three dear children Blanca, Cäcilie and Cornelie, my little grandson Fritz, my son-in-law Emanuel, to Wilhelm's children and to myself. Beseech the eternal God that He keep us on the path of virtue, honor and justice our whole life long and that He protect us from the temptation to do wrong, and that He shield us from sickness and misfortune . . .

Almighty God! Ennoble and purify my heart and my soul. Cleanse my character of the many blemishes which disfigure it: transform me into a man of religious, virtuous, energetic and benevolent character. Give me as many years of life as you gave to my late mother, and even more. Let me enjoy them in health, virtue, joy, domestic harmony, peace of mind, prosperity, and artistic productivity and fame. Above all, most merciful God, give your blessing to my beloved Minna, my three children Blanca, Cäcilie and Cornelie, and my beloved little grandson Fritz.

Almighty God, may you, in your great mercy, allow me to see Cäcilie and Cornelie happily married in the near future. Allow me to keep all of my senses until my death, in particular my sight and my hearing: may they not become weaker than they already are at this time. May I remain robust and clear of mind. Preserve my artistic creativity and effectiveness. Preserve the prosperity you have so generously given me. Preserve, increase, and ennoble my artistic fame. Let my fame spread throughout the world and transform my enemies into supporters and admirers. Preserve the five French operas I have composed and let them be part of the repertoire of all theaters throughout my lifetime and 50 years beyond my death. Allow me to complete *Vasco* [L'Africaine] within a few months. Let *Vasco* be performed at the Paris Opéra in 1864 and allow me to witness this event in health and happiness . . . Make *Vasco* an overwhelming success at its first performance at the Paris Opéra, and make its success a deserved and lasting one. Make *Vasco* quickly become part of the general theater repertoire the world over as was the case with "Robert" and "Huguenots," and let it remain a part of the repertoire as long as "Robert" and "Huguenots" have been and will continue to be. Almighty God, let the success of *Vasco* be so great that it will fill my old age with fame and joy and will preserve my name and fame for posterity. Amen.

Almighty and merciful God, grant me a gentle, easy and painless hour of death, free of fear and a guilty conscience. Allow me to die without fear, devoutly confident of what awaits me in the hereafter. Do not let my death be preceded by a long and painful illness. Instead, may death come softly, quickly and unexpectedly. Before that, allow me to settle wisely all my earthly affairs. Do not let me die abroad but at home, surrounded by my dear wife and my three beloved children. And, almighty God, please let my last will and testament be a *wise* one, assuring the same prosperity to my wife, my three children, my grandchild and closest descendants that you have mercifully granted me and allowed me to maintain.
Amen.

*   *   *

Meyerbeer arrived in Paris on September third, 1863 to begin rehearsals for L'Africaine. *In the following letter he confirms once again—as Blaze de Bury also states in his biography of Meyerbeer—his firm intention to arrange for the performance of* La Jeunesse de Goethe *at the Odéon after the premier of* L'Africaine.

114. To Karl Kaskel

Paris, December 30, 1863

Dearest brother,

The moment when a year of life breaks away from the present and sinks into the past, when a new year rises, containing events which are unknown to us, is always a moment of both fear and solemnity. The heart instinctively turns to God beseeching him to protect those who are dear to us and whose love is our greatest source of joy. When I pray to God to

Illus. 24: *L'Africaine,* premier April 28, 1865: Act III, Scene 6. Drawing
by Auguste Anastasi (*L'Illustration,* Paris, May 6, 1865).

watch over my beloved wife, my children and my grandchild, I also say a prayer in my heart for the happiness and welfare of you and yours, and for our continued friendship which I have greatly cherished over these many years. I pray to God that, for you and yours, everything may remain as it is, for I could not wish you anything better. You are a highly respected, honorable and wealthy man, rich in spirit and compassionate; all prerequisites for *noble* partaking of the joys of life. You have kind, decent children who are all very happily married. How could anyone wish anything more for you except that everything remain as it is?

I have been in Paris for a few months because the powers that be encouraged me to see that my *L'Africaine* is finally performed at the Paris Opéra. Naturally, this has always been my wish, However, with the current roster of singers at the Opéra, I still need two singers (of the highest caliber) for two leading roles. The management believes they have just recently found them, however they are both currently under contract and will not be available until spring. As a result, the rehearsals could not begin until then which means that *L'Africaine* will not be performed until next fall, for a summer performance run is undesirable. By that time, or even before, I will have completed another major work. A year and a half ago I finished the music for a major play for the Odéon theater, but I do not think it wise for me to initiate the performance of another dramatic composition before *L'Africaine* has been given. Since I know how interested you are in my artistic activities, I am telling you these small details no matter how unimportant they may be for anyone else. And now my dear brother, let me wish you health and happiness for the New Year and give my regards to dear Felix.

Your eternally devoted friend
and brother,
Meyerbeer

*   *   *

This is the last birthday letter to Meyerbeer's 27-year-old daughter. Meyerbeer's heartfelt wishes for his daughter were more than fulfilled: in 1869, Cäcilie married the Austrian diplomat Baron Andrian zu Werburg. Her son, a boyhood friend of Hugo von Hofmannsthal was a very talented writer and became director of the Vienna Burgtheater in 1918. When Cäcilie died in Salzburg at the ripe old age of 94, the Berlin "Illustrierte Nachtausgabe" devoted an extensive article, entitled "Die Ahnfrau in Salzburg" [Ancestress in Salzburg], to her:

> *When, after a performance of* Everyman *in front of the Salzburg Cathedral, the world's wealthy were searching for a sumptuous dinner, happily overindulging at the tables of the luxury hotel, an ancient and venerable matron would descend from her widow's quarters, a small hotel room, and walk into the magnificent dining room wearing a black silk dress and graceful high-heeled shoes. Her face was dark and weather-beaten, mummy-like; it seemed to consist of nothing but lines and deep wrinkles. She would stride among*

the rows of people who would first gaze upon the unusual guest with some
fear and then with curiosity. It was Meyerbeer's daughter, and she brought
into the lively and frivolous present the cold breath of a past long since part
of history.

115. To Cäcilie Meyerbeer

Paris, March 8, 1864

My dearest beloved Cäcilie,

Accept my heartfelt congratulations and fatherly blessing on the occasion of your birthday. I hope that these lines will arrive in Wiesbaden on the morning of the tenth and that they will find you in the best of health, both physically and spiritually. May these precious gifts be yours for an entire lifetime which, I pray, the almighty God will extend to your 100th birthday. May God soon grant you a kind and good husband whom you love and who will love and cherish you. When this day comes, it will be the happiest day of my life. As for me, all I ask of your husband is that he be a decent and understanding man who is lovingly devoted to you. May his love for you be true and not influenced by the dowry which I have set aside for you and your sisters. Above all, may he make you happy. Whether he comes from high society or a middle-class family, is rich or poor, occupies an important or modest position in the world is of no importance to me. If you have the proper attitude when choosing a husband, you will not place any importance on the above-mentioned details.

As for my birthday presents to you, dearest child, you already know what they are because, as Mamma wrote in her letter, you have already picked them out. Therefore I can assume that you will be pleased with them. I would like, however, to make an additional present for you and Cornelie; the *nervus rerum* (meaning money) for a one-month trip in May when Mamma begins her cure. It may come to pass that I present my opera in Paris, but unfortunately this is still not definite: of the many promised singer debuts, only two materialized, one of which was bad. The other was good, but negotiations broke down due to exaggerated salary demands. Therefore, I will most likely have to travel to Vienna next month to hear the tenor Mongini, whom the opera management is now considering. As I was saying, if my opera is presented next month in Paris, you could both come to Paris to stay with your father and Gaichen. If this is not the case, you can spend the month traveling through northern Italy where you will not be very far from Mamma, who will probably go to Switzerland, pour qu'elle puisse promptement mettre la main sur vous [so that she will be able to keep track of you], should you want to run away. In the event that you come to Paris, moi, je pourrais vous tenir sous clef, mauvaises sujettes [I could keep an eye on you two rascals].

George Sand wrote a five-act play based on her beautiful novel *Le Marquis de Villemer* with which you are familiar. The play was performed a few days ago at the Odéon theater and was very enthusiastically received. There is talk of it everywhere. When my cough is better, I, too, would like to see it. The weather here is very unhealthy: very hot, but with lots of rain and storms. Once again, dear Cäcilie, I wish you a happy and blessed birthday and embrace you in spirit. Give my love to Mamma and Cornelie.

Your devoted father,
Meyerbeer

* * *

With the exception of his "Stabat mater," Rossini composed only smaller occasional works after the tremendous success of his Guillaume Tell *in 1829. In 1863 he composed the* Petite Messe Solennelle, *the most important of his later works, scored for four solo voices, double quartet, two pianos, and harmonium; it was performed for the first time on March 14, 1864 only a few weeks before Meyerbeer's death. It was heard by a small audience at the town house of Count Pillet-Will and was dedicated to his wife, Countess Louise. Although the doctor had ordered Meyerbeer to stay in bed, he did not want to miss the performance. He is said to have been deeply moved and to have burst into tears. He also supposedly gave Rossini an enthusiastic embrace and attended the second performance on the following day. He was still affected by the performance when he wrote the following letter to Rossini; it indicates some of the feelings which may have moved the already weakened Maestro upon hearing the Mass.*

116. To Gioacchino Rossini

[Paris, March 15, 1864]

To Jupiter Rossini
Divine Master,

I cannot let this day end without once again thanking you for the immense pleasure I experienced during each of the two performances I attended of your latest sublime creation. May God keep you among us until your 100th birthday so that you can create other masterpieces of this type. May God also see fit to grant me an equally long life so that I may hear and admire the new products of your immortal genius.

Your constant admirer and old
friend,
G. Meyerbeer
Paris, March 15, 1864

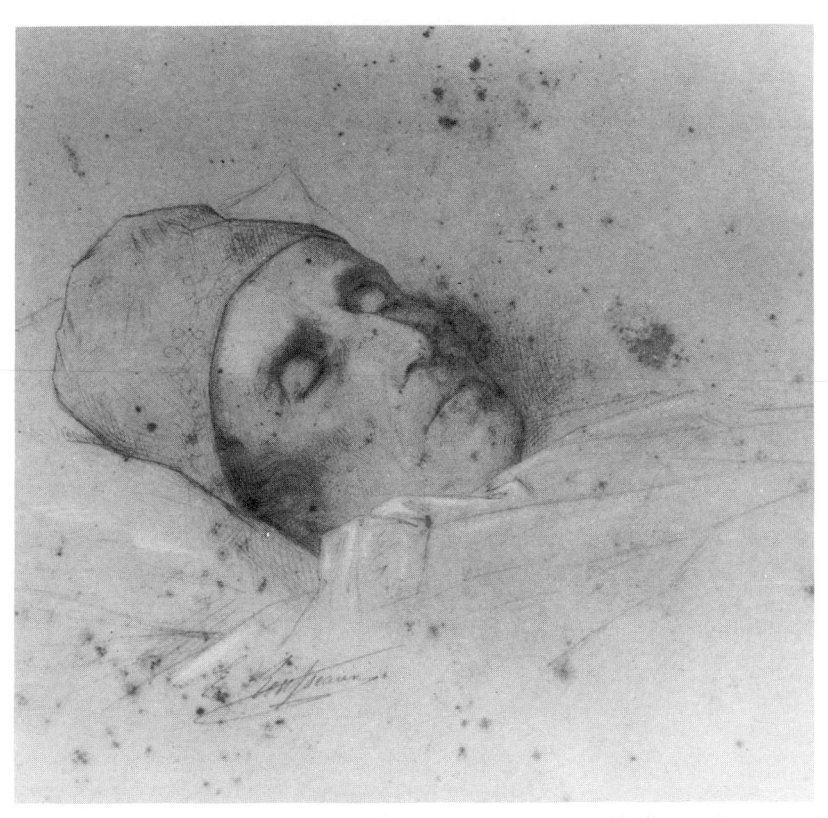

Illus. 25: Meyerbeer on his death bed, Paris, May 2, 1864. Illustration
by E. Rousseau (Meyerbeer Archives, Berlin).

*   *   *

Postscript: The tiring rehearsals for the premier of L'Africaine *had undermined Meyerbeer's health. In April he began to have dizzy spells. Meyerbeer had his two younger daughters, Cäcilie and Cornelie, come to Paris, but did not dare worry his wife who was staying with his eldest daughter, Blanca, in Berlin. He died unexpectedly on May second at 5:40 A.M. When, on the following day, Rossini wanted to pay Meyerbeer a visit, he learned of the tragic event. Deeply shocked, he fainted and was unconscious for ten minutes. Afterwards, he sat down at the piano and composed a "Chant funèbre" [hymn of mourning]: "Pleure! Pleure! muse sublime" [Weep! Weep! sublime muse]. Rossini wrote the following words on the autograph score: "a brief song of mourning for my poor friend Meyerbeer. G. Rossini."*

The entire world was shocked. The rehearsals for L'Africaine *had to be interrupted because there were still several versions of sections of the score. Meyerbeer always made last-minute changes during the rehearsals, once he was able to see the effect of individual pieces, François Joseph Fétis, the Belgian music theorist, was well acquainted with Meyerbeer and had followed his career as a*

181

Illus. 26: Arietta "Soave istante" for the tenor Giovanni Battista Rubini (unpublished, private collection).

critic. He agreed to undertake the revisions of the score. The premier of L'Africaine *took place on April 28, 1865 in the presence of the French emperor and empress as well as prominent European figures from the world of politics and culture. The event was a brilliant posthumous tribute to the deceased.*

me un pegno cortese di grato mercè — o! pegno beato bramato bramato da

me O pegno beato.... bramato ...... da me.

All Eco abbellito di Rubini;
all Usignolo del Nord;
alla soave speranza;

Omaggio

Francofort 6 Mayo 33.   Giacomo Meyerbeer

Illus. 27: Meyerbeer's burial at the Jewish cemetery in Berlin,
Schönhauser-Allee, on May 9, 1864. Drawing by M. L. Loeffler
(*L'Illustration*, Paris, May 28, 1864).

Chronological Table

1791 Jakob Liebmann Meyer Beer is born on September five in Vogelsdorf or Tasdorf near Berlin.

1798 Begins piano lessons with Franz Lauska.

1801 October 14: first public performance as a pianist with Mozart's D Minor Piano Concerto.

1803 Enrolls in the Berlin Academy of Voice. Instruction in composition with Carl Friedrich Zelter. December 12: completion of first piano sonata.

1807 Aron Wolfssohn takes charge of Meyer Beer's education. Beginning of studies with Bernhard Anselm Weber.

1810 Contraction of the two names to 'Meyerbeer'. Move to Darmstadt. Lessons with Abbé Vogler. Founding of the 'Harmonischer Verein'[Harmonic Society] with friends and fellow classmates, Carl Maria v. Weber, Gottfried Weber, Johann Baptist Gänsbacher, Alexander von Dusch.

1811 May eighth: premier of the lyrical rhapsody "Gott und die Natur" [God and Nature] (Schreiber) in the Royal National Theater in Berlin.

1812 Meyerbeer arrives in Munich on April 25 and completes his studies with Vogler. December 23: premier of *Jephta's Gelübde* [Jephta's Vow] (Schreiber) in the Munich Royal Court and National Theater.

1813 January third: trip to Stuttgart, where the comedy with music entitled *Wirth und Gast* [Host and Guest, also known as "Alimelek"] (Wohlbrueck) is performed. February 12: Appointment as court composer for the Archduke of Hesse-Darmstadt. March: trip to Vienna.

1814 Meyerbeer arrives in Paris at the end of December.

1815 Stay in London from November 30 to December 31.

1816 Trip to Italy—Verona (March)—Rome (May)—Naples (June)—Sicily.

1817 July 19: premier of the opera *Romilda e Costanza* (Rossi) in Padua.

1819 March: premier of the opera *Semiramide* (Rossi) in Turin. June 26: premier of the opera *Emma di Resburgo* (Rossi) in Venice.

1820 November 14: premier of the opera *Margherita d'Anjou* (Romani) in Milan.

1822 March 12: premier of the opera *L'Esule di Granata* (Romani) in Milan.

1824 March seventh: premier of the opera *Il Crociato in Egitto* (Rossi) in Venice.

1825 Return to Paris on February 23. October 27: Meyerbeer's father Jacob Herz Beer dies in Berlin.

1826 Meyerbeer marries his cousin Minna Mosson on May 25. June fifth: Carl Maria v. Weber dies in London—Meyerbeer promises to complete Weber's opera *Die Drei Pintos*.

1827   Beginning of collaboration with Eugène Scribe.

1831   November 21: Premier of the opera *Robert le Diable* (Scribe) in Paris.

1832   January 19: Appointment as corresponding member of the Academy of Arts in Paris and as knight of the Legion of Honor. August 11: Friedrich Wilhelm III grants Meyerbeer the title of court conductor.

1833   May first: appointment as full member of the Prussian Academy of Arts. Meyerbeer pays a 30,000 franc breach-of-contract penalty to opera director Louis Véron due to a delay in the production of *Les Huguenots*. Travels to Italy with his wife Minna.

1836   February 29: premier of the opera *Les Huguenots* (Scribe) in Paris.

1837   Scribe writes the libretto for Meyerbeer's *L'Africaine*. Work begins on the opera *Cinq Mars* (Saint-Georges), but is stopped on December fifth.

1838   September: work begins on *Le Prophète* (Scribe).

1840   Maurice Schlesinger in Paris publishes a "Collection des mélodies de Giacomo Meyerbeer," containing 22 songs.

1841   March: the first version of the score for *Le Prophète* is completed and is given to a notary in Paris.

1842   May 31: Meyerbeer receives the order Pour le mérite in the peace category from Friedrich Wilhelm IV. June 11: Meyerbeer is appointed Prussian Music Director General.

1843   February 28: premier of the festival production with live scenes [tableaux vivants] entitled *Das Hoffest von Ferrara* [The Court Festival of Ferrara] (Raupach).

1844   December seventh: premier of the festival production *Das Feldlager in Schlesien* (Scribe—Rellstab) on the occasion of the reopening of the Berlin opera house which had been destroyed by fire in 1843.

1846   February: Meyerbeer is made a member of the Academy of Arts in Brussels. September 19: premier of the play *Struensee* by Michael Beer with music by Meyerbeer. December 6: journey to Vienna.

1847   February 18: premier in Vienna of the new version of *Feldlager in Schlesien*, now entitled *Vielka*, with Jenny Lind in the title role.

1848   Return to Paris in October.

1849   April 16: premier of the opera *Le Prophète* (Scribe) in Paris.

1850   January 28: Friedrich August of Saxony grants Meyerbeer the Knight's Cross of the Royal Saxon Order of Merit. February 28: premier of *Le Prophète* in Vienna; on April 28 in Berlin. July 10: honorary doctorate in philosphy from the University of Jena. November first: appointment as knight of the Austrian Order of Franz Joseph.

1851   Premier in Berlin of the ode to Christian Rauch (Kopisch) on the occasion of the May 31 celebration for the unveiling of Rauch's monument of Frederick the Great. Member of the senate of the

Berlin Academy of Arts.

1852   January 27: Meyerbeer returns the unfinished opera *Die Drei Pintos* by Carl Maria v. Weber to Weber's family after paying them a total compensation of 4000 thalers. May 26: premier of the festival cantata *Marias Genius* to celebrate the silver wedding anniversary of Prince Karl. July 18: appointment as honorary member of the Akademie der Tonkunst in Vienna.

1854   February 16: premier of the opéra comique *L'Étoile du Nord* (Scribe) in Paris. June 27: Meyerbeer's mother Amalia Beer dies in Berlin. September 30: Meyerbeer is granted the commander's cross of the Order of the Wuerttemberg Crown, the recipient of which becomes a member of the nobility. Meyerbeer, however, does not take advantage of this.

1855   February ninth: the Commander's Cross, first class, of the Ernestin House Order in Hannover is conferred.

1857   February 24: appointment as member of the Academy of Arts in Florence.

1859   April fourth: premier of the opera comique *Le Pardon de Ploërmel* (Barbier and Carré) in Paris.

1861   February 21: death of Eugène Scribe. Spring: performance of "Krönungsmarsch" for Wilhelm I.

1862   April 20: journey to London where the overture for the opening of the Universal Exposition is performed on May first.

1864   May second: Meyerbeer dies in Paris; the body is brought to Berlin where Meyerbeer is buried on May ninth.

1865   April 28: premier of the opera *L'Africaine* (Scribe) in Paris.

Recipients and Sources of Letters

Abbreviations:
MA   Meyerbeer Archives (Staatsbibliothek West Berlin, Stiftung
     Preussischer Kulturbesitz, Music Division)
BN   Bibliothèque Nationale Paris, Départment de la musique

Letters published here for the first time are indicated by an *

1. August 9, 1810 to Ambrosius Kühnel in Leipzig: Stockholm, Stiftelsen
   Musikkulturens främjande*
2. May 22, 1811 to Gottfried Weber in Mannheim: privately owned;
   present location unknown. Printed in *Die Musik* 1908, vol. 28, p. 73 f.
3. January 8, 1812 to Carl Maria von Weber in Leipzig: MA (draft)
4. August 30, 1812 to Amalia Beer in Berlin: MA
5. January 16, 1813 to Johann Baptist Gänsbacher in Prague: Vienna,
   Gesellschaft der Musikfreunde
6. September, 1814 to Aron Wolfssohn in Berlin: MA (draft)
7. October 15, 1814 to Count Ferdinand Palffy von Erdöd in Vienna: MA*
8. November 1814 to Jacob Herz Beer in Berlin: MA (draft, fragment)
9. June 27, 1819 to Franz Sales Kandler in Venice: Vienna, Austrian
   National Library
10. May 21, 1823 to Nicolas Prosper Levasseur in Paris: BN
11. July 5, 1823 to Nicolas Prosper Levasseur in Paris: BN
12. June 3, 1824 to Francesco Pezzi in Milan: Stockholm, Stiftelsen
    Musikkulturens främjande*
13. July 10, 1825 to Francesco Pezzi in Milan: Stockholm, Stiftelsen
    Musikkulturens främjande*
14. December 11, 1825 to Count Karl von Brühl in Berlin: Original lost;
    printed in *Sammelbände der Internationalen Musikgesellschaft* IV (1903),
    p. 519 f.
15. March 9, 1826 to Heinrich Joseph Baermann in Munich: Berlin (DDR),
    Deutsche Staatsbibliothek, Music Division*
16. July 16, 1828 to Friedrich Wilhelm III of Prussia in Berlin: Merseburg
    (DDR), Deutsches Zentralarchiv, Königliche Haussachen
17. July 20, 1830 to Marie Patzig in Baden-Baden: original unknown; sold
    by auction in 1954 by Meyer & Ernst in Berlin
18. June 25, 1831 to Heinrich Heine in Paris: BN, olim Collection
    Schocken
19. December, 1831 to Heinrich Heine in Paris: BN, olim Collection
    Schocken
20. February 4, 1832 to Count Friedrich Wilhelm von Redern in Berlin:
    original unknown; printed in *Sammelbände der Internationalen
    Musikgesellschaft* IV (1903), p. 524
21. Spring 1832 to Alexandre Dumas in Paris: Berlin, Staatliches Institut
    für Musikforschung, SPK
22. May 4, 1832 to Minna Meyerbeer in Baden-Baden: MA

23. May 23, 1832 to Alexandre Dumas in Paris: BN
24. June 24, 1832 to Minna Meyerbeer in Baden-Baden: MA
25. October 10, 1832 to Minna Meyerbeer in Frankfurt-Main: MA
26. July 22, 1833 to Minna Meyerbeer in Bad Ems: MA
27. September 5, 1833 to Minna Meyerbeer in Baden-Baden: MA
28. March 29, 1834 to the Akademie der Künste in Berlin: Berlin, Archiv der Preussischen Akademie der Künste
29. May 1, 1834 to Minna Meyerbeer in Milan: MA
30. July 2, 1834 to Eugène Scribe in Paris: BN
31. September 1, 1834 to Louis Gouin in Paris: MA
32. October 6, 1834 to Minna Meyerbeer in Baden-Baden: MA
33. November 26, 1834 to Minna Meyerbeer in Baden-Baden: MA
34. January 28, 1835 to Wilhelm Speyer in Frankfurt-Main: Berlin, Staatliches Institut für Musikforschung SPK
35. December 24, 1835 to Minna Meyerbeer in Frankfurt: MA
36. March 1, 1836 to Minna Meyerbeer in Frankfurt: MA
37. March 6, 1836 to Minna Meyerbeer in Frankfurt: MA
38. March 10, 1836 to Minna Meyerbeer in Frankfurt: MA
39. June 4–5, 1836 to Minna Meyerbeer in Baden-Baden: MA
40. June 10, 1837 to Eugène Roger de Bully, *alias* Roger de Beauvoir in Paris: MA
41. October 20, 1837 to Gottfried Weber in Darmstadt: privately owned; printed in *Die Musik,* vol. 28 (1908), p. 158 ff.
42. September 23, 1838 to Heinrich Heine in Paris: original unknown; photographic copy Weimar (DDR), Nationale Forschungs- und Gedenkstätten der klassischen Literatur
43. August 29, 1839 to Heinrich Heine in Paris: source as for 42 above
44. October 19, 1839 to Gustav Schilling in Stuttgart: MA
45. December 4, 1839 to Conradin Kreutzer in Vienna: New York, Pierpont Morgan Library, Mary Flagler Music Collection
46. January 28, 1840 to Gustav Schilling in Stuttgart: original unknown; unsigned draft: Berlin (DDR), Deutsche Staatsbibliothek, Music Division
47. March 18, 1841 to Baron August von Lüttichau in Dresden: original unknown; printed in Richard Wagner, *Gesammelte Briefe,* ed. by Julius Kapp and Emmerich Kastner, Leipzig, 1914, vol. 1, p. 182
48. September 28, 1841 to Heinrich Heine in Paris: original unknown; printed in Friedrich Hirth *Heinrich Heine, Bausteine zu einer Biographie,* Mainz, 1950, p. 64
49. December 9, 1841 to Count Friedrich Wilhelm von Redern in Berlin: original unknown; printed in Richard Wagner, *Gesammelte Briefe,* ed. by Julius Kapp and Emmerich Kastner, Leipzig, 1914, vol. 1, p. 211
50. August 31, 1842 to Ernst Raupach in Berlin: Berlin, Staatliches Institut für Musikforschung SPK
51. Fall 1842 to Heinrich Heine in Paris: original unknown; photographic copy: Weimar, Nationale Forschungs- und Gedenkstätten der klassischen Literatur
52. December 1842 to Heinrich Joseph Baermann in Munich: Berlin

(DDR) Deutsche Staatsbibliothek, Music Division
53. April 29, 1843 to Prince Wilhelm zu Sayn und Wittgenstein in Berlin: Berlin (DDR) Deutsche Staatsbibliothek, Music Division (draft)
54. November 12, 1843 to Eugène Scribe in Paris: Berlin, Staatsbibliothek SPK
55. December 5, 1843 to Jean Auguste Ingres in Paris: original in anonymous private collection; sold spring 1985 at auction by Erasmus-Haus, Basel, catalogue 831*
56. April 19, 1844 to Heinrich Börnstein in Paris: original unknown; draft in Minna Meyerbeer's hand: Berlin (DDR), Deutsche Staatsbibliothek, Music Division
57. December 21, 1844 to Friedrich Wilhelm IV of Prussia: MA
58. February 5, 1845 to Friedrich Wilhelm IV of Prussia: Merseburg (DDR), Deutsches Zentralarchiv, Königliche Haussachen
59. February 20, 1845 to Louis Spohr in Kassel: Berlin (DDR), Deutsche Staatsbibliothek, Music Divsion
60. February 28, 1845 to Jenny Lind in Berlin: anonymous private owner; sold at auction by Ingo Nebehey, Vienna*
61. August 20, 1845 to Princess Augusta of Prussia in Berlin: original unknown; draft: Berlin (DDR), Deutsche Staatsbibliothek, Music Division*
62. August 31, 1845 to Heinrich Heine in Paris: Düsseldorf, Heinrich Heine-Institut
63. April 21, 1846 to Eugène Scribe in Paris: BN*
64. June 14, 1846 to Carl Heine in Hamburg: Düsseldorf, Heinrich Heine-Institut, Sammlung Strauss
65. September 19, 1846 to Louis Gouin in Paris: MA*
66. November 13, 1846 to Louis Brandus in Paris: BN*
67. November 23, 1846 to Alexander von Humboldt in Berlin: Berlin (DDR), Deutsche Staatsbibliothek, Music Division (draft)*
68. February 5, 1847 to Amalia Beer in Berlin: MA*
69. March 28, 1847 to Amalia Beer in Berlin: MA*
70. July 24, 1847 to Jenny Lind in London: Berlin (DDR) Deutsche Staatsbibliothek, Music Division (draft)*
71. September 25, 1847 to Franz Grillparzer in Berlin: Vienna, Stadtbibliothek*
72. August 11, 1848 to Louis Gouin in Paris: MA*
73. October 10, 1848 to Amalia Beer in Berlin: MA*
74. February 6, 1849 to Amalia Beer in Berlin: MA*
75. April 14, 1849 to Narcisse Girard in Paris: original unknown: printed in Revue et gazette musicale de Paris, June 29, 1849, p. 131*
76. April 16, 1849 to Amalia Beer in Berlin: MA*
77. May 4, 1849 to Minna Meyerbeer in Berlin: MA*
78. February 6, 1850 to Amalia Beer in Berlin: MA*
79. March 28, 1850 to Karl Kaskel in Dresden: Washington, Library of Congress*
80. October 10, 1850 to Amalia Beer in Berlin: MA*
81. May 27, 1851 to Cornelie Meyerbeer in Bad Ischl: MA*

82. June 16, 1851 to Adolphe Sax in Paris: MA*
83. October 27, 1851 to Eugène Scribe in Paris: MA*
84. November 25, 1851 to Herrmann Sillem & Co. in London: original unknown; sold at auction by Hans Schneider, Tutzing, catalogue 192, no. 105*
85. January 30, 1852 to Louis Gouin in Paris: MA*
86. February 8, 1852 to Franz Liszt in Weimar: Weimar (DDR) Nationale Forschungs- und Gedenkstätten
87. May 30, 1852 to Louis Gouin in Paris: MA*
88. March 24, 1853 to Louis Gouin in Paris: MA*
89. April 23, 1853 to Louis Gouin in Paris: MA*
90. May 29, 1853 to Dr. Joseph Bacher in Vienna: MA*
91. July 3, 1853 to Princess Anna of Hesse in Berlin: MA*
92. February 9, 1854 to Louis Véron in Paris: original unknown; printed in Louis Véron, *Mémoires d'un Bourgeois de Paris*, Paris, 1856, vol. 3, p. 150 ff
93. July 18, 1854 to Louis Brandus in Paris: BN*
94. December 19, 1854 to Rosine Stoltz in Paris: MA*
95. December 22, 1854 to Bonard in London: MA*
96. May 21, 1855 to Pietro Romani in Florence: original sold in 1977 at auction by R. Macnutt, Ltd, London; now in private collection of Max Reis, Zürich*
97. January 5, 1856 to Baron Franz von Dingelstedt in Munich: MA*
98. January 6, 1856 to Aloys Ander in Vienna: MA*
99. April 25, 1856 to Giovanni Velluti in Venice: Padua, Museo civivo*
100. March 29, 1857 to Louis Brandus in Paris: BN*
101. April 30, 1857 to Louis Brandus in Paris: BN*
102. December 13, 1857 to Louis Brandus in Paris: BN*
103. April 5, 1859 to Minna Meyerbeer in Berlin: MA*
104. February 4, 1860 to Franz Liszt in Weimar: Weimar (DDR), Nationale Forschungs- und Gedenkstätten der klassischen Literatur*
105. June 5, 1860 to Princess Augusta of Prussia in Berlin: original unknown; sold at auction by Stargardt Auctioneers (catalogue 699), June, 1972*
106. June 28, 1860 to Baron Franz von Dingelstedt in Weimar: MA*
107. January 28, 1861 to Henri Blaze de Bury in Paris: MA*
108. April 30, 1861 to Baron Friedrich von Flotow in Schwerin: MA*
109. September 29, 1861 to Louis Brandus in Paris: MA*
110. November 5, 1862 to Carl Altmüller in Vienna: MA*
111. June 12, 1863 to Louis Brandus in Paris: BN*
112. August 3, 1863 to Louis Brandus in Paris: BN*
113. December 8, 1862 Daily Prayer: MA
114. December 30, 1863 to Karl Kaskel in Dresden: Washington, Library of Congress*
115. March 8, 1864 to Caecilie Meyerbeer in Wiesbaden: Reinbek, private collection H. Becker*
116. March 15, 1864 to Gioacchino Rossini in Paris: original unknown; printed in G. Radiciotti, *G. Rossini*, Tivoli, 1929, vol. 2, p. 444

List of Works

1. Operas

Jephtas Gelübde, opera in three acts, libretto by A. Schreiber (December 23, 1812, Munich Court Opera).

Wirth und Gast, or, *Aus Scherz Ernst,* comedy in two acts, libretto by J. G. Wohlbrück (January sixth, 1813, Stuttgart Court Theater).

Romilda e Costanza, melodramma semiserio in two acts, libretto by Gaetano Rossi (July 19, 1817, Padua, Teatro Nuovo).

Semiramide riconosciuta, dramma per musica in two acts, libretto by Gaetano Rossi, based on Metastasio (March 1819, Turin, Teatro Reggio).

Emma di Resburgo [Emma di Leicester], melodramma eroico in two acts, libretto by Gaetano Rossi (June 26, 1819, Venice, Teatro S. Benedetto).

Margherita d'Anjou, opera semiseria in two acts, libretto by Felice Romani based on work by Guilbert de Pixérécourt (November 14, 1820, Milan, La Scala). Revision of Thomas de Sauvage (March 11, 1826, Paris Théâtre Odéon).

L'Esule di Granata, opera seria in two acts, libretto by Felice Romani (March 12, 1822, Milan, La Scala).

Il Crociato in Egitto, Opera seria in two acts, libretto by Gaetano Rossi (March seventh, 1824, Venice, La Fenice), Revision for Paris (September 25, 1825, Paris, Théâtre Italien).

Robert le Diable, opera in five acts, libretto by Eugène Scribe and Germain Delavigne (Novembe 21, 1831, Paris, Opéra).

Les Huguenots, opera in five acts, libretto by Eugène Scribe and Emile Deschamps (February 29, 1836, Paris Opéra).

Ein Feldlager in Schlesien, Opera in three acts, libretto by Eugène Scribe and Ludwig Rellstab (December seventh, 1844, Berlin, Royal Opera House). Revised by Charlotte Birch-Pfeiffer and entitled *Vielka* (February 18, 1847, Vienna, Theater an der Wien).

Le Prophète, opera in five acts, libretto by Eugène Scribe (16 April 1849, Paris, Opéra).

L'Étoile du Nord, opéra comique in three acts, libretto by Eugène Scribe based on his ballet *La Cantinière* (February 16, 1854, Paris, Opéra comique).

Le Pardon de Ploërmel (also under the titles *Die Goldsucher; Die Wallfahrt nach Ploërmel; Dinorah*), opéra comique in three acts, libretto by Jules Barbier and Michel Carré (April fourth, 1859, Paris, Opéra comique).

L'Africaine, opera in five acts, libretto by Eugène Scribe, final version by F. J. Fétis (April 28, 1865, Paris Opéra).

2. Opera Fragments and Plans

Abu Hassan, Singspiel in two acts, libretto by F. K. Hiemer?; Plan, Darmstadt, 1810.

Der Admiral oder Der verlorene Prozess, Plan, Darmstadt, 1811.

Le bachelet de Salamanque, sketches, 1815?

L'Almanzore, opera, libretto by Gaetano Rossi, planned for the Teatro
Argentino in Rome, 1821.

Ines de Castro, melodramma tragico, libretto by Gaetano Rossi for Naples,
1825, outline.

Malek Adel, melodramma, libretto by Gaetano Rossi, outline, 1824.

La Nymphe de Danube, Pasticcio, libretto by Thomas de Sauvage, outline,
Paris, 1826–1829.

Le Portefaix, opéra comique, libretto by Eugène Scribe outline, Paris, 1831.

Les Brigands, opera, libretto by Alexandre Dumas, outline, Paris, 1832.

Cing Mars, opera, libretto by H. Saint-Georges and François de Planard,
sketches, Paris, 1837.

Noëma ou le repentir [*L'ange au exil*], opera, libretto by Eugène Scribe and
Henry Vernoy de Saint-Georges, outline, Paris, 1846.

Die Drei Pintos, opera based on sketches by Carl Maria v. Weber. Sketches
and fragments, Berlin—Paris, 1826–1852.

3. Stage Compositions

Der Fischer und das Milchmädchen oder Viel Lärm um einen Kuss [the fisher-
man and the milk maiden, or much ado about a kiss] (Le passage de
la rivière ou la femme jalouse) [the passage of the river, or the
jealous woman], divertissement, libretto by I. E. Lauchery (March
26, 1810, Berlin Court Opera).

Das Brandenburger Tor, [The Brandenburg Gate] lyrical drama, libretto by
E. Veith, Vienna, 1814 (performance not documented).

Gli amori di Teolindu [Teolinda's loves], dramatic cantata, libretto by
Gaetano Rossi, for solo soprano, solo clarinet, chorus and orchestra
(Verona, March 18, 1816).

Das Hoffest von Ferrara, [The Court Festival of Ferrara] masque, libretto by
Ernst Raupach based on Tasso (February 28, 1843, Berlin, Palace).

Struensee, play with music, tragedy by Michael Beer (September 19, 1846,
Berlin, Schauspielhaus).

La Jeunesse de Goethe [L'Etudiant de Strassbourg], play with music, text by
Henri Blaze de Bury, Paris, 1860–1862 (performance not
documented).

4. Instrumental Music

Many unpublished youth works, piano sonatas, fantasies, variations,
piano concertos.

Torch Dance in B-flat major for large orchestra, for the marriage of
Princess Marie and the Crown Prince of Bavaria (Berlin, 1842).

Torch Dance in E-flat major for large orchestra, for the marriage of
Princess Charlotte and the heir to the throne of Saxony-Meiningen
(Berlin, 1850).

Torch Dance in C minor for large orchestra, for the marriage of Princess Anna and Prince Friedrich of Hessen (Berlin, 1853).

Torch Dance (with "God save the King") in C major for large orchestra, for the arrival of the recently married Crown Prince Friedrich Wilhelm and Princess Victoria of England (Berlin, 1858).

Festival March for large orchestra, for the celebration of Schiller's 100th birthday (Berlin 1859).

Coronation March for two orchestras, for the coronation of Wilhelm I of Prussia (Königsberg, during the coronation procession to the church, 1861).

Festival Overture in March Style, for the London World Exposition (London, 1862).

5. Compositions for Special Occasions

Several early cantatas for festivities in the Meyerbeer parents' home were never published.

Bayerischer Schützenmarsch [Bavarian Riflemen's march], cantata for four solo voices and wind ensemble, text by King Ludwig I of Bavaria (Munich, 1829).

Festival song on occasion of the erection of the Gutenberg monument in Mainz, for solo voices and men's chorus (Mainz, 1834).

Friendship, four-part song for men's voices, text by Emile Deschamps (L'Amitié, Gloire, Gloire) for the founding of the Berlin Singakademie (Berlin, 1842).

To the Fatherland ("A la Patrie") for four-part men's chorus, two tenors and two basses (Berlin, 1842).

The Joyous Hunters ("Les Joyeux Chasseurs") for men's chorus (Berlin).

A Song for the Master of German Song, for men's chorus, for the reception for Louis Spohr (Berlin, 1845).

The Wanderer and the Spirits at Beethoven's Grave, "Was schwebet durch die Räume" [What floats through the Heavens], for bass solo and three sopranos, text by Ferdinand Braun, French text by M. Bourges (Vienna, 1845).

Festival hymn, "Du, Du, der über Raum und Zeit" [Thou, Thou throughout Time and Space] for solo voices and a cappella chorus, text by Karl Winkler, for the 25th wedding anniversary of Their Majesties the King and Queen of Prussia (November 29, 1848, Berlin).

Friedericus Magnus, "Für solchen König Blut und Leben" [Blood and Life for such a King], song for chorus and orchestra, text by Ludwig Rellstab, inserted into the opera *Ein Feldlager in Schlesien* on the day of the unveiling of the monument to Frederick the Great by Rauch (Berlin, May 31, 1851).

Ode to Rauch "Steht auf und empfangt mit Feiergesang" [Stand up and Receive with Festive Song] for solo voices, chorus and orchestra, text by E. Kopisch, for the academy celebration for Rauch (June ninth, 1851, Berlin), a new text written later by L. Rellstab: "Opferhymne an den Zeus" [Hymn of Sacrifice to Zeus].

"Maria und ihr Genius" [Maria and Her Guardian Spirit], "Erschienen ist der freudenreiche Tag" [The Joyous Day has Come], cantata for soprano, tenor, mixed chorus and orchestra, text by Goldtammer, for the celebration of the silver wedding anniversary of Prince Carl (May 26, 1852, Berlin-Glienicke).

Bridal Procession from the Homeland, song for eight-part mixed chorus, text by Ludwig Rellstab, French text "Adieux aux jeunes mariés" [Farewell to the Young Newlyweds] by Émile Deschamps for marriage of Princess Luise of Prussia to the reigning Prince of Baden (Berlin, July 1856).

Nice à Stephanie, cantata for solo soprano and chorus, text by Pillet, for the birthday of Archduchess Stephanie of Baden (December 26, 1857, Nice).

Festival cantata, "Wohl bist du uns geboren, gestorben bist du nicht" [You Were Born unto Us, you have never died], for solo voices, mixed chorus and orchestra, for the 100th birthday of Friedrich Schiller (November 10, 1859, Paris).

Song of the Union [Bundeslied], based on "God save the King," French text "Invocation à la terre natale" [Invocation to the native land], for men's chorus, piano ad lib.

Festive hymn, cantata of homage for six solo voices, chorus and orchestra, text by Dr. Köster (October 24, 1861, Berlin).

Das Lied vom blinden Hessen (The Song of the Blind Hessian), "Ich weiss ein theuerwerthes Land" (I know of a Precious Land), for tenor solo and four-part male chorus, text by Carl Altmüller, dedicated to the Hessian Male Choral Society, French text "Le Chant des Exilés", text by Duesberg (Berlin, July 1862).

6. Sacred Music

98th Psalm, for mixed chorus a cappella (March 17, 1811, Berlin), unpublished.

Gott und die Natur [God and Nature], oratorio for solo voices and chorus, text by Aloys Schreiber (May eighth, 1811, Berlin), unpublished. Includes *Chor der Elemente* and *Choral No. 10* mentioned in letter 2.

Gott ist mein Hirt [The Lord is My Shepherd], psalm for solo voices and double chorus (1813, Berlin), unpublished.

Hallelujah, small cantata for four mixed voices, organ ad lib. (1815), unpublished.

An Gott [To God], hymn for four mixed voices, piano ad lib., text by Friedrich Wilhelm Gubitz (1817).

Prière d'enfants [Children's Prayer] "Le souverain maître" [The Almighty Lord] for three women's voices (supplement no. six to the Allgemeine Musikalische Zeitung, 1839).

Two religious poems, "Gloria in der Höhe" [Glory to the Highest]; "Hallelujah, der Herr ist da" [Hallelujah, the Lord is Here], for two sopranos and alto, organ ad lib., text by J. Neuss (Mainz, 1853).

The 91st Psalm. Trost in Sterbensgefahr [Comfort in the Face of Death], for solo voices and eight-part chorus (Berlin, 1853).

Pater noster, motet for mixed four-part chorus a cappella (November 15, 1857, Berlin).

Penitential hymn "Qui sequitur me" for solo bass and mixed chorus, text by Corneille and Ludwig Rellstab (Berlin, 1859).

Seven Spiritual Songs, "Morgenlied" [Morning Song], "Dem Dreieinigen" [To the Holy Trinity]; "Vorbereitung zum Gottesdienst" [Preparation for the Service]; "Danklied" [Song of Thanks]; "Nach dem Abendmahl" [After the Lord's Supper]; "Wach auf mein Herz" [Awake, My Heart]; "Liebster Jesu wir sind hier" [Dearest Jesus, We are Here], for four voices with piano accompaniment ad lib.; text by Friedrich Gottlieb Klopstock (1841, Berlin and Paris).

Prière du Matin, [morning prayer], for eight-part double chorus with piano accompaniment ad lib. (1864, Paris).

7. Mélodies, Songs, Romances, Elegies, Canzonets

Many songs were published individually, in journals or in collections. Publication: 40 mélodies, Paris 1850, M. Schlesinger.

Bibliography

(Selection) Arranged chronologically.

Meyerbeer, Giacomo: Briefwechsel und Tagebücher, edited by Heinz and Gudrun Becker. I: Berlin, 1960; II: Berlin, 1970; III: Berlin, 1975; IV: Berlin, 1985.

Blaze de Bury, Henry: Meyerbeer Paris, 1865.
Mendel, Hermann: Giacomo Meyerbeer, sein Leben und seine Werke Berlin, 1869.
Schucht, Jean F.: Meyerbeers Leben und Bildungsgang . . . Leipzig, 1869.
Body, Albin: Meyerbeer aux eaux de Spa Brussels, 1885.
Destranges, Etienne: L'oeuvre théâtral de Meyerbeer Paris, 1893.
Weber, Johannes: Meyerbeer, Notes et souvenirs d'un de ses Secrétaires, Paris, 1898.
Eymieu, Henry: L'oeuvre de Meyerbeer Paris, 1910.
Curzon, Henri de: Meyerbeer Paris, [n.d.] 1910.
Abert, Hermann: Giacomo Meyerbeer, in: Jahrbuch Peters 1918, p. 37–52.
Dauriac, Lionel: Meyerbeer Paris, 3d ed. 1930.
Kapp, Julius: Giacomo Meyerbeer, Berlin, 1932.
Crosten, William L.: French Grand Opera, an Art and a Business, New York, 1948, p. 106–128.
Becker, Heinz: Meyerbeers Ergänzungsarbeit an Webers nachgelassener Oper "Die Drei Pintos", in: Die Musikforschung, 1954, p. 300–312.
Noske, Frits: La mélodie française de Berlioz à Duparc, Amsterdam-Paris, 1954, Presses universitaires de France.
Heinz Becker: Meyerbeers Beziehungen zu Louis Spohr, in: Musikforschung, X, 1957, pg. 479–486.
Cooper, Martin: Giacomo Meyerbeer, in: Fanfare for Ernest Newman, London, 1958, p. 38–57.
Becker, Heinz: Der Fall Heine—Meyerbeer, Berlin, 1958.
_____ , Giacomo Meyerbeer, in: Year Book IX of the Leo Baeck Institute, London, 1964, p. 178–201.
Frederichs, Henning: Das Rezitativ in den "Hugenotten" G. Meyerbeers, in: Beiträge zur Geschichte der Oper, edited by H. Becker, Regensburg, 1969, p. 55–76.
Becker, Heinz: Meyerbeers Mitarbeit an den Libretti seiner Opern, in: Kongress-Bericht Bonn, 1970, p. 155–160.
Bose, Fritz, ed.: Meyerbeer. Sizilianische Volkslieder, Berlin, 1970.
Frese, Christhard: Dramaturgie der grossen Opern Giacomo Meyerbeers, Berlin, 1970.
Gibson, Robert Wayne: Le Prophète. A Study in Operatic Style. Diss., Northwestern University, 1972.

Thomson, Joan Lewis: Meyerbeer and his contemporains, Diss., Columbia University, 1972.

Böhmel, Bernd: Thesen zu Meyerbeer, in: Meyerbeer, *Les Huguenots*, Materialien zum Werk, Edition Peters, Leipzig, 1974, p. 15ff.

Gülke, Peter: Versuch mit Meyerbeer, ibid., p. 17ff.

Rienäcker, Gerd: Gedanken zum Opernschaffen von Giacomo Meyerbeer, ibid., p. 20ff.

Döhring, Sieghart: Les oeuvres tardives de Meyerbeer in: Schweizerische Musikzeitung, 1975, p. 57–65.

Becker, Heinz, ed.: Die "Couleur locale" in der Oper des 19. Jahrhunderts, Regensburg, 1976.

Cohen, H. Robert: On the Reconstruction of the visual elements of French Grand Opera: Unexplored sources in Parisian collections, in: Kongressbericht der IGfMw., Berkeley, 1977, p. 463–481.

Döhring, Sieghart: Multimediale Tendenzen in der französischen Oper des 19. Jahrhunderts, in: Kongressbericht der IGfMw., Berkeley 1977, p. 497–500.

Love, Harold: Lyster's 1862 "Huguenots": a milestone of musical theatre in Australia, in: Studies in music 11, 1977, p. 49–59.

Roberts, John Howell: The Genesis of Meyerbeer's "L'Africaine", Diss., University of California, Berkeley, 1977.

Bloom, Peter Anthony: Friends and admirers: Meyerbeer and Fétis, in: Revue Belge de Musicologie 32/33, 1978/79, p. 174–187.

Dahlhaus, Carl: Motive der Meyerbeerkritik, in: Jahrbuch des Staatlichen Instituts für Musikforschung 1978, Berlin, 1979, p. 35–42.

Pendle, Karin: Eugène Scribe and French Opera of the 19th Century, Ann Arbor, 1979.

Becker, Heinz: ". . . der Marcel von Meyerbeer", in: Jahrbuch des Staatlichen Instituts für Musikforschung 1979, Berlin, 1980, p. 79–100.

————, Meyerbeer und seine Vaterstadt Berlin, in: Studien zur Musikgeschichte Berlins im frühen 19. Jahrhundert, ed. by Carl Dahlhaus, Regensburg, 1980, p. 429–450.

Chabot, C.: Ballet in the operas of Eugène Scribe: an apology for the presence of dance in opera, in: Studies in music from the University of Western Ontario 5, 1980, p. 7–14.

Dahlhaus, Carl: Musikalischer Realismus, München, 1980 (p. 105ff. with information on *Le Prophète*).

Join-Dieterle, C.: *Robert le Diable*, Le premier opéra romantique, in: Romantisme, 1980, no. 28–29, p. 147–166.

Becker, Heinz: Giacomo Meyerbeer in Selbstzeugnissen und Bilddokumenten, Reinbek 1980.

Walsh, T. J.: Second Empire Opera, The Théâtre lyrique, Paris 1851–1870, London/New York 1981.

Budden, Julian: Verdi and Meyerbeer in relation to "Les Vêpres Siciliennes", in: Studi Verdiani 1, 1982, p. 11–20.

Döhring, Sieghart: Die Autographen der vier Hauptopern Meyerbeers: Ein erster Quellenbericht, in: Archiv für Musikforschung, 1982, p. 32–63.

_____, Réminiscences. Liszts Konzeption der Klavierparaphrase, in: Festschrift Heinz Becker, Laaber, 1982, p. 131–151.

Schneider, Herbert: Die Bearbeitung des *Pardon de Ploërmel* von G. Meyerbeer im Jahre der Uraufführung, in: Festschrift Heinz Becker, Laaber, 1982, p. 152–161.

Dahlhaus, Carl: Französische Musik und Musik in Paris in: lendemains 31/32 VIII, 1983, p. 5–10

Döhring, Sieghart: Giacomo Meyerbeer: Grand Opéra als Ideendrama: ibid., p. 11–22.

Rienäcker, Gerd: Finali in Opern von E. T. A. Hoffmann, Louis Spohr, Heinrich Marschner und Carl Maria von Weber—Gedanken zur Theorie und Geschichte des Opernfinales. Berlin, 1984 (dissertation).

Becker, Heinz: Setkáni v Boulogne-sur-mer: Wagner a Meyerbeer (encounter in Boulogne-sur-mer: Wagner and Meyerbeer) in: Hudebni veda XXI, 1984, p. 293–302.

Ottlová, Marta and Posbísil, Milan: Smetanüv Meyerbeer (Smetana's Meyerbeer), ibid, p. 355–364.

Ludvová, Jitka: Meyerbeer na prazském nemeckém jevisti 1815–1935 (Meyerbeer on the German stage in Prague, 1815–1935), ibid., p. 365–374.

Srba, Borivoj: Scénické výpravy Meyerbeerových oper da ceském jevisti (the sets for Meyerbeer operas at the Czech Theater), ibid., p. 376–385.

Becker, Heinz: Meyerbeers Wiener Reisetagebuch 1813 in: Festschrift für Rudolf Elvers zum 60. Geburtstag, Tutzing 1985, p. 29–47.

Dahlhaus, Carl: Wagner, Meyerbeer und der Fortschritt. Zur Opernästhetik des Vormärz: ibid., p. 103–116.

Becker, Heinz: Zwischen Oper und Drama. Zu Meyerbeers Konzeption der dramatischen Szene in: Wagner Literatur und Wagnerforschung, Bericht über das Wagner-Symposium München 1983, edited by Carl Dahlhaus and Egon Voss, Mainz, 1985, p. 86–94.

Döhring, Sieghart: Meyerbeers Konzeption der historischen Oper und Wagners Musikdrama, ibid., p. 95–100.

Hirsbrunner, Theo: Ernest Reyer, ein Komponist zwischen Meyerbeer und Wagner, ibid., p. 109–113.

Günther, Ursula: Wagnerismen in Verdis *Don Carlos* von 1867: ibid., p. 101–108.

Walter, Michael: Zwei Hugenotten-Bearbeitungen des 19. Jahrhunderts, in: Jahrbuch für Opernforschung, 1985, p. 122–143.

Miller, Norbert: Grosse Oper als Historiengemälde. Überlegungen zur Zusammenarbeit von Eugène Scribe und Giacomo Meyerbeer [exemplified by the first act of *Les Huguenots*], in: Oper und Opertexte, edited by Jens Malte Fischer, Heidelberg, 1985, p. 45–79.

Becker, Heinz: Eine "Undine"—Oper Meyerbeers für Paris, in: Festschrift Martin Ruhnke, Neuhausen-Stuttgart, 1986, p. 31–44.

Schläder, Jürgen: Das Opernduett, Ein Szenentypus des 19. Jh. und seine Vorgeschichte. Bochum, 1986 (in press).

Walter, Michael: Hugenotten Studien (diss., Mainz, 1985) Frankfurt, 1987 (Hochschulschriften Reihe 36—Musikwissenschaft, vol. 24).

Everett, Andrew: "Bewitched in a magic garden". Meyerbeer in Italy, in: The Donizetti Society Journal 6, Oxford 1988, p. 163–192.

Weinland, Helmuth: Wagner und Meyerbeer in: Musik-Konzepte 59, p. 31–72 (1988).

Becker, Heinz: Habent sua fata documenta (Zum Erwerb des Meyerbeer-Archivs) in: Jahrbuch Stiftung Preussischer Kulturbesitz, vol. 24, 1987 Berlin, 1988.

New Editions

G. Meyerbeer, Lieder, volume I, edited by Reiner Zimmermann, Leipzig, 1982 (VEB Edition Peters No. 9783a).

G. Meyerbeer, *Les Huguenots*, vocal score edited by Reiner Zimmermann. Original version. German translation Bernd Böhmel. Version produced in Leipzig by Bernd Böhmel, Joachim Herz, Hans-Jörgen Leipold and Eginhard Rölig, Leipzig, 1975.

G. Meyerbeer, *Les Huguenots*, libretto. Translation by Bernd Böhmel, Leipzig, 1979 (VEB Edition Peters No. 10015).

Reprints

Early Romantic Opera (Series)
New York and London, Garland:
no. 18 *Il Crociato in Egitto* (based on a contemporary manuscript)
no. 19 *Roberto le Diable* (facsimile of the orchestral score)
no. 20 *Les Huguenots* (dto.)
no. 21 *Le Prophète* (dto.)
no. 22 *L'Etoile du Nord* (dto.)
no. 23 *Le Pardon de Ploërmel* (dto.)
no. 24 *L'Africaine* (dto.)

Recordings

Il Crociato in Egitto BJRS 128 (3).

Robert il Diavolo (Scotto, Malagu, Merighi, Christoff) Sansogno MRF 20 (3).

Les Huguenots (Sutherland, Arroyo, Vrenios, Ghiuselev) Decca 460 (4).

Le Prophète (Horne, Scotto, McCracken, Hines) CBS 79 400.

Dinorah (Cook, du Plessis, Oliver) Opera Rara OR 5.

Lieder—Mélodies (D. Fischer-Dieskau, K. Engel) Archiv 2533 295.

"Gli amori di Teolinda" (Julia Varady, Jörg Fadle), Conductor Gerd Albrecht, Orfeo S054831 A.

Coronation March for two orchestras (1861) Conductor Caspar Richter, Capriccio CD 10186.

Index of Persons

tion, he played a major role in the effort to emancipate the Jews in Prussia. 9, 30, 32, 41

Beer, Julius, son of Wilhelm Beer. 116

Beer, Michael, 1800–1833, Meyerbeer's youngest brother, became well known as a writer. In his major work *Der Paria* (1828), he called attention to the problems of his fellow Jewish citizens by using the example of a Paria in India. 45, 51f, 57, 108, 109, 115

Beer, Wilhelm, 1797–1850, brother, banker, business official in Berlin and representative in the German national assembly (Frankfurt, 1848), amateur astronomer who, with Mädler, published the first lunar map. 15, 25, 33, 57, 60, 70, 103, 106, 111, 115, 116, 120, 126, 127, 128, 129, 131, 175

Beethoven, Ludwig van, 1770–1827, composer, met Meyerbeer in 1815 and knew him only as one of the musicians in a performance of his "Schlacht von Vitforia". 14, 30

Belletti, male singer. 155

Bellini, Vincenzo, 1801–1835, one of Italy's most distinguished opera composers whose opera *Norma* greatly influenced Meyerbeer. 59

Benedict, Julius, Sir, 1804–1885, composer and conductor, conductor at Covent Garden in London in 1835. 172

Berlioz, Hector, 1803–1869, composer and music critic for several Parisian newspapers. Like Meyerbeer, with whom he enjoyed a friendly relationship of mutual respect, he placed special emphasis in his works on new and colorful instrumentation.71, 91, 92, 100, 121, 140

Bertin, Armand, 1801–1854, journalist and owner of the "Journal des Débats" which was very renowned in Paris; was one of Meyerbeer's major supporters in Paris. 59, 60

Betourné, writer. 52

Bignardi, tenor. 172

Blahetka. 85

Blaze de Bury, Ange Henry, 1813–1888, music essayist, writer for the "Revue des Deux Mondes" and "Le Menestrel". 76, 167, 169, 170, 174, 176

Bluethendorn, Dr. 85

Blume, Heinrich, 1788–1856, singer and actor at the royal theater in Berlin. In 1821 he created the role of Caspar in Weber's "Freischütz".55

Börnstein, Heinrich, 1805–1892, journalist. In 1844 he founded "Vorwärts, Journal allemand de Paris" and wrote reports for the "Frankfurter Conversationsblatt" and the "Allgemeine Theaterzeitung" in Vienna as well as for other papers. 98

Boieldieu, François Adrien, 1775–1834, composer; achieved lasting recognition with his opéra comique *La dame blanche*. 57

Bonard, French lawyer in London. 152

Borghi-Mamo, Adelaide, 1826–1901, one of the greatest altos of her time, first sang at the Italian opera house (1854), then achieved great success at the Opéra in Paris (1856). 160

Brandus, Gemmy, 1823–1873, music publisher and dealer in Paris. 110, 149, 152

Brandus, Louis (Ludwig), 1816–1887, music publisher and dealer in Paris. 110, 158, 159, 161, 170, 172, 173

Brühl, Karl, Count von, 1772–1837; 1815–1828 general director of the theaters in Berlin. 39f

Bully, Eugène Auguste Roger de, 1806–1866, novelist and dramatist. 76

Burguis, secretary to Meyerbeer's mother, Amalia Beer. 116, 120

Busch, Wilhelm, 1832–1908, cartoonist, painter, and writer; published his first illustrated stories in the "Fliegende Blaetter" in 1859. 162, 163

C

Cabel, Marie Josephe, née Dreulette; born 1827, studied voice at the Paris Conservatoire on Meyerbeer's advice. The dizzying virtuosity of the title role in Meyerbeer's opera *Dinorah* (1859), which he wrote for her, provides evidence of this coloratura soprano's extraordinary abilities. 149, 150, 159, 160

Calzados. 160

Campe, Julius, 1792–1867, publisher in Hamburg who distinguished himself by publishing the works of Heine and others. 104

Castellan, Jeanne Anais, born 1819, premier dramatic singer of the Italian opera in Paris since 1848. 124

Castelli, Ignaz Franz, 1781–1862, court dramatist of the Kärtnertor Theater in Vienna, librettist, translator of foreign opera texts, also occasional editor of the "Allgemeiner musikalischer Anzeiger". 23, 85

Cerf, Carl Friedrich (Hirsch), 1782–1845, originally a horse dealer, then Kommissionsrat and proprietor of the Königstädter Theater in Berlin. 57

Chollet, Jean Baptiste Marie, 1798–1892, distinguished singer at the Paris Opéra comique for whom Hérold composed the title role of his *Zampa*. 64

Chopin, Frédéric François, 1810–1849, composer; lived in Paris after 1830. 139

Chorlei = Chorley, Henry Fothergill, 1808–1872, music critic and essayist. 150

Cicéri, Pierre Luc Charles, 1782–1868, set designer for several Parisian theaters. 48

Clapisson, Antonin Louis, 1808–1866, composer and violinist at the Paris Opéra. 120

Clementi, Muzio, 1752–1832, piano virtuoso and composer, lived in England after 1766 and undertook numerous concert tours on the continent. 9

Corneille, Pierre, 1606–1684, French playwright. 171

Cramer, Johann Baptist, 1771–1858, piano virtuoso and composer, music publisher, spent most of his life in London, lived in Paris 1832–1845. 33

Crémieux, Isaac Adolphe, 1796–1880, lawyer in Paris, member of the provisional French government in 1848, 1870/71 Minister of Justice. 76

Crivelli, Gaetano, 1774–1836, tenor, 1811–1817 member of the Italian opera in Paris. 35ff

Czerny, Carl, 1791–1857, piano virtuoso and composer, lived in Vienna and was a very sought after piano teacher. His etudes and studies are still part of the instructional literature. 139

D

Dabadie, Henry Bernard, 1797–1853, baritone at the Paris Opéra. 148

Damoreau–Cinti, Laure Cynthie, née Montalant, 1801–1863, singer, made her debut at the Paris Opéra in 1825. Meyerbeer composed the role of Isabelle in *Robert le Diable* for her. 54

Degas, Edgar, 1834–1917, painter, one of the major figures in French impressionism. 47

Dehn, Siegfried Wilhelm, 1799–1858, librarian of the Royal Library in Berlin, music theorist. 133

Delavigne, Germain, 1790–1868, writer and librettist in Paris, collaborated with Scribe on the librettos for Meyerbeer's *Robert le Diable* and *Les Huguenots*. 106

Deligny. 142, 143

Demerie (Glossop-Demerie), female singer. 54

Dessauer, "Der alte Dessauer" *See:* Leopold I.

Diabelli, Anton, 1781–1858, composer, primarily known as a publisher of works by Franz Schubert and others. Beethoven composed variations on a waltz by this Viennese publisher. 139

Dingelstedt, Franz, 1814–1881, raised to the status of a Baron in 1867, writer and dramatist, director of the Court and National Theater in Munich, general manager in Weimar in 1857, then became director of the Vienna Court Opera and the Hofburg Theater. 155, 166, 169

Donizetti, Gaetano Domenico Maria, 1797–1848, composed approx. 70 operas. His masterpiece, *Lucia di Lammermoor* (1835) is especially popular today in opera houses the world over. 87, 97, 172

Doris. *See* Beer, Doris

Duisberg, Julius, historian and journalist in Paris. 158, 159, 160, 161

Dumas, Alexandre (senior), 1802–1870, dramatist and novelist who helped with the breakthrough of romantic drama in France. Today he is known primarily for his adventure novels such as *The Three Musketeers* and *The Count of Monte Christo*. 17, 49, 52f, 111

Duponchel, Charles, 1795–1868, architect and painter, was first a stage director and then at times director of the Paris Opéra. 56, 68, 73, 74, 118, 119, 120

Duprez, Gilbert Louis, 1806–1896, premier tenor at the Paris Opéra, professor of voice at the Paris Conservatoire and editor of a very important voice method. 61, 64

Dusch, Alexander von, 1789–1876, state minister, wrote many treatises on music for such publications as the "Allgemeine musikalische Zeitung" in Leipzig and the "Morgenblatt für gebildete Stände". 22, 23, 28

E

Eberty, Mathilde, daughter of Felix Eberty, a cousin of Minna Meyerbeer. 132

Elisabeth Ludovika, Queen of Prussia, 1801–1873, daughter of Maximilian I of Bavaria, married Friedrich Wilhelm IV. 141

Elssler, Fanny, 1810–1884, dancer who gave special preference to the character dance. She went to Berlin in 1832 and later also celebrated triumphs in Paris, London and the United States. 69

Engel, Carl, 1818–1882, German music scholar, moved to London in 1850, did research on the history of musical instruments and the music of Non-European peoples. 172

Engel, David Hermann, 1816–1877, composer, after 1848 cathedral organist and teacher at the cathedral school in Merseburg. 172, 174

Epée, Charles Michel, Abbé de l', 1712–1789, clergyman, founded the first school for the deaf and mute in Paris and developed the finger and sign language; he taught the mute to speak thereby enabling them to perceive and participate in their environment. 115

Ernst August, King of Hannover, 1771–1851. 108

Eugénie Marie de Guzman, 1826–1920, married Napoleon III in 1853. 164

Eunike, Friedrich, 1764–1844, premier tenor of the Royal Theater in Berlin from 1796–1823. 22

F

Falcon, Maria Cornélie, 1812–1897, singer, member of the ensemble of the Paris Opéra 1832–1837. 71, 72, 73, 133

Faubel, Joseph, born 1801, clarinetist in the Munich court orchestra. 42m

Faure, Jean Baptiste, 1830–1914, came to the Opéra Comique in Paris as a baritone in 1852, then went to the Opéra in 1861 where he became very celebrated. 156, 172

Ferriere, Marquis de la. 140

Fétis, François Joseph, 1784–1871, important Belgian music theorist and music critic, founder of the "Revue musicale" in Paris. 45, 74, 181

Flécheux, Louise Marie, 1813–1842, singer at the Paris Opéra. 71

Flotow, Friedrich von, Baron, 1812–1883, lived most of his life as a composer in Paris, was later director of court music for the Grand Duke of Mecklenburg. Of his operas, only *Alessandro Stradella* and *Martha* enjoyed lasting success. 169

Friedrich II, King of Prussia, 1712–1786. In the wars of 1740/41 and 1744/45 he expanded the territory of Prussia. An episode from these campaigns served as the subject of Meyerbeer's festival opera *Ein Feldlager in Schlesien*. 97, 152

Friedrich Wilhelm III, King of Prussia, 1770–1840, married Luise von Mecklenburg-Strelitz who died at an early age. His reign encompassed Napoleon's march into Berlin (1806). Napoleon was responsible for lifting the restrictive laws which applied to Jews and were still in effect at that time. He is remembered for having developed his country culturally by founding the university and reorganizing the Berlin theaters. 9, 39, 41, 43f, 54, 77

Friedrich Wilhelm IV, King of Prussia, 1795–1861, was considered a "romantic ruler," was very receptive to artists and the arts and demonstrated his strong support for Meyerbeer by appointing him general music director and director of court music. 12, 57, 77, 88, 89, 99, 100, 104 112, 119, 126, 137, 141, 165, 173

Friedrich Wilhelm Karl, Prince of the Netherlands, 1797–1881, second son of Wilhelm I of the Netherlands. In 1825 he married Luise, one of the daughters of Friedrich Wilhelm III of Prussia. 141, 165

G

Gänsbacher, Johann Baptist, 1778–1844, studied with Meyerbeer under Abbé Vogler in Darmstadt and was a member of the "Harmonische Verein" (Harmonic Society); later became director of music at St. Stephen's Cathedral in Vienna. 11, 27

Gaichen, probably a governess or companion of Meyerbeer's daughters. 179

Gardoni, Italo, 1821–1882, singer at the Paris Opéra and at the Théâtre italien, also sang later in London, Vienna, Petersburg and Madrid. 105, 106, 130, 156

Gareis, Gottlieb, died 1859, violist,

member of the royal orchestra in Berlin. 94

Gautier, H., lawyer in Paris. 161

Georg. *See* Beer, Georg

Gern, Johann Georg, 1757–1830, singer, bass at the Berlin Court and National Theater. 22

Geymard, male singer. 173

Girard, Narcisse, 1797–1860, professor of violin at the Paris Conservatoire, conductor at the Paris Opéra. 121, 122

Girardin, Émile de, 1806–1881, politician, writer and publisher of the Parisian newspaper "La Presse", married the writer Delphine Gay. 73

Giulini = Giuglini, Antonio, 1833–1865, for but a few years one of the most celebrated tenors, greatly acclaimed at the Scala in Milan as well as in London, Berlin and finally in Vienna. 160

Gluck, Christoph Willibald, 1714–1787. Gluck's operas were very popular in Germany until the middle of the 19th century. His operatic reforms were directed against the formal schematism and pure virtuosity of Italian opera seria. Meyerbeer was particularly influenced by the structure of his recitatives. 95, 99, 137

Goethe, Johann Wolfgang von, 1749–1832. It was Michael Beer, whose "Paria" Goethe had recommended to Eckermann for review, and Goethe's friend Zelter who brought Meyerbeer to Goethe's attention. As a result, Goethe stated in reference to a possible composer for *Faust*: "It would have to be a someone . . . who, like Meyerbeer, has spent a long period of time in Italy, so that his German nature is combined with an Italian perspective . . ." 10, 88, 165, 166, 167

Goldschmidt, Benny, London banker. 120

Gomis, José Melchor, 1791–1836, originally director of military music in Valencia, later composer and voice teacher in Paris and, from time to time, in London, published a very respected vocal method in 1825. 62

Gouin, Louis, 1780–1856, administrative director of the Paris postal service and Meyerbeer's confidant. 63, 64, 65, 83, 109, 110, 119, 120, 133, 136, 138, 140, 142, 144, 150, 151, 159, 162

Gounod, Charles, 1818–1893, composer, director of the Paris Orphéon, 1852–1893. 173

Grillparzer, Franz, 1791–1872, writer (*Die Ahnfrau* 1817, *Sappho* 1818), director of archives in Vienna, retired early from the stage (in 1838) after the failure of his comedy *Weh dem der lügt*. 117, 118

Guerber, Samuel, banker in Florence. 35

Guhr, Karl Wilhelm Ferdinand, 1787–1848, conductor at the Frankfurt opera and director of the Frankfurt museum concerts, composer. 69

Guidi, Giovanni Gualberto, 1817–1883, music publisher in Florence, published the first pocket scores (*Guillaume Tell, Les Huguenots, Robert le Diable*).153

Gye. 160

H

Härtel, Gottfried Christoph, 1763–1827, music publisher—publishing house of Breitkopf & Härtel—publisher of the "Allgemeine musikalische Zeitung". 23, 25

Halévy, Jacques Fromental Elie, 1799–1862, achieved his greatest success in 1835 with his two operas *La Juive* and *Léclair*. He then fell into the shadow of Meyerbeer whose worldwide fame eclipsed his own. 14, 67, 76, 81, 138, 150

Hannover, King of. *See* Ernst August

Hanslick, Eduard, 1825–1904, Dr. of Jurisprudence, music critic in Vienna since 1846, first for the "Wiener Musikzeitung", then the "Wiener Zeitung", the "Presse" and the "Neue Freie Presse", professor at the University of Vienna since 1861 (history of music and esthetics), known primarily for his work "Vom Musikalisch-Schönen, written in 1854. 75

Harlas, Helene, 1785–1818, singer at the Munich Court Opera, companion of Heinrich Baermann. Meyerbeer dedicated the cantata for clarinet, soprano and chorus *Gli amori di Teolinda* (1816) to them. 91

Heine, Carl, 1810–1865, banker in Hamburg, cousin of the writer Heinrich Heine. 104, 105, 107

Heine, Heinrich, 1797–1856, writer. Meyerbeer was a central figure in Heine's featured music articles written in Paris for the "Allgemeine Zeitung" in Augsburg. 11, 17, 37, 45f, 80, 81, 88, 91, 104, 108, 119, 120, 136, 158, 159

Heine, Mathilde Crescence Eugénie, née Mirat, 1815–1883, married Heinrich Heine in 1841. 81, 82, 88, 158, 159, 161

Heine, Salomon, 1767–1844, banker in Hamburg, uncle of the writer. 80, 104, 105

Hell, Theodor. *See* Winkler, Karl

Heller, Stephen, 1813–1888, pianist and composer, protégé of Robert Schumann; after 1838 lived in Paris as a piano teacher. 75

Henning, Karl Wilhelm, 1784–1867, violinist, royal conductor in Berlin. 21, 94

Henri, one of Meyerbeer's servants. 132

Hérold, Louis Joseph Ferdinand, 1791–1833, composer, chorus director at the Opéra comique and the Opéra in Paris, achieved major success with his opera *Zampa* in 1831. 14, 64

Herz, Henri (Heinrich), 1803–1888, piano virtuoso, piano manufacturer in Paris, professor at the Conservatoire. 139

Hesse, Prince of, married to Anna of Prussia. 146

Heugel, Jacques Léopold, 1815–1883, music publisher in Paris. 172

Hiller, Ferdinand, 1811–1885, composer and conductor in Leipzig (Gewand-haus concerts), Dresden, Düsseldorf and Cologne (Gürzenich concerts). 45, 100

Hofmannsthal, Hugo von, 1874–1929, writer. 178

Holbein, Franz Ignaz von, 1779–1855, actor and playwright, was the director of several theaters before becoming the director of the Vienna Hofburg Theater and the Court Opera in 1849. 128, 146

Holding, theatrical agent in Vienna. 156

Holzmiller, Eduard, born approx. 1806, singer at the Berlin Königstädter Theater from 1830–1836, was then employed in Hannover. 57

Horn, Ernst, 1774–1848, professor, health official in Berlin. 56

Hoven. *See* Vesque von Püttlingen

Humann, Adolph, 1794–1853, first bassoonist of the Royal Orchestra in Berlin. 94

Humboldt, Alexander von, Baron, 1769–1859, naturalist. Between 1845–1858, he published his four-volume work entitled *Kosmos* which contained the wealth of knowledge and experiences he gathered on his journeys through-out the world. Humboldt was very close to the Meyerbeer family, especially to the composer's mother. He was always very supportive of Meyerbeer and of the efforts to eman-cipate the Jews in Prussia. 60, 109, 111, 112, 117, 118

I

Iffland, August Wilhelm, 1759–1814, actor and general director of the Royal Theater in Berlin, was also director of the Opera House during the same period. 21

Ingres, Jean Auguste Dominique, 1780–1867, painter. 98

Isabella II, Maria Luise, Queen of Spain, 1830–1904, succeeded her father, Ferdinand VII, to the throne in 1833—albeit initally under guardianship. 131

J

Jaeger, Franz, 1796–1852, tenor at the Königstädter Theater in Berlin. 57

Julliat, writer. 159

Julius. *See* Beer, Julius

K

Kaiser, Georg Felix, 1883–1918, wrote a doctoral thesis on "Beiträge zur Characteristik C. M. v. Webers als Musikschriftsteller" (concerning Carl Maria von Weber's characteristics as a music essayist) and published Weber's collected writings. 24

Kalkbrenner, Friedrich Wilhelm Michael, 1785–1849, piano virtuoso, composer, lived in London 1814–1823, then in Paris and was a part owner of the Pleyel Piano Company. 33, 139

Kandler, Franz Sales, 1792–1831, navy clerk in Venice and Naples, 1815–1828; writer on music. 33, 34

Karl (Charles) IX, King of France, 1550–1574. At the beginning of his reign (1560), he was still under the regency of his mother, Catherine di Medici. Due to her influence thousands of Huguenots in Paris and in the coun-tryside lost their lives during the "blood wedding" or "St. Bartholomew Day's Massacre," on the occasion of the marriage of her daughter Margarete to King Henry of Navarra in 1572. 56

Karl, Prince of Prussia (Friedrich Karl Alexander of Prussia), 1801–1883, third son of Friedrich Wilhelm III. 137, 146

Kaskel, Karl, Baron von, banker in Dresden, probably a grandchild of the banker, wine dealer and Saxon court agent Jakob Kaskel (Jakob Dresden) who died in 1788. 129, 176

Kindermann, August, 1817–1891, began his singing career in Berlin, went to Leipzig in 1839 and to Munich in 1846 where he was very popular. 156

Kinsky, Georg, 1882–1951, musicologist, compiled a catalog of the Heyer collection in Cologne and, in addition to many other musicological works, an index of Beethoven's works (completed by H. Halm). 15

Klengel, August Alexander, 1783–1852, pianist and composer, lived 1815/16 in London, was then royal organist at the Saxon court in Dresden. 33

Korff, Emanuel Karl Heinrich, Baron von, 1826–1903, officer, in later years Major General and frequent guest of the Kaiser, Meyerbeer's son-in-law. 12

Korff, Fritz, Baron von, Meyerbeer's grandson. 175

Kotzebue, August von, 1761–1819, writer, wrote approx. 200 works for the stage. In 1819, he was stabbed to death by Karl Sand for political reasons. 100

Kreutzer, Conradin, 1780–1849, composer and conductor in Stuttgart, Donaueschingen, Vienna, Cologne, and Riga. Of his 30 operas, only *Das Nachtlager in Granada* has remained in the repertory of German opera houses. 84

Kriehuber, Joseph, 1801–1876, important Viennese lithographer and painter. 114

Kühnel, Ambrosius, 1770–1813, publisher, founded the "Bureau de Musique" with Franz Anton Hoffmeister in 1800. After Kühnel's death, the publishing house was taken over by Carl Friedrich Peters in 1813. 19

Kullak, Theodor, 1818–1882, pianist and composer, co-founder of Berlin Conservatory, music instructor of the royal princes and princesses of Prussia. 165

Küstner, Karl Theodor von, 1784–1864, general manager of the Royal Theater in Berlin 1842–1851. 102, 111, 131

L

Labarre, Theodore (=Berry, Théodore François Joseph), 1805–1870, harpist, occasionally also conductor at the Opéra comique in Paris, 1851 director of the private orchestra of Napoleon III. Labarre was also highly esteemed as a composer of romances and ballets. 52

Lachner, Franz, 1803–1890, composer and conductor, first in Vienna and Mannheim, since 1836 court conductor and conductor of the Court Opera in Munich. 102, 156

Ladenberg, Adalbert von, 1798–1855, Prussian statesman, 1848–1850 Minister of Culture. 111

Lafont, Marcelin, 1800–1838, male singer. 60

Lagrun, female singer. 141

Lanner, Joseph, 1801–1843, composed countless Ländler, galops, waltzes ("Die Schönbrunner", "Hofball-Tänze"). Johann Strauss, Sr. also played in his Viennese orchestra before the ensemble was divided. 139

La Rochefoucauld, François, Vicomte Sosthène de, in 1825 he earned the derision and scorn of Paris journalists when he wanted to teach dramatists as well as composers of operas and ballets to incorporate moral and monarchistic beliefs into their works, for which he even promised prizes. The "Académie royale de musique" (the Opéra) was jokingly referred to as the "académie morale de musique". 38

Lassalle, Ferdinand (until 1846 Lassal), 1825–1864, writer. After studying philosophy, philology and archeology, he lived in Paris, Düsseldorf and Berlin. After meeting Karl Marx he became very active in establishing the social democrats in Germany. 107, 108

Laube, Heinrich, 1806–1884, writer and journalist, editor of the widely circulated "Zeitung für die elegante Welt," 1849–1867 artistic director of the Vienna Hofburg Theater, later artistic director of the Vienna Stadttheater. 92, 109

Lauska, Franz, 1764–1825, since 1798 piano teacher at the Prussian court. 9

Lauters, female singer. 160

Lehmann, Heinrich, 1814–1882, painter, later professor at the Ecole des Beaux-Arts in Paris. 98

Lehmann, Rudolf, 1819–1905, painter in Paris. 98

Leo, Auguste, banker in Hamburg, moved to Paris, relative of composer Ferdinand Hiller. 98

Leopold I, King of Belgium, 1790–1865, son of Duke Franz of Sachsen-Koburg. 141

Leopold I., Prince of Anhalt-Dessau, 1676–1747, "the old Dessauer", Field Marshal to Friedrich Wilhelm I, introduced marching in step to the Prussian troops. This was the beginning of the era of military marches. 97

Le Sueur, Jean François, 1760–1837, conductor at Notre Dame in Paris, court conductor to Napoleon, composer. 12

Levasseur, Nicolas Prosper, 1791–1871, one of the most renowned French basses of the 19th century. Meyerbeer composed the role of Bertram in *Robert le Diable* and of Marcel in *Les Huguenots* for him. 34ff, 54, 68, 71, 73, 148

Lichtenthal, Peter (Pietro), 1780–1853, doctor, composer and writer, composed and arranged many ballets for La Scala in Milan, as a correspondent wrote articles for the Leipzig Allgemeine musikalische Zeitung, author of a major music dictionary. 33

Liebmann, Meyer Wulff, 1745–1812, manager of the Prussian postal delivery service, general concessionaire of the Prussian lottery, banker, Meyerbeer's grandfather. 9, 25

Lind Jenny, 1820–1887, soprano, achieved her first major triumph in 1844 in Berlin in Meyerbeer's *Ein Feldlager in Schlesien*. She renounced the stage in 1849, after which she did concert tours exclusively, including concerts in America. 96, 99, 102, 103, 104, 113, 114, 115, 116, 117, 119, 166

Liszt, Franz, 1811–1886, piano virtuoso, composer, since 1842 court conductor in Weimar. 139, 164

Lucca, Pauline, 1841–1908, Viennese singer, 1861–1872 member of the ensemble of the Berlin Court Opera where, in 1865, she was very successful in the role of Selica in Meyerbeer's opera *L'Africaine*. 174

Lucchesini, Marquis. 146

Lüttichau, August, Baron von, 1786–1863, general director of the Dresden Court Theater 1824–1862. 87

Lumley, Benjamin, London theater director. 160

Luther, Martin, 1483–1546, leader of the Reformation. 79, 84

Lutzer, Jenny, 1816–1877, renowned coloratura singer at the Vienna Court Opera, married to Franz Baron von Dingelstedt. 166, 167

M

Mädler, Johann Heinrich von, 1794–1874, astronomer. In 1824 he encouraged Meyerbeer's brother Wilhelm to build an observatory on the roof of the Beer villa in the Tiergarten section of Berlin. Together with Wilhelm Beer, he published a large lunar map. 129

Mahler, Gustav, 1860–1911, composer, in 1877 completed sketches by Carl Maria v. Weber for the opera *Die Drei Pintos*. The work, however, was unsuccessful. 75

Malibran, Maria Felicità, née Garcia, 1808–1836, singer, sister of Viardot-Garcia. After her debut in London in 1825, the alto was engaged by the Paris Opéra in 1827. 61

Maria Anna, Empress of Austria, married to Ferdinand I of Austria. 84

Marot, Clement, 1496–1544, French writer, in later years was persecuted as a Huguenot. In 1541 and 1543 he published "The Psalter of the Huguenots". 56

Marschner, Heinrich August, 1795–1861, court conductor in Hannover. He and C. M. v. Weber were the major composers of German romantic opera. 100

Marx, conductor. 151

Marx, Karl, 1818–1883, philosopher, founder of "Marxism". In 1844 he, Börnstein and others published the journal "Vorwärts" in Paris; in 1848 he published "The Communist Manifesto" with Friedrich Engels. 98

Mason. *See* Monck Mason

Massol, Jean Étienne Auguste, alias Eugène, 1802–1887, was member of the ensemble at the Paris Opéra 1825–1858. 148

Massow, von, Privy Counselor, general manager of the gardens in Prussia. 96

Mathilde. *See* Eberty, Mathilde

Mecklenburg, Archduchess of. 141

Méhul, Etienne Nicolas (1763–1817), important French composer of operas.

Vossische Zeitung in Berlin, father of Ludwig Rellstab. 22

Remont, Court Counsellor von. 146

Remorini, Ranieri, 1783–1873, Italian singer and buffo, was very celebrated in the role of the Pharaoh in Rossini's *Mosè*. 36

Reynoldsen, representative of the management of the Drury Lane Theater in London. 152

Richter, Gustav, 1823–1884, court painter, married Cornelie Meyerbeer. 12, 163

Richter, Hans, 1876–1955, son of Cornelie Meyerbeer. 15

Ricordi, Milan publishing house. 145

Riem, Wilhelm Friedrich, 1779–1837, organist, since 1807 active in the reformed church in Leipzig, at the Thomas School after 1814. After 1822 also director of the Singakademie in Bremen. 20

Ries, Ferdinand, 1784–1838, pianist and composer, conductor of the Frankfurt Cäcilienverein. 33, 69

Ries, Hubert, 1802–1886, violinist and concertmaster of the Royal Orchestra in Berlin. 94

Ristori, Adelaide, 1822–1906, Italian actress, after 1855 performed in many European cities as well as in America and Australia. 167

Rochefoucauld. *See* La Rochefoucauld

Rock (Röck), Carl Ludwig, 1790–1869, jurist, fraternity brother of A. v. Dusch, returned to Lübeck in 1814 where he became a member of the senate in 1833 and mayor in 1855. 23

Röckel, Joseph August, 1783–1870, music director and composer, occasionally director of a touring German Opera troupe. 100

Roger, Gustave Hippolyte, 1815–1879, singer, had his debut at the Paris Opéra comique in 1838 and went to the Opéra in 1848 where he sang the title role of Meyerbeer's *Le Prophète* in 1849. 119, 123, 124, 125 127, 141

Romani, Pietro, 1791–1877, composer and conductor in Florence. 153

Roqueplan (Rocoplan), Louis Victor Nestor, 1804–1870, journalist, editor of "Le Figaro" in Paris, director of the Théâtre des Variétés, then 1847–1854 director of the Opéra, in 1847 as co-director with Duponchel. 1857–1860 director of the Opéra comique. 14, 118, 125, 138, 140, 141, 142, 143, 144, 161

Rossi, Gaetano, 1780–1855, librettist, wrote the libretti for Meyerbeer's Italian operas *Romilda e Costanza, Emma di Resburgo, Il Crociato in Egitto* and the never completed *Almanzore*. 33, 62

Rossini, Gioacchino Antonio, 1792–1868. In 1816 he achieved his decisive success in Italy as an opera composer with his *Barber of Seville*. In 1823 he became director of the Italian opera in Paris; two years later he became the royal general director of music. He wrote his last opera, *Guillaume Tell*, in 1829, in the style of French grand opera. 11, 12, 13, 33, 38, 76, 138, 139, 173, 180, 181

Rothschild, Salomon, Baron (as of 1822) von, one of the sons of Mayer Amschel Rothschild, the founder of the banking dynasty in Frankfurt, went to Vienna in 1821 where he soon attained a prominent position as a banker and ousted Arnstein & Eskeles as well as Sina and Geymüller from their previously dominant positions. 114

Rounat, de la, director of the Odéon in Paris. 167 168

Rubini, Giovanni Battista (1794–1854), "the king of tenors," "the nightingale of Europe." He earned great successes in operas by Rossini, Bellini, and Donizetti. Through these appearances and through concert tours he became a millionaire. 182f.

Rungenhagen, Karl Friedrich, professor, 1778–1851, director of the Berlin Singakademie. 102

Russia, Emperor of. *See* Nikolaus I.

Russia, Empress of. *See* Alexandra Feodorowna

S

Saint-Georges, Henry Vernoy de, 1799–1875, librettist, wrote numerous librettos for Auber, Bizet (*La Fille de Perth*), Donizetti (*La fille du regiment*), Halévy, Hérold and, among others, Flotow (*Martha*). 76

Saling, Marianne (Mirjam), born 1785 in Berlin, daughter of the Berlin court jeweler Salomon Hannover and Cheile Eger. Her sister Julie (Gela) was married to the language professor Karl Heyse and was the mother of the writer Paul Heyse. 58

Sand, George = Amandine Aurore Lucie

Baronne de Dudevent, née Dupin, 1804–1876, French writer. She not only created a sensation with her novels, some of which appeared in the "Revue des deux mondes" and the "Revue indépendante," but also as the result of her relationships with Alfred de Musset, Liszt, Chopin and with the Saint Simonists. 62, 65, 71, 179

Santini, Vincenzo Felice, died 1836, buffo singer in Munich. 41, 42

Sax, Adolphe (originally Antoine Joseph), 1814–1894, one of the most important instrument makers of his time, maintained a workshop in Paris, developed the bass clarinet, cylinder trumpet, saxophone, and other instruments. 131, 133, 150

Sax, Marie Constance (=Sass, Marie), 1838–1907, had her debut at the Théâtre lyrique in Paris in 1859, went to the Opéra in 1860 where she was very celebrated, and later went to Italy. 174

Sayn and Wittgenstein and Count of Stolberg-Wernigerode, Wilhelm, 1770–1851, minister of the royal household in Berlin. 93

Schätzell, Pauline von, born 1812 in Berlin, member of the Berlin Court Opera 1828–1832. 51, 55

Schechner-Waagen, Nanette, 1806–1860, singer, engaged in Vienna in 1825, became very successful in Berlin in 1827, returned to Munich in 1827. 42

Schelble, Johann Nepomuk, 1789–1837, singer, conductor and composer, founder of the "Cäcilienverein" in Frankfurt-on-the-Main. 69

Schelling, Friedrich Wilhelm Joseph von, 1775–1854, philosopher, from 1806 general secretary of the Academy in Munich where he met Meyerbeer in 1812. 24

Schiller, Johann Christoph Friedrich von, 1759–1805, writer. 164, 165, 166, 171

Schilling, Gustav, Dr., 1803–1881, music essayist, director of the Stoepel Music School in Stuttgart. 82, 83, 85

Schlesinger, Maurice Adolphe (Moritz), 1798–1871, music publisher in Paris. 59, 110, 139, 165

Schmalz, Amalie Auguste, 1771–1848, actress and royal chamber singer in Berlin. 22

Schnyder von Wartensee, Xaver, 1786–1868, composer, music teacher and writer on music in Frankfurt. 69

Schreiber, Aloys Wilhelm, Dr., 1761–1841, professor of esthetics at the University of Heidelberg, wrote lyrics for songs and opera librettos. 20, 22

Schubert, Franz, 1797–1828, composer. Meyerbeer never met Schubert personally. 169

Schucht, Jean F., 1822–1894, Dr. phil., at first music teacher and writer on music in Berlin, later consultant for the "Neue Zeitschrift für Musik" in Leipzig; published a biography of Meyerbeer in 1869. 15

Schumann, Robert, 1810–1856, composer. Meyerbeer considered him to be his most relentless opponent who published a critique of Les Huguenots in 1837 which severely damaged Meyerbeer's reputation, especially in later years—almost up to the present day, especially since Wagner's verdict against Meyerbeer seemed to confirm the view of the 26-year-old Schumann. 13, 14

Scribe, Eugène, 1791–1861, alone and in collaboration with others, he wrote approx. 400 stage works, including many successful comedies and numerous opera librettos for the most renowned composers of his time. 14, 17, 43, 48f, 52, 56, 62, 70, 82, 96, 105, 120, 134, 138, 141, 142, 149, 152, 173

Scudo, Pietro (Pierre, Paul), 1806–1864, music critic in Paris, published his reviews in several volumes. 144

Seidler, Caroline, née Wranitzki, c.1790–1872, singer at the Berlin Court Opera. 55

Semler, Franz Xaver, 1772–1875, violist, royal chamber musician in Berlin. 94

Shakespeare, William, 1564–1616. Numerous composers of the 19th century chose his works as a basis for their opera librettos. 169

Sillem, Hermann, London banker. 136

Spain, Queen of. See Isabella

Speyer, Wilhelm, 1790–1878, merchant and composer of numerous songs and choral works for men's voices which earned him great popularity. 68, 74, 92

Spezia, female singer. 160

Spohr, Louis, 1784–1859, violin virtuoso, composer, conductor at the Theater an der Wien, then in Frankfurt, from 1822 conductor of the court orchestra in Kassel. 30, 69, 100, 101

Spontini, Gaspare Luigi Pacifico, 1774–1851, composer, 1820–1841 court composer and Prussian Director General of Music in Berlin under Friedrich Wilhelm III. 12, 23, 49, 88, 90

Springer, Julius, 1817–1877, publisher and Berlin city councilman(?). 85

Staudigl, Joseph, 1807–1861, premier bass at the Vienna Court Opera. 116

Stegmeyer, Mattaeus, 1771–1820, Viennese actor, composer, writer, author of "Rochus Pumpernickel" which was very popular in his day. 30

Stieglitz, Johann (Israel), Dr., 1767–1840, in 1802 became court doctor and personal physician for the King of Hannover, was considered one of Germany's most prominent physicians. 57

Stoltz, Rosine (=Nöb, Victorine), 1815–1903, mezzo soprano, 1837–1847 member of the Paris Opéra. 106, 151

Strauss, Johann (senior), 1804–1849, composer of waltzes. 116, 139

Strauss, Richard, 1864–1949, composer. 9

Strodtmann, Adolf, 1829–1879, writer and publicist, 1861–1866 published Heine's works in 21 volumes. 158

T

Taglioni, Marie, 1804–1884, dancer, 1827–1832, prima ballerina of the Paris Opéra. Later she danced at the Scala in Milan and in Turin. She created the role of "Sylphide". 47f, 55, 69

Taglioni, Filippo, 1777–1871, father of Marie Taglioni, maître de ballet and major choreographer at the Paris Opéra, creator of many successful ballets. Taglioni also worked in Stockholm, Kassel, Vienna and Munich. 48

Taxis, Countess. 27

Thomas a Kempis, Thomas von Kempen (actual name Thomas Hamerken, lat. Malleolus), 1379 or 1380–1471, theologian. "De Imitatione Christi" was his most important work. 171

Thomas, Charles Louis Ambroise, 1811–1896, composer, 1856 professor of composition at the Paris Conservatoire where he became director in 1871. Thomas' major work, *Mignon,* was not performed until 1866, after Meyerbeer's death. 159, 160

Tichatscheck, Joseph Aloys, 1807–1886, tenor, member of the ensemble at the Dresden court opera 1838–1872 where he became famous as a Wagnerian tenor: he sang the roles of Rienzi and Tannhäuser. 155, 156

Tietjens, Therese Johanna Alexandra, 1831–1877, singer, had her debut in 1849 in Hamburg and was a member of the Vienna Court Opera 1856–1858. After this until her death she performed in London. 174

Tollmann, Johannes, 1775–1829, violinist, music director in Basel. 23

Tomaschek, Johann Wenzel = Tomásek, Václav Jan, 1774–1850, Czech composer, wrote many songs, symphonies, chamber music and piano works. 30

Tosi, Adelaide, ca. 1797–1859, Italian singer, had her debut in 1821 at La Scala in Milan, performed later on several Italian stages as well as in Madrid and London. 37

Tuczeck, Leopoldine, singer in Berlin. 96

U

Ugalde, female singer. 150

Ungher, Caroline, 1803–1877. After her debut in Vienna she sang on many stages in Italy, 1833 in Paris, 1839 in Dresden. Bellini, Donizetti, Mercadante and others wrote for her. 61

Unknown = Dusch, Alexander von.

V

Valentin, Nanette. Börne, Heine, Humboldt and many famous artists frequented the Valentin household in Paris. The elegant balls and receptions given by this family were very well known at that time. 45

Velutti, Giovanni Battista, 1780–1861, the last great Italian castrato, sang the lead role in Meyerbeer's opera *Il Crociato in Egitto* (1824, in Venice). 37, 39, 157

Verdi, Giuseppe, 1813–1901, the most important Italian opera composer in the second half of the 19th century. The period of his great successes began in 1851 with *Rigoletto.* In 1855, he composed *Les Vêpres Siciliennes* for Paris; later he revised *Macbeth* and *Don Carlos* for the French stage. 12, 14, 138, 156, 173

Véron, Louis Désiré, Dr., 1798–1867, physician and journalist, 1831–1835 director of the Paris Opéra, founder of the "Revue de Paris", later was director of the "Constitutionel". 49, 52f, 54, 56, 59, 60, 62, 63, 64, 65, 67, 68, 69, 147, 148

Vespermann, Katharina, born 1802, singer from Munich. 42

Vesque von Püttlingen, Johann (pseudonym J. Hoven), Dr. jur., 1803–1883, department head in the Foreign Ministry in Vienna, composer. 101

Viardot, Louis, died 1883, director of the Théâtre italien in Paris, then impresario for his wife, Pauline Viardot-Garcia. 118, 119

Viardot-Garcia, Pauline, 1821–1910, singer, daughter of Manuel Garcia, had her debut in 1839 in London and in 1849—at Meyerbeer's continued insistence—came to the Paris Opéra where she sang the role of Fides in Meyerbeer's opera *Le Prophète*. 118, 119, 123, 124, 125, 130

Victoria, Queen of England, 1819–1901, crowned in 1837. 104, 118

Villaret, male Parisian singer. 173

Vogler, Georg Joseph, 1749–1814, Abbé, composer and theorist, organ virtuoso, conductor of court orchestra in Darmstadt, Meyerbeer's teacher. 9, 11, 19, 20, 21, 25, 26, 28

W

Wagner, Albert, 1799–1874, opera singer and director, brother of Richard Wagner. 142

Wagner, Carl Jacob, 1772–1822, conductor and composer in Darmstadt. 25

Wagner, Johanna (Jachmann-Wagner), 1828–1894, singer, sang the role of Elisabeth in Richard Wagner's *Tannhäuser* in 1845, appointed chamber singer in Berlin in 1853. In 1861, she lost her singing voice for several years; during this period she was a very respected tragic actress. 142, 143

Wagner, Minna, née Planer, 1809–1866, Richard Wagner's first wife. 89

Wagner, Richard, 1813–1883, composer, originally sought Meyerbeer's protection. Although Meyerbeer supported Wagner both financially and by giving him personal references, he later became Meyerbeer's opponent ("Opera and Drama", "Jews in the World of Music"). With the creation of so-called music drama, Wagner intro-

duced a rival concept to that of the Grand Opéra. 12, 14, 15, 17, 87, 89, 100, 142

Weber, Bernhard Anselm, 1766–1821, conductor at the National Theater in Berlin, briefly served as Meyerbeer's composition teacher. See letter 1. 10, 20, 23, 31

Weber, Carl Maria von, 1786–1826, composer, together with Meyerbeer he founded the "Harmonische Verein" while they were both studying under (Abbé) Vogler. As a result of Meyerbeer's stay in Italy and the success of his Italian operas, the former friends became estranged. 11, 15, 19, 21, 23 24, 26, 75, 76, 83, 94, 99

Weber, Caroline, née Brandt, 1794–1852, married Carl Maria v. Weber. 75

Weber, Gottfried, 1779–1839, composer and music theorist, publisher of "Cäcilia, Zeitschrift für die musikalische Welt." He was a member of the "Harmonische Verein" and also a jurist and ducal district attorney. 20, 21, 24, 25, 28, 33, 76, 77, 78, 79

Weber, Johann (biographer) 144

Weill, Alexander (Abraham), 1811–1899, journalist, Paris correspondent for the "Zeitung für die elegante Welt". 82

Weimar, Grandduke of. 141

Werner, Zacharias, 1768–1823, clergyman and writer, originally Protestant minister, converted to Catholicism in 1811 and became a priest in 1814; he was considered an excellent preacher. 79

Westenholz, Friedrich, 1778–1840, oboist, member of the Royal orchestra in Berlin. 94

Wette, Wilhelm de (De Wette, W.), 1780–1849, Protestant theologian, professor in Heidelberg, Berlin and Basel. 86

Wieprecht, Wilhelm Friedrich, 1802–1872, Prussian military music director, composer. 94

Wilhelm, Princess. *See* Augusta, Princess of Prussia

Wilhelm Friedrich Heinrich, Prince of the Netherlands, 1820–1879, second son of King Wilhelm II, after 1850 governor of the Grand Duchy of Luxembourg. 141

Wilhelm Friedrich Ludwig, Prince of Prussia, 1797–1888, in 1858 became prince regent, in 1861 King of Prussia, was crowned German Emperor in

1871. 57, 58, 103, 137, 165
Winkler, Karl Gottlieb Theodor, 1775–1856, Russian and Saxon court councillor, writer, deputy director of the Dresden court theater, director and publisher of the Dresden Abendzeitung. 47, 75, 76, 120
Wittgenstein, Princess. 78, 140
Wohlbrück, Johann Gottfried, 1770–1822, court actor and director, wrote the libretto for Meyerbeer's *Abimelek.* 25
Wolff. *See* Beer, Wilhelm. Meyerbeer's brother kept his original given name of Wolff until 1818.
Wolfssohn, Aron, ca. 1754–1835, professor and director of the Wilhelm School in Breslau, went to Berlin in 1807 to tutor the Beer brothers. His Hebrew reader for Jewish young people was published in 1790; later he wrote numerous works on religious themes and, together with others, published the journal "Meassef". 9, 19, 28, 31
Worms de Romilly, prominent Parisian banker, later president of the Jewish Consistory in Paris. 28

Z

Zelter, Carl Friedrich, 1758–1832, composer, close friend of Goethe, since 1800 director of the Berlin Singakademie, founded the Royal Institute for Sacred Music in Berlin in 1822, taught Meyerbeer at various times. 10
Zuccoli=Zucchelli, Carlo, 1793–1879, distinguished Italian bass. 36

215